GIFTED CHILDREN

FRANK LAYCOCK

Oberlin College

SCOTT, FORESMAN AND COMPANY

Glenview, Illinois

Dallas, Tex.   Oakland, N.J.   Palo Alto, Cal.   Tucker, Ga.   London, England

Library of Congress Cataloging in Publication Data

Laycock, Frank, 1922–
  Gifted children.

  Bibliography: p. 173
  Includes index.
  1. Gifted children—Education. I. Title.
LC3993.L37   371.9'5   78-26875
ISBN 0-673-15142-5

12345678910–RRC–8584838281807978

For Lenore, and for our children: Vera, Christopher, Deirdre, and Megan

Respect a child's faculties from the moment it inhales the clear air.

Confucius

Photo Credits

Chapter 1: John Arms/Image, Inc.
Chapter 2: © Eric Kroll/Taurus
Chapter 3: Scott, Foresman staff
Chapter 4: Ken Murray/Image, Inc.
Chapter 5: Scott, Foresman staff
Chapter 6: Scott, Foresman staff
Chapter 7: Marjorie Pickens, from *Beginning Experiences in Architecture* by George Trogler, Van Nostrand Reinhold Co., 1972

Literary Credits

p. 6   Abridged from "Child E", Chapter Eight of CHILDREN ABOVE 180 IQ, STANFORD BINET ORIGIN AND DEVELOPMENT, by Leta S. Hollingworth. Copyright 1942 by World Book Company. Reprinted by permission of Mr. Benjamen H. Florence, Executor for the estate of Henry L. Hollingworth.

p. 10   From "Three Gifted Children: A Developmental Study" by Gertrude Hildreth, from THE JOURNAL OF GENETIC PSYCHOLOGY: Child Behavior, Animal Behavior and Comparative Psychology, Volume 85, Second Half, December, 1954. Copyright 1954 by The Journal Press, Provincetown, Massachusetts. Reprinted by permission of The Journal Press and Dr. Gertrude Hildreth.

p. 15   Excerpt from "The Eternal Apprentice". Reprinted by permission from TIME, The Weekly Newsmagazine; Copyright Time Inc. 1948.

p. 18   From "Evening with a Gifted Child," by Joseph Mitchell. Reprinted by permission; ©1940, 1968 Joseph Mitchell. Originally in The New Yorker.

p. 24   From ABLE MISFITS: A STUDY OF EDUCATIONAL AND BEHAVIOUR DIFFICULTIES OF 103 VERY INTELLIGENT CHILDREN (I.Q.s 120-200) by M. L. Kellmer-Pringle, 1970, Longman Group Limited in association with The National Bureau for Co-operation in Child Care, London. © M. L. Kellmer Pringle 1970. Reprinted by permission of Longman Group Limited.

p. 34   From "The Discovery and Encouragement of Exceptional Talent" by Lewis M. Terman in The American Psychologist, Volume 9, 1954. Copyright 1954 by The American Psychological Association. Reprinted by permission.

p. 36   Adaptation of table, "Structure-of-Intellect Components" by Marcella R. Bonsall and Mary M. Meeker as it appeared in James M. Dunlap, "The Education of Children with High Mental Ability" in EDUCATION OF EXCEPTIONAL CHILDREN AND YOUTH, Cruickshank and Johnson, eds., © 1955, 1967, 1975, p. 147. Reprinted by permission of Prentice-Hall, Inc., Englewood Cliffs, New Jersey and the Los Angeles County Division of Program Evaluation, Research, and Pupil Services.

p. 37   Adapted from The Gifted Child in the Elementary School (What Research Says to the Teacher, No. 17, 1st ed.) by James J. Gallagher, 1959, American Educational Research Association, N.E.A., Association of Classroom Teachers. Cited in Samuel A. Kirk, EDUCATING EXCEPTIONAL CHILDREN, Houghton-Mifflin, 1972. Reprinted by permission of the National Education Association, Washington, D. C.

p. 66   Adapted from Chapter II, pages 22-23 of THE STRUCTURE OF HUMAN ABILITIES by Philip E. Vernon. New York and London: John Wiley & Sons, Inc. and Methuen & Co. Ltd., 1961. Reprinted by permission.

p. 68   From "Three Faces of Intellect" by J. P. Guilford, from THE AMERICAN PSYCHOLOGIST, 1959. Copyright 1959 by the American Psychological Association. Reprinted by permission of the American Psychological Association and Dr. Joy P. Guilford.

PREFACE

Gifted children are any society's prime asset. They are born at every social and economic level, but they do not all get proper nurture. Now that we are caught up in crises that threaten other resources, I hope that these children, too, will get the attention they must have. I have therefore brought together basic information about gifted children: who they are, why we need them, how we spot them, and what we can do for them.

I believe this is a timely enterprise. John Curtis Gowan, in a 1975 address honoring Terman's major research on gifted children (Stanley, George, & Solane, 1977) pointed out that we may soon see major progress in studying our brightest children. In the past there has been little systematic analysis of what constitutes giftedness. Now specialists from many fields are becoming interested in the gifted. Psychologists are concerned about behavioral differences among people; experts in cognition are examining anew problem solving and creativity; and neurologists are looking for the basic mechanisms of thought. Educators and sociologists, linguists and lawyers, are also working together to determine how we can make a fresh commitment to individual development and fair play, free of the constraints that prejudice and unequal opportunity have imposed on the selection and education of the gifted.

This book offers general background on the subject rather than specific and detailed instructions about how to identify bright children or how to develop practical plans for teaching them. This information is available in other books, most recently those by Gallagher (1975) and Newland (1976). Here I have assembled facts that ought to be considered before we confront individual children or design curricula for them: patterns of traits, the behavior we can expect, traditional ways of providing help, and issues and proposals presently under study.

As compared to other discussions of bright children, this book refers more to practices in several countries. I have drawn heavily on work that was originally reported in English, because most of the systematic research has come from the United States, Britain, and the Commonwealth countries. But I find it useful and provocative to look also at how other countries, notably China, have treated their most promising children. This international *ambiance* emphasizes the global scope of the challenge posed by gifted children.

An important segment of this book examines historic and current statements about how and why we must watch closely over the gifted. There is a peculiar urgency, now, to look squarely at the gifted. There are critics who argue for egalitarian treatment, who point to the pitfalls in standardized testing, who insist that children must be allowed to be free spirits, or who concentrate upon the prejudice directed against minority children; these critics often oppose programs designed for the brightest. Special attention, the argument goes, is undemocratic, unfair to the disadvantaged, and unevenly distributed. If, as a result of these arguments, bright children are left to themselves, or if they are everywhere merged with the mass, they and we alike will suffer.

The book betrays some of my bias. I begin with biographical excerpts because I believe many arguments about gifted children would subside if everyone really looked hard at individual children who unmistakably demonstrate their keen minds and special abilities. Their divergence from most children—not to mention the impressive differences among the bright themselves—would then strike us all, as it has careful observers from Plato to Terman.

I also believe that we can best understand bright children if we use a perspective that goes beyond individual experiences, and this belief is reflected in the book. Our limited, idiosyncratic contacts with children need the complement of systematic investigation. Well-documented research corrects the bias of personal observation. It offers us general themes we can examine to see how they fit our own children. To be most useful in a book like this, however, references to research should be parsimoniously chosen. Discussion here will center on only a few specific studies, with reference to the host of other corroborating investigations.

Systematic generalizations about children—even the most carefully derived—rarely turn into foolproof recipes. Particular situations demand particular decisions, and these must be assessed on the spot. In a book belong the measured considerations that should inform decisions. It would be foolish to write as though gifted children were so similar that we could say beforehand exactly what to expect of them, what to do with them, and why. Rather we want to present them in the richness of their variety and in the many different settings that societies have seen fit to establish for them.

This, then, is a book that offers an individual perspective, enhanced with empirical information—systematically gathered and cautiously generalized. It is selective, not encyclopedic. It discusses psychological data, social issues, and educational patterns—each at the level of general principle rather than immediate prescription.

Acknowledgments

Many people have influenced me in writing this book. I should like to acknowledge here with respect and thanks the unusual stimulation and support that several of them have offered.

Years ago, Harold Carter, Luther Gilbert, Harold Jones, and Noel Keys opened my eyes to cognitive development and gifted children. Later, Robert Havighurst and Bernice Neugarten schooled me in the power of environmental contributions to development. In Switzerland, Bärbel Inhelder and Eric Lunzer were thoughtful guides to Piaget's work and influence. In Sweden, Torsten Husén and Eve Malmquist helped me to follow educational reforms in Scandinavia and Europe. In Britain, several persons have been generous with advice and shrewd observations about education for gifted children there: A. H. Halsey, Brian Holmes, H. B. Miles, E. A. Peel, Jean Russell-Gebbett, and Alfred Yates. In Asia, Mark Thelen, Hwang Chien-hou, and—while at Oberlin—Tadahiko Inagaki encouraged me to trace the relation between Eastern and Western education. At home and in Asia, William McNaughton has for many years informed and stimulated me regarding oriental cultures. In Ohio, Charles Jordan and Jean Thom introduced me to the Cleveland Major Work Program and led me to work with them and the Ohio Association for Gifted Children.

I have a heavy debt to Wilhelm Sjöstrand, who has provided counsel and friendship for many years. Daniel Keating, Lloyd Lovell, and Julian Stanley gave specific advice and criticism regarding the manuscript. At Scott, Foresman, Joanne Tinsley, Margaret Prullage, and Patricia Nerenberg have been sharp-eyed and supportive editors. At Oberlin College, the Research and Development Committee, administration, and Shansi Memorial Association have supplied funds for various projects related to this book.

Above all, my special gratitude to my wife and family are expressed in the dedication.

F.L.

CONTENTS

Some Gifted Children

... a local habitation and a name.
William Shakespeare,
A Midsummer Night's Dream, V:*i*:17

What is it like to be gifted? There are two ways to answer this question: we could describe particular persons who were or are extraordinarily bright, or we could list a group of traits characteristic of most gifted individuals. Each reply is useful, and in Chapters 1 and 2 we will do both.

Because the gifted are scarce, few of us are likely to know many or to have any dependable impression of gifted children as a group. This chapter, then, will offer excerpts from biographies of several very intelligent young persons, and Chapter 2 will summarize what gifted children have in common. The sequence is intentional. The summaries come second because lists of characteristics are bloodless, never recreating the children to whom they refer. Generalizations organize experience, pointing out patterns, but they are awkward substitutes for direct experience. A few sharp vignettes of children, chosen to be representative, can both amplify whatever acquaintance with "the gifted" you might already have and vivify the subsequent descriptions of them.

We shall begin with an excerpt from the autobiography of J. S. Mill—a first-person narrative that preserves the integrity of the whole person. Then we shall look at a report on Leta Hollingworth's "Child *E*," one of the best-known (to psychologists) of the very brightest of children—those who are farthest from the norm. We shall follow with several brief excerpts from a clinical study that demonstrated that the gifted are not only different from the "average" but also strikingly different among themselves. After these children, who span the full range of brightness, we will look at some persons who illustrate special interests that the gifted often develop: literary, aesthetic, scientific. Finally, we will present some illustrations of the problems the gifted must solve as they deal with their own emerging lives and their relations to others.

JOHN STUART MILL

John Stuart Mill is a secure example to start our study of the gifted because he was not only a precocious child but also became a powerful influence upon nineteenth-century social thought. We can examine his early years knowing that we encounter a child whose remarkable brilliance will not fade. He is an archetypal genius: he showed great gifts in childhood and made remarkable contributions in maturity. He is an especially fortunate choice for study, too, because we have his own words, the record of his childhood as he remembered it.

Mill gives a striking display of native talent responding to a strict regimen. His father, a recognized intellectual himself, took unusual and strict personal charge of his child's education. From the start, the younger Mill was held to very high standards of intellectual attainment. There was no quarter given for immaturity or incompetence. We cannot know how far he might have gone had he spent a more relaxed childhood, with a broader mix of friendship and childish fun. The following excerpt is from his respectful account of a childhood aimed steadily at mental development.

. . . I have no remembrance of the time when I began to learn Greek, I have been told that it was when I was three years old. My earliest recollection on the subject, is that of committing to memory what my father termed vocables, being lists of common Greek words, with their signification in English, which he wrote out for me on cards. Of grammar, until some years later, I learnt no more than the inflexions of the nouns and verbs, but, after a course of vocables, proceeded at once to translation; and I faintly remember going through Æsop's Fables, the first Greek book which I read. The Anabasis, which I remember better, was the second. I learnt no Latin until my eighth year. At that time I had read, under my father's tuition, a number of Greek prose authors, among whom I remember the whole of Herodotus, and of Xenophon's Cyropædia and Memorials of Socrates; some of the lives of the philosophers by Diogenes Laertius; part of Lucian, and Isocrates ad Demonicum and Ad Nicoclem. I also read, in 1813, the first six dialogues (in the common arrangement) of Plato, from the Euthyphron to the Theoctetus inclusive: which last dialogue, I venture to think, would have been better omitted, as it was totally impossible I should understand it. But my father, in all his teaching, demanded of me not only the utmost that I could do, but much that I could by no possibility have done. What he was himself willing to undergo for the sake of my instruction, may be judged from the fact, that I went through the whole process of preparing my Greek lessons in the same room and at the same table at which he was writing: and as in those days Greek and English lexicons were not, and I could make no more use of a Greek and Latin lexicon than could be made without having yet begun to learn Latin, I was forced to have recourse to him for the meaning of every word which I did not know. This incessant interruption, he, one of the most impatient of men, submitted to, and wrote under that interruption several volumes of his History and all else that he had to write during those years.

The only thing besides Greek, that I learnt as a lesson in this part of my childhood, was arithmetic: this also my father taught me: it was the task of the evenings, and I well remember its disagreeableness. But the lessons were only a part of the daily instruction I received. Much of it consisted in the books I read by myself, and my father's discourses to me, chiefly during our walks. From 1810 to the end of 1813 we were living in Newington Green, then an almost rustic neighbourhood. My father's health required considerable and constant exercise, and he walked habitually before breakfast, generally in the green lanes towards Hornsey. In these walks I always accompanied him, and with my earliest recollections of green fields and wild flowers, is mingled that of the account I gave him daily of what I had read the day before. To the best of my remembrance, this was a voluntary rather than a prescribed exercise. I made notes on slips of paper while reading, and from these in the morning walks, I told the story to him; for the books were chiefly histories, of which I read in this manner a great number . . . . In these frequent talks about the books I read, he used, as opportunity offered, to give me explanations and ideas respecting civilization, government, morality, mental cultivation, which he required me afterwards to restate to him in my own words. He also made me read, and give him a verbal account of, many books which would not have interested me sufficiently to induce me to read them of myself . . . . Of children's books, any more than of playthings, I had scarcely any, except an occasional gift from a relation or acquaintance: among those I had, Robinson Crusoe was preeminent, and continued to delight me through all my boyhood. It was no part, however, of my father's system to exclude books of amusement, though he allowed them very sparingly. Of such books he possessed at that time next to none, but he borrowed several for me; those which I remember are the Arabian Nights, Cazotte's Arabian Tales, Don Quixote, Miss Edgeworth's Popular Tales, and a book of some reputation in its day, Brooke's Fool of Quality.

In my eighth year I commenced learning Latin, in conjunction with a younger sister, to whom I taught it as I went on, and who afterwards repeated the lessons to my father: and from this time, other sisters and brothers being successively added as pupils, a considerable part of my day's work consisted of this preparatory teaching. It was a part which I greatly disliked; the more so, as I was held responsible for the lessons of my pupils, in almost as full a sense as for my own: I, however, derived from this discipline the great advantage, of learning more thoroughly and retaining more lastingly the things which I was set to teach: perhaps, too, the practice it afforded in explaining difficulties to others, may even at that age have been useful. . . .

In the same year in which I began Latin, I made my first commencement in the Greek poets with the Iliad. After I had made some progress in this, my father put Pope's translation into my hands. It was the first English verse I had cared to read, and it became one of the books in which for many years I most delighted: I think I must have read it from twenty to thirty times through. I should not have thought it worth while to mention a taste apparently so natural to boyhood, if I had not, as I think, observed that the keen enjoyment of this brilliant specimen of narrative and versification is not so universal with boys, as I should have expected both *à priori* and from my individual experience. Soon after this time I commenced Euclid, and somewhat later, Algebra, still under my father's tuition.

. . . During the same years I learnt elementary geometry and algebra thoroughly, the differential calculus, and other portions of the higher mathematics far from thoroughly: for my father, not having kept up this part of his early acquired knowledge, could not spare time to qualify himself for removing my difficulties, and left me to deal with them, with little other aid than that of books: while I was continually incurring his displeasure by my inability to solve difficult problems for which he did not see that I had not the necessary previous knowledge.

As to my private reading, I can only speak of what I remember. History continued to be my strongest predilection, and most of all ancient history. . . . A voluntary exercise, to which throughout my boyhood I was much addicted, was what I called writing histories. I successively composed a Roman History, picked out of Hooke; an Abridgment of the Ancient Universal History; a History of Holland, from my favourite Watson and from an anonymous compilation; and in my eleventh and twelfth year I occupied myself with writing what I flattered myself was something serious. This was no less than a History of the Roman Government . . . . A few years later, in my contempt of my childish efforts, I destroyed all these papers, not then anticipating that I could ever feel any curiosity about my first attempts at writing and reasoning. My father encouraged me in this useful amusement, though, as I think judiciously, he never asked to see what I wrote; so that I did not feel that in writing it I was accountable to any one, nor had the chilling sensation of being under a critical eye. . . .

During this part of my childhood, one of my greatest amusements was experimental science; in the theoretical, however, not the practical sense of the word; not trying experiments—a kind of discipline which I have often regretted not having had—nor even seeing, but merely reading about them. I never remember being so wrapt up in any book, as I was in Joyce's Scientific Dialogues . . . .

From about the age of twelve, I entered into another and more advanced stage in my course of instruction; in which the main object was no longer the aids and appliances of thought, but the thoughts themselves. . . . my father made me read the whole or parts of several of the Latin treatises on the scholastic logic; giving each day to him, in our walks, a minute account of what I had read, and answering his numerous and searching questions. . . . It was his invariable practice, whatever studies he exacted from me, to make me as far as possible understand and feel the utility of them: and this he deemed peculiarly fitting in the case of the syllogistic logic, the usefulness of which had been impugned by so many writers of authority. I well remember how, and in what particular walk, in the neighbourhood of Bagshot Heath (where we were on a visit to his old friend Mr. Wallace, then one of the Mathematical Professors at Sandhurst) he first attempted by questions to make me think on the subject, and frame some conception of what constituted the utility of the syllogistic logic, and when I had failed in this, to make me understand it by explanations. The explanations did not make the matter at all clear to me at the time; but they were not therefore useless; they remained as a nucleus for my observations and reflections to crystallize upon; the import of his general remarks being interpreted to me, by the particular instances which came under my notice afterwards. My own consciousness and experience ultimately led me to appreciate quite as highly as he did, the value of an early practical familiarity with the school logic. I know of nothing, in my education, to which I think myself more indebted for whatever capacity of thinking I have attained. The first intellectual operation in which I arrived at any proficiency, was dissecting a bad argument, and finding in what part the fallacy lay: and though whatever capacity of this sort I attained, was due to the fact that it was an intellectual exercise in which I was most perseveringly drilled by my father, yet it is also true that the school logic, and the mental habits acquired in studying it, were among the principal instruments of this drilling. I am persuaded that nothing, in modern education, tends so much, when properly used, to form exact thinkers, who attach a precise meaning to words and propositions, and are not imposed on by vague, loose, or ambiguous terms. . . .

. . . I do not believe that any scientific teaching ever was more thorough, or better fitted for training the faculties, than the mode in which logic and political economy were taught to me by my father. Striving, even in an exaggerated degree, to call forth the activity of my faculties, by making me find out everything for myself, he gave his explanations not before, but after, I had felt the full force of the difficulties; and not only gave me an accurate knowledge of these two great subjects, as far as they were then understood, but made me a thinker on both, I thought for myself almost from the first, and occasionally thought differently from him, though for a long time only on minor points, and making his opinion the ultimate standard. At a later period I even occasionally convinced him, and altered his opinion on some points of detail: which I state to his honour, not my own. It at once exemplifies his perfect candour, and the real worth of his method of teaching.

At this point concluded what can properly be called my lessons: when I was about fourteen I left England for more than a year; and after my return, though my studies went on under my father's general direction, he was no longer my schoolmaster. . . .

There was one cardinal point in this training, of which I have already given some indication, and which, more than anything else, was the cause of whatever good it effected. Most boys or youths who have had much knowledge drilled into them, have their mental capacities not strengthened, but overlaid by it. They are crammed with mere facts, and with the opinions or phrases of other people, and these are accepted as a substitute for the power to form opinions of their own . . . . Mine, however, was not an education of cram. My father never permitted anything which I learnt to degenerate into a mere exercise of memory. He strove to make the understanding not only go along with every step of the teaching, but, if possible, precede it. Anything which could be found out by thinking I never was told, until I had exhausted my efforts to find it out for myself. . . . A pupil from whom nothing is ever demanded which he cannot do, never does all he can.

One of the evils most liable to attend on any sort of early proficiency, and which often fatally blights its promise, my father most anxiously guarded against. This was self-conceit. He kept me, with extreme vigilance, out of the way of hearing myself praised, or of being led to make self-flattering comparisons between myself and others. From his own intercourse with me I could derive none but a very humble opinion of myself; and the standard of comparison he always held up to me, was not what other people did, but what a man could and ought to do. He completely succeeded in preserving me from the sort of influences he so much dreaded. I was not at all aware that my attainments were anything unusual at my age. If I accidentally had my attention drawn to the fact that some other boy knew less than myself—which happened less often than might be imagined—I concluded, not that I knew much, but that he, for some reason or other, knew little, or that his knowledge was of a different kind from mine. My state of mind was not humility, but neither was it arrogance. I never thought of saying to myself, I am, or I can do, so and so. I neither estimated myself highly nor lowly: I did not estimate myself at all. If I thought anything about myself, it was that I was rather backward in my studies, since I always found myself so, in comparison with what my father expected from me. I assert this with confidence, though it was not the impression of various persons who saw me in my child-hood. They, as I have since found, thought me greatly and disagreeably self-conceited; probably because I was disputatious, and did not scruple to give direct contradictions to things which I heard said. I suppose I acquired this bad habit from having been encouraged in an unusual degree to talk on matters beyond my age, and with grown persons, while I never had inculcated on me the usual respect for them. My father did not correct this ill-breeding and imperti-nence, probably from not being aware of it, for I was always too much in awe of him to be otherwise than extremely subdued and quiet in his presence. Yet with all this I had no notion of any superiority in myself; and well was it for me that I had not. I remember the very place in Hyde Park where, in my fourteenth year, on the eve of leaving my father's house for a long absence, he told me that I should find, as I got acquainted with new people, that I had been taught many things which youths of my age did not commonly know; and that many persons would be disposed to talk to me of this, and to compliment me upon it. What other things he said on this topic I remember very imperfectly; but he wound up by saying, that whatever I knew more than others, could not be ascribed to any merit in me, but to the very unusual advantage which had fallen to my lot, of having a father who was able to teach me, and willing to give the necessary trouble and time; that it was no matter of praise to me, if I knew more than those who had not had a similar advantage, but the deepest disgrace to me if I did not. . . . (Mill, 1873, pp. 5–34)

E, A PRODIGIOUS CHILD

The young Mill did not have an ordinary childhood as we know it. With no regular schooling and constant association with adults and adult expectations, he led a rarefied, protected life. But obviously, he was no ordinary child. Let us turn to another extremely intelligent boy, immortalized—at least among psychologists—by Leta Hollingworth in the early twentieth century. *E* went to school, but in many other ways he was not unlike Mill, despite the difference in time and culture. Hollingworth found *E's* measured IQ to be 187 and called him a "prodigious child."

Child *E* when first seen was a boy 8 years 4 months of age. He was born June 17, 1908, and the first psychological measurements were made November 4, 1916. The circumstances that led to acquaintance with him were as follows:

A child of exceptional intelligence was desired for demonstration before a class at Teachers College, Columbia University, engaged in the study of the psychology and treatment of exceptional children. *E* was suggested because of his remarkable school record. The consent of the parents was secured and the psychological examination was made before a class of about thirty students.

This was not, of course, the ideal circumstance under which to perform a mental test for scientific record. The presumption would be that the audience would tend to reduce the child's performance, so that whatever error there might be from this source would be in the direction of making the child appear less exceptional than he really was. . . .

Early History
E was his parents' fourth child, three girls having been born before him, all having died. Birth was difficult. He was bottle fed. His parents were both in middle life at the time of his birth. He cut his first tooth at 8 months—a lateral incisor. He walked at thirteen months.

Up to the age of 2 years *E* did not say a word. He then began to talk, and before he was 3 years old was able to read such books as *Peter Rabbit.* Conversation with him was carried on in German, French, Italian, and English equally. When he did begin to talk he could say in these four languages all the words he knew.

E's health has been exceptionally good from infancy. . . .

School Achievement
E went to kindergarten from the age of 3 years to the age of 5 years. From 5 to 6 he was out of school on account of school organization (he could not be accepted in the first grade). From 6 to 7 years he attended an open-air, ungraded school and did the work of the second to the fourth grades. From 7 to 8 years

he was in the fourth grade in regular school classes, and at the time of first observation by the writer, when he was 8 years old, he was in the sixth grade.

He was thus three full years accelerated in school grading, according to age-grade norms, but was still three years retarded in school according to his Mental Age. (Terman makes special note of the fact that superior children are almost invariably retarded in school grading according to Mental Age.) His mother stated that under private tutors *E* had at this time covered the work of the seventh and nearly all the work of the eighth grade. . . .

In addition to his regular school work *E,* by the time he was 8 years old, had covered the following special work in language and mathematics, either with a tutor or with his mother:

Mathematics: Algebra as far as equations; geometry.
Latin: Partial knowledge of the four declensions (he has been taught by the direct, informal method, and reads easy Latin).
Greek: Worked out the alphabet for himself from an astronomical chart, between the ages of 5 and 6 years.
French: Equal to about two years in the ordinary school.
German: Ordinary conversation.
Spanish: Attended class with his mother—reads and understands.
Italian: Reading knowledge and simple conversation.
Portuguese: Asked his mother to take this course at the Columbia Summer School because he could not be registered himself.
Hebrew: A beginning.
Anglo-Saxon: A beginning.
Astronomy: He has worked out all the constellations from MacCready, and displays a very great interest in this subject. One evening this winter he noticed a new planet near the Twins. He said it was Saturn but his mother thought it was Mars. *E* went home, worked the position out from the chart and found it to be Saturn.
Miscellaneous: He has a great interest in nature, wherever found, and is already able to use Apgar intelligently. His writing is not equal to his other accomplishments. He is very slow at it and for this reason dictates most of his "home work" to a stenographer. History is his chief and absorbing interest among school subjects.

As a demonstration before her class at Teachers College, Hollingworth gave *E* the Stanford-Binet intelligence test. Her analysis of the results follows. In this analysis, "Average Adult" and "XVIII, 6" refer to levels of the test associated, respectively, with adult and eighteen-year-old performance standards.

Mental Measurements

. . . An analysis of his performance shows that *E* has extraordinary appreciation of the exact use of words and of the shades of difference between words. He gave correct meanings for 64 words out of the 100 in the vocabulary test. His vocabulary thus includes 11,520 words. The score of the Average Adult is 65 words. Thus he just missed scoring on this Average Adult test. Samples of his definitions are as follows:

scorch—is what happens to a thing when exposed to great heat.
quake—is a kind of movement, unintended.
ramble—is a walk taken for pleasure.
nerve—is a thing you feel by—for instance, cold.

majesty—is a word used to address a king—your majesty.
Mars—is a planet.
peculiarity—is something you do that nobody else does.
mosaic—is a picture made of many small pieces of marble.
bewail—is to be extremely sorrowful.
tolerate—is to allow others to do what you don't like yourself.
lotus—is a kind of flower.
harpy—is a kind of half-bird, half-woman, referred to in Virgil.
fen—is a kind of marsh.
laity—is *not* clergy.
ambergris—it comes from a whale.
straw—the stalk of a cereal plant.
lecture—someone giving a very long talk about something to an audience.

E also has a prodigious ability for comprehending and formulating abstract ideas, and for working with symbols. He gave the differences between the abstract concepts under Average Adult as follows:

a—laziness and idleness. Laziness is that you don't *want* to work; idleness is that you *can't*, for a while.
b—evolution and revolution. Evolution is making things from the beginning; revolution is changing them.
c—poverty and misery. Poverty is when you don't have anything; misery is how you feel when someone insults you.
d—character and reputation. Character is what he *really* is; reputation is what they *think* he is. . . .

During the examination he showed neither embarrassment nor any tendency to "show off." He was alert, interested, and gave his attention strictly to the business in hand. He always knew when he had failed on a test, and gave up with great reluctance. For example, he was unable to solve the problems under XVIII, 6, in the time allotted; but he carried these data away in his head, and held to them tenaciously till he had solved the problems. In several instances after he had given his reply he recast it in better form. . . .

Social Habits, Tastes, etc.

E does not care to play, and would never do so unless forced. He is very impersonal and agreeable in his attitude toward other children. His chief diversion is reading and his favorite book at the age of 8 is *Ivanhoe*. He has no hobbies at this age. In the spring of 1916, after careful and thoughtful preparation, he was confirmed in the Episcopal church. His desire is to be a clergyman and to become a missionary. When asked what he would consider the most fun in life, he replied, "To have statistics of my imaginary country." This country is on Venus. It is inhabited by people and has a navy like ours. *E* does not volunteer much information about his interests. All these items had to be elicited by questioning. . . .

Later Scholastic Records

In the spring of 1917 *E* finished the sixth, seventh, eighth, and ninth grade work at the Horace Mann School, New York City. He was then just 9 years old. Thereafter he attended the Friends Seminary, New York City, and was graduated from the high school there in the spring of 1920, with an excellent record and excess credits, at the age of 11 years 10 months.

. . . *E* expressed a desire to attend Columbia and received permission to take the mental tests with the applicants of 1920. He was admitted to Columbia

College with the freshmen of 1920, with 14 points of advance credit toward a B.A. degree. . . .

Extracurricular Activities

E was of course a conspicuous freshman because of his extreme youth, and he was hazed by the sophomores for refusing to wear a prescribed necktie. One of the New York newspapers commented on his conduct under hazing as follows:

> He has demonstrated that he is nevertheless a regular fellow. He did it first by bringing about a conflict in which he himself was the much buffeted prize of battle, and then by glorying in his bruises instead of making them the basis of a grievance. He is a good sport as well as a good scholar, and being both he ought to go far.

E also participated in the class play, given in 1921, humorously consenting to impersonate himself. . . .

Eventual Scholastic Records

In June, 1923, *E* was graduated from Columbia College, with the degree of B.A. He took general honors, Phi Beta Kappa honors, and the English Seminary Prize, awarded by the Society for Promoting Religion and Learning "for the best essay in sermon form on an assigned topic." He was within eleven days of his fifteenth birthday when he was graduated. He was elected to Phi Beta Kappa at the age of 14 years, probably the youngest person ever elected to that organization.

E was graduated with excess credit (8 points) toward the M.A. degree. This degree was awarded him in June, 1924, when he was not quite 16 years of age, more than enough work for it having been accomplished. He was matriculated for the Ph.D. degree before he was 16 years old, and by the age of 18 years 9 months had practically finished all the requirements for that degree except completing the dissertation. The dissertation topic had been then approved, in the field of history, and *E* was at work on the material.

In October, 1926 (aged 18 years 4 months), *E* entered upon his professional studies for the ministry in the theological seminary of his choice. Since the age of 15 he had done special work at the seminary. He had read prayers in one of the city churches as a lay reader since the age of 16 and was at this time a candidate for ordination as deacon, but this ordination could not take place before the twenty-first birthday. . . .

Researches of *E*

When *E* was 10 years old he made an original contribution in connection with the Pentateuch, and was made a member of The Oriental Society of Research in Jerusalem.

At 13 years of age *E* was first admitted to the Bodleian Library, at Oxford, for purposes of research.

In 1923 *E* presented his M.A. essay—"Appolonius, Diocetes of Egypt"—which pertains to Egyptian history of the third century B.C. and is on file in the Library of Columbia University.

E has also done research (1924–1925) on the order of Pliny's letters; on Irish constitutional history (1924–1925); and was in 1926 and 1927 reading Greek papyri.

The subject of his dissertation for the Ph.D. was reported as "Feudal Estates in Byzantine Egypt." (Hollingworth, 1942, pp. 134–156)

E was ordained at age twenty-one, completed the Ph.D. at twenty-two, and married several years later. He has not become eminent, as Mill did. But Leta Hollingworth's early IQ reading of 187 proved reliable, and she said of *E* that his tested ability put him in a position "occupied by but one child in more than a million . . . as far removed from the average, in the direction of superiority, as an idiot stands removed in the direction of inferiority" (pp. 141–42).

THREE GIFTED BOYS IN A PRIVATE SCHOOL

Another psychologist, Dr. Gertrude Hildreth, made a longitudinal report of three gifted boys attending the Lincoln School of Teachers College, Columbia University, and a fourth boy of average ability but comparable background attending the same school. The three gifted boys were referred to as *A, B,* and *C;* the average boy as *D.* Hildreth wrote of her investigation in a 1954 article excerpted below and later in her book entitled *Introduction to the Gifted* (1966).

> . . . The four boys came from homes of similar economic and social status. The parents of all four children, both fathers and mothers, were professional people, doctors, musicians, teachers, and clergymen being represented among them; all were college and university graduates. Each of the four mothers had achieved professional status in her own right, and during the years of the study they were engaged in their professions. All the parents were native born except *A*'s father, who had a European background. Due to his father's foreign background and because of having lived abroad in early childhood, *A* was bilingual, but the other children knew and used only English. *D* developed left-handedness at an early age, but the other three boys were consistently right-handed from their early school years. *A* was an only child, *B* had an older brother, *C,* an older brother and younger sister, *D,* an older sister. . . .
>
> The Stanford-Binet test . . . was administered to each boy several times . . . . The resulting IQs . . . are shown graphically [:] . . .

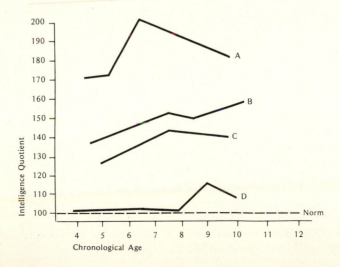

When the boys were about nine-and-a-half years old they were given a series of standardized manual dexterity tests by the originator of the test series, Dr. Marie Van der Lugt, a psychologist from Rotterdam, Holland, who was at that time demonstrating the tests in the United States. . . .

In commenting on the results, Dr. Van der Lugt observed that A made the highest rating on these manual dexterity tests of all the seven-year-olds she had ever examined here or abroad.

The impression is widespread that gifted children are superior in verbal reasoning and symbolical learning but comparatively backward in manual dexterity. The contrary proved to be the case with these gifted children, all of whom showed good or superior ability in manual skills, who proved to be well above average in dealing with concrete situations, and in creating things with their hands. Even in kindergarten A showed superiority in arts and crafts. A boat he made and painted bright pink and blue was placed on display in the school exhibit cases. . . .

A was the most precocious of the three gifted boys in literary productivity, for he began very early telling stories which his mother jotted down; and as soon as he himself gained sufficient spelling and writing skill (between the age of five and six) he began to record ideas for himself. The other boys were less advanced in story telling and writing, but as they progressed through the elementary grades all did some writing as class exercises, for the school paper, or as a recreational activity. . . .

The four boys were decidedly different in personal characteristics, temperament, and intellectual qualities. Each has his own idiosyncrasies and personal problems of adjustment. The following brief sketches are based upon voluminous records kept for each child.

Characteristics of A

Teachers quickly discovered that A was a bright child, full of vitality, enthusiastic, humorous and playful, always doing things with vim and gusto. The other children respected his intelligence and admired his vast abilities. He proved to be a leader in dramatic play, with a head full of fertile ideas and language expression equal to any occasion. With adults he was thoroughly at ease. . . .

A proved to have an amiable disposition, to be friendly toward other children, but he was not able to plan or work with them very well because he was always so far ahead of the others in his grasp of a situation. . . .

A enjoyed "clowning" and amusing people. He tended to lampoon other children who were slow and clumsy. When he was five he dubbed his awkward partner in folk dancing "Mr. Hippopotamus." Although the children enjoyed his sense of humor, they resented the tricks he was forever playing on them and the way he used his cleverness to wriggle out of difficult situations when he was caught. . . .

Very early he tended to dominate any situation, shoving others aside in dictatorial fashion saying, "You can't do that," or laying down the law to his classmates. At the age of eight he was described as dictatorial, insistent on having his own way, inclined to precipitate a fight when controversy arose. His high shrill voice frequently had a note of irritation as he tried to argue his side of the case, and he was not always inclined to take the blame when he should.

One day when he irritated the children by being too bossy, they gave him the "Heil Hitler" salute and dubbed him "Adolf Mussolini." Later he learned to be more diplomatic in handling his associates. . . .

Teachers confessed that they were baffled to know what to do for a child with a mind so mature. They would say with a note of despair: "He knows all the work we're having, yet he is so young and even immature in some respects." When the boy was nearing 11 teachers observed that he was a curious mixture of keen intellect and infantile emotional reactions. They recognized that this boy needed a more challenging program, but they were at a loss as to how to provide for a child so extremely gifted. Teachers recognized that this boy offered a challenge that even the best of them were unable to meet in regular school classes even when most of the children were rapid learners. Acceleration in grade placement did not take care of this remarkable boy's need for advanced school work.

Characteristics of B

At an early age B showed ability to make adjustments easily, to accept suggestions from the teacher, to be responsible in following routines, and dependable in carrying out instructions. He was exceedingly agile and nimble in his movements, able to work with high concentration of attention, tending to continue on a job until it was completed. He worked with purpose and planning, showed evidences of leadership, and found a place for himself in a group of like-age children with little effort. He proved to be at ease with adults, companionable in the family circle. During the elementary school years he appeared to have more ability than he actually put to use. He tended to be a gay, happy youngster, inclined to laugh easily. As he developed, his leadership traits stood out more and more. He was decisive as he went about his affairs with a serious purpose, but his face easily lighted up over some joke or nonsense. His strong traits were his tolerance of others and definite standards of right and wrong, his indignation at anything that was not fair. He proved to be well-liked and respected by everyone. B often showed more interest in helping other children than in working on his own projects, and enjoyed helping his classmates out of their difficulties. He tended to be a well-balanced child, popular with the group.

B showed leadership qualities in his ability to organize and to plan well, to lead in some activity without appearing to dominate, and he was always reasonable in letting others take turns in leading. He showed an early interest in ethics and religion which grew out of hearing Bible stories read to him by his mother.

By the age of eight B had become quiet and solemn, tending to be inconspicuous in the group and not inclined to volunteer to act or speak. Although the other children liked having him as a friend, they commented, "He concentrates too much, he's too quiet." "When he gets angry he walks away to get rid of it. He's a good sport and not cranky."

By the age of nine he had become somewhat dogmatic and was inclined to make blunt direct comments to other children, but he was still considered a "regular fellow," fitting easily into the group. To the end of the fifth grade when B's family moved away, the boy continued to be a leader and an outstanding contributor to class projects.

Characteristics of C

From the age of five when teachers first began to make reports, C was described as an intelligent, good-looking, well-balanced, friendly child. He was inclined to be rather bossy toward other children, but to show maturity in taking responsibility and in thinking out the right course of action. He proved to be well-liked by both children and adults. His whole expression radiated happiness for he wore a smile most of the time, and was usually chatting with someone in his enthusiasm over work or play. He greeted teachers in a friendly way. Sometimes he tended to question the reason for some request made of him, but accepted the explanation with a good spirit. He worked at things with high enthusiasm and a fine power of perseverance. He enjoyed praise for good accomplishment, but never showed a tendency toward selfish rivalry. His fondness for one little girl in the class, first shown in kindergarten, continued throughout the school years.

C was described as having an alert, happy, sensitive face with eyes that glowed with friendliness and humor. He proved to be one of the most naturally friendly children with boys, girls, and adults that his teachers had ever seen; and his joy in life was unbounding. At times he was inclined to go to greater lengths in hilarity and fun than was helpful, but he responded well to quieting down. As he matured he was sought after by the girls and greeted eagerly by the boys because of his sunny, happy disposition, gay, charming manner, his good looks and quick responsiveness. He always caught the humor in any situation. He proved to be fair-minded and tolerant, able to stick to a task with no diminution in interest, showing in this respect unusual maturity for his years. However, his great friendliness and many interests tended to make him more popular than was sometimes good for him, for he was inclined to fool around, to be distracted by all the attention he received, and to waste his time. The boy was creative and original, stimulating others in his enthusiasm for art, woodwork, writing stories, and the like.

C's personal attractiveness made him so popular that the group tended to elect him for responsibility on major committees. All these responsibilities he took very seriously. He was unanimously re-elected by his class as a school council member for a second term when he was in the sixth grade. The children also chose him to play the leading part of the handsome prince in the class play. He proved in emergency situations to be tactful, quick, and resourceful. He was natural in his manner, genuine, and affectionate. He was generous and sincere in praising others for accomplishing a good job.

The findings for the three gifted boys suggest that some degree of relationship exists between the extent of deviation from the average in mental development and difficulties in adjustment. Boy A's extreme degree of mental deviation tended to remove him too far from others of his age to insure the best personal relations.

Characteristics of D

Early reports were made of D's behavior by his nursery school teacher when he was three years old. . . . In contrast with the other children in the group, who tended to be precocious, D proved to be little aware of his environment, and to play alone, manipulating materials in a monotonous way, accompanying his play with noisy vocalizations. The teacher noted his difficulties in readjusting after an absence and his solitariness which made him seem strange compared with the others. He was little inclined to join other children in group play, showed unfriendly behavior toward other children, disregarded or gave negative reactions toward the teacher's suggestions. . . .

At the age of seven some of these earlier tendencies still persisted. D tended to stand off, surveying the other children instead of joining them in play. He was inclined to disrupt their play by grabbing blocks and running off with them. The boy seldom paid attention to group instructions, but had to be told everything over again individually. Often he resented the children's avoidance of him and would come to the teacher with complaints about them. He was slow in taking up any new activity and showed a lack of skill in using materials.

Toward the close of the second grade, *D* had improved in social adjustments, he seemed happier and was pleased to be included more frequently by the other children. About this time teachers became more concerned about the boy's slow progress in reading and recommended remedial work which was carried on regularly the following year.

By the age of eight *D* had become more active and happy in school, but he continued to be slow and deliberate in his movements. He ceased to be an onlooker, becoming cooperative and friendly with other children. There was unfriendly rivalry shown between *D* and another boy in the group who, like *D,* was large and strong for his age. Though the boy's sister frequently showed impatience with his slowness, the two children were fond of each other and *D* was inclined to brag about the things his sister could do. *D* responded well to praise and teachers encouraged his efforts as much as possible by commending him before the group. He tended to become antagonistic when criticized by the other children.

Because of his prowess in sports, *D* gained the admiration of the children and assumed some degree of leadership. The children had affectionate regard for him although they never left off criticizing him. He was inclined to become sullen and discouraged when appreciation was withheld.

Sympathetic and understanding teachers did much for the boy during the time he was in the middle grades in their effort to draw out and develop his abilities. During his last year in the school when he was nine he did good work, taking a prominent part in a class play.

During this year teachers noted that *D* continued to be slow and lethargic, not as alert as the rest of the children, but trustworthy and dependable. His teachers observed that intellectually he showed less promise than the rest of the group, his memory for facts was relatively poor, and his reasoning less effective.

Both teachers and parents agreed that *D* would probably get along better in a school enrolling children with learning abilities more nearly comparable to his own, where the pace in learning would not be so swift as in a school enrolling brighter than average children.

From these individual reports it is apparent that among children in the gifted category wide variations in personal traits are to be expected. These three gifted boys did not show equally well-rounded development; furthermore they showed differences in the effectiveness with which they used their intelligence. *B* and *C* showed better all-round development than *A*, and both *B* and *C* made better social adjustments in relation to other children than *A*. *C* was the best liked and most socially adept of the three gifted boys. *B* appeared to make more effective use of his high mental ability than *A*, for he could meet practical situations more competently. *A*'s extreme degree of intellectual deviation placed him too far above other children in his school group (average IQ 120) to achieve a high degree of popularity with them. Obviously, gifted children have their own adjustment problems. *D*'s slowness was a definite handicap to the achievement of satisfactory adjustments in his association with children who, on the whole, were considerably brighter than himself.

There were differences in the children's home backgrounds that accounted for the variations shown by these children in character and personal development. *C*'s congenial home environment with understanding parents and a brother and sister contributed greatly to his happy, wholesome development. The fact that *A* was an only child who had little association with other children outside of school must be taken into account in evaluating his personality. His attachment to his parents was so strong that he became more accustomed to dealing with adults than with children. His mother, a highly intellectual woman, maintained closer contacts with her boy and gave him more direct teaching than the other mothers. *B*'s parents, both intellectual persons, were inclined to take their task of child raising very seriously. *B*'s older brother no doubt contributed much to his social adjustments, for there were times when it seemed that otherwise *B* might have become self-centered and intellectually isolated from other children. *D*'s home life was complex. Responsibility for his care was assumed much of the time by persons other than his parents. (Hildreth, 1954, pp. 240-61)

SPECIAL TALENTS: SCIENCE AND AESTHETICS

Very bright children, whose facile minds can learn virtually anything well, often concentrate rather soon upon one field. Past child prodigies such as Gauss, the mathematician, and Mozart, the musician and composer, exemplify early accomplishment in special areas. Here we shall present biographical sketches of three individuals in the twentieth century who not only have shown early and remarkable talents in science, music, and mathematics, but also have developed wide-ranging interests and abilities in other fields.

J. Robert Oppenheimer, Student and Physicist

Consider J. Robert Oppenheimer (1904–1967), the theoretical physicist. Not long after World War II, the American news magazine, *Time,* made him the subject of a cover story that described his work on the development of the atomic bomb and his subsequent appointment as Director of the Institute for Advanced Study at Princeton. In the article, Oppenheimer reminisced about his growing fascination from the age of five with the world of science. Over the years he made serious forays into other domains, from Sanskrit and archaeology to Dante and ethics, but physics was his enduring passion.

> . . . His father was a bluff, warmhearted German-Jewish immigrant who had achieved his principal ambition—to become an American. Julius Oppenheimer had also made a very considerable success as a Manhattan textile importer: the Oppenheimers had a country house at Islip, N.Y., a sunny, nine-room apartment on Riverside Drive with three Van Gogh originals hanging in the living room. Julius doted on his son, took him to Europe four times and asked only that the boy be "a decent character."
>
> His mother was kind in a very strict way and every inch a lady. In the Oppenheimer household, it was possible to think something rude, harsh or improper, but never possible to say it. "My life as a child," Robert recalls, "did not prepare me in any way for the fact that there are cruel and bitter things." He remembers himself unfondly as "an unctuous, repulsively good little boy." The trouble, he thinks, was that his home offered him "no normal, healthy way to be a bastard."
>
> School was the same. Manhattan's Ethical Culture Schools tried to find a moral equivalent for religion (credo: "Deed, not Creed") and went in for the

production of quiz kids. By the time he graduated, Robert could read Caesar, Virgil, and Horace without a Latin dictionary, had read Plato and Homer in the Greek, composed sonnets in French, and tackled treatises on polarized light.

So long as schoolboy conversations were intellectual Robert got along fine, a classmate remembers, but surrounded by small talk, Robert sat morose, "exactly as though he weren't getting enough to eat or drink." The boy told his favorite English teacher, Herbert Winslow Smith: "I'm the loneliest man in the world."

His interest in science had been kindled by accident: at five, visiting his grandfather in Germany, Robert got a little box of minerals as a gift. In time, a collection of rocks from many countries filled the Oppenheimer hallway.

It was Augustus Klock, a cheerful little Ethical teacher, who first introduced Robert to a laboratory. Klock wore Herbert Hoover collars, had a fund of jokes and a communicable delight in chemistry and physics. Julius Oppenheimer—who had begun to consider his son as a kind of public trust—arranged for Klock to give Robert a special, intensive summer course in chemistry. They brought their lunches to the laboratory. While Klock brewed strong tea in beakers over a Bunsen burner, Robert turned out "a bushel of work" that never failed to rate the coveted Klock rubber stamp: "OK-AK." In six weeks, Robert completed a year's course. Says Klock: "He was so brilliant that no teacher would have been skillful enough to prevent him from getting an education." Robert got his introduction to the atomic theory ("A very exciting experience . . . beautiful, wonderful regularities!"). . . .

Then came Harvard, "the most exciting time I've ever had in my life. It was like the Goths coming into Rome." Oppenheimer rampaged through the Widener Library stacks: he read Dante in Italian, got a "working knowledge" of French literature, dipped into Chinese, philosophy, mathematics. In his third year, he took six courses and attended four more (normal quota: five). He liked exams—"the definiteness and excitement"—and got A's. One Oppenheimer remark is a Harvard legend: "It was so hot today the only thing I could do all afternoon was lie on my bed and read Jeans's *Dynamical Theory of Gases.*"

At Harvard, Oppenheimer sought out and apprenticed himself to two great teachers: Physicist Percy Williams Bridgman and the late Philosopher Alfred North Whitehead. He had already made an important discovery: the best way to learn is to find the right person to learn from.

Gruff, honest Bridgman assigned Robert to a project involving a copper-nickel alloy. Oppenheimer built a furnace, made his alloy, completed the study with sufficient precision for Bridgman to publish the findings. Says Bridgman: "A very intelligent student. He knew enough to ask questions." After hours, at the Bridgman home, the conversation ranged far and wide, giving Oppenheimer chances to display his often irritating erudition. Once Bridgman identified a picture as a temple at Segesta, Sicily, built about 400 B.C. Young Oppenheimer quickly set his professor straight: "I judge from the capitals on the columns that it was built about 50 years earlier."

In those days he wrote poems and stories ("an attempt to make peace with the world"), wore his hair long, liked to debate hours with highbrow friends, and took solitary walks. Says Oppenheimer, who discusses his own life as dispassionately as he does Archimedes' Law: "My feeling about myself was always one of extreme discontent. I had very little sensitiveness to human beings, very little humility before the realities of this world." He was, in fact, an intellectual snob.

He graduated *summa cum laude* in three years. . . .

Robert sailed for England and another apprenticeship, this time under Lord Rutherford and Sir J. J. Thomson at Cambridge University. Before he left, Bridgman told him: "You cannot be satisfied with just measuring up with other people. You can consider yourself a failure unless you stand out in front." . . .

At Cambridge, he was "a complete failure in the lab" but a success at theory: "Quantum mechanics had just begun to come into existence. It was a very exciting time in physics. Anyone could just get in there and have fun." . . .

But without the friendships he had painfully made at Harvard, Oppenheimer was soon deep in depression and doubt. He convinced himself that he could no longer postpone "the problem of growing up." He read Dostoevsky, Proust, and Aquinas and explored the defects in his own character. At Christmas time, walking by the shore near Cancale in Brittany, "I was on the point of bumping myself off. This was chronic." He came out of this period of self-examination, he now feels, "much kinder and more tolerant—able to form satisfactory, sensible attachments."

Max Born invited him to Göttingen, where he earned his Ph.D. (at 23) three weeks after enrolling. Oppenheimer's Ph.D. thesis was a brilliant paper on quantum mechanics: *Zur Quantentheorie kontinuierlicher Spektren.* After the oral exam, a colleague asked Physicist James Franck (now at the University of Chicago) how it had gone with Oppenheimer. Replied Franck: "I got out of there just in time. He was beginning to ask me questions." . . .

It was Oppenheimer's good fortune that in 1928 a center of the world's ablest and most vigorous physicists was also in the west—at the California Institute of Technology . . . . At that time, by contrast, the University of California seemed to have "a hick school of science." Both wanted him: he arranged to oscillate between the two.

The newcomer's scientific standing and what admirers call his "genius look" won him an instant audience on both campuses. But the theater almost emptied after the first act. Professor Tolman wryly congratulated Oppenheimer on his first lecture: "Well, Robert, I didn't understand a damn word." He had lectured at a breakneck pace, in abstract prose punctuated by a dozen distracting mannerisms.

Oppenheimer was tolerated only because his brilliance was as evident as his impatience. (Says CalTech's Professor Charles Lauritsen: "The man was unbelievable! He always gave you the right answer before you formulated the question.") Gradually and painfully, coached by colleagues and profiting by errors, Oppenheimer learned to put a check-rein on his galloping mind, to raise his voice, and to save his sarcasms for showoffs and frauds. In time, Cal and CalTech realized that Oppenheimer (like Whitehead and Bridgman) was "a man to whom you could be an apprentice." . . .

What made him so good a teacher was that he was still a student—and always would be. In seminars he was forever reading aloud the latest letter from a top physicist friend in Denmark or England, reporting a hot tip just telephoned from Harvard, or commenting on a physical journal fresh from a Japanese press. Privy to this latest scientific gossip ("the lifeblood of physics," Oppenheimer calls it), his students felt themselves in the vanguard of advancing knowledge. . . .

At Berkeley, Oppenheimer also apprenticed himself to the late Professor Arthur Ryder, greatest Sanskrit student of his day. In the long winter evenings, he and a handful of other students visited Ryder's house to share his Sanskrit learning and his Stoic faith.

Ryder taught Oppenheimer to read the Hindu scriptures in Sanskrit, his eighth language. Oppie still reads them, for his "private delight" and sometimes for the public edification of friends (the *Bhagavad-Gita,* its worn pink cover patched with Scotch tape, occupies a place of honor in his Princeton study). He is particularly fond of one Sanskrit couplet: "Scholarship is less than sense, therefore seek intelligence." . . . (*Time Magazine,* 1948, pp. 70–72, 75)

Philippa Duke Schuyler, a Musical Prodigy

Philippa Duke Schuyler presents us with another example of precocity that embraces a wide range of intellectual and artistic activity. She first came to general public notice in a 1940 *New Yorker* profile written by Joseph Mitchell. Apart from a description of her astonishing talents and accomplishments, we are also given an intimate picture of Philippa as an exuberant nine-year-old who liked to tell riddles and eat ice cream.

Philippa Duke Schuyler is probably the best example in the city of what psychologists call a gifted child. Physically, she is nine years old. Her mental age, according to the Clinic for Gifted Children at New York University, which tests her periodically, is sixteen. She has an IQ of 185. Philippa reads Plutarch on train trips, eats steaks raw, writes poems in honor of her dolls, plays poker, and is the composer of more than sixty pieces for the piano. Most of these compositions are descriptive, with such titles as "Spanish Harlem," "Men at Work," "The Cockroach Ballet," and "At the Circus." She began composing before she was four, and has been playing the piano in public, often for money, since she was six. She has an agreement with the National Broadcasting Company by which she plays new compositions for the first time in public on a Sunday-morning broadcast called "Coast to Coast on a Bus," and she frequently plays on other radio and television programs. A Schuyler album, "Five Little Pieces," was published two years ago by her mother, and three thousand copies have been sold. This summer she played compositions by Bach, Rimsky-Korsakoff, Debussy, Schumann, and herself in Grand Rapids, Indianapolis, Cincinnati, Columbus, Youngstown, Atlantic City, and Trenton. . . .

. . . A child psychologist who examined her last winter said that she could easily do ninth-grade work, but her parents decided she shouldn't do any skipping. "She isn't in a hurry," Mrs. Schuyler told the psychologist. "Furthermore, ninth-grade children might baby her, and that wouldn't be healthy."

The Schuylers recently invited me to come and hear Philippa play. I went up one evening around eight o'clock. Mrs. Schuyler met me at the door and said that Philippa was in her own room transcribing a composition called "Caprice No. 2," which she had finished just before dinner. We went into the living room, where Mr. Schuyler, in shirtsleeves, was hunched over a desk. At his elbow was a stack of clippings about Philippa from newspapers in the cities in which she had recently played. He was pasting these in a large scrapbook. "We have nine scrapbooks full of stuff about Philippa, one for each year," he said. "She's never seen them. In fact, so far as we know, she's never seen a clipping about herself. We're afraid it might make her self-conscious. When she gets to be a young woman, we'll bring out all her scrapbooks and say, 'Here are some things you might find interesting.' " . . .

Mr. Schuyler looked up from the scrapbook. "She has radio fans all over the world, not only in Africa," he said. "On her last birthday she received six sable skins and a black pearl from Alaska, a jewel box from Japan, a scarf from Portugal, and a doll from the Virgin Islands."

While we were looking at an ebony elephant, Philippa came into the room. Mr. Schuyler unobtrusively closed the scrapbook and put it in a drawer of the desk. Then he introduced me to Philippa. She shook hands, not awkwardly, as most children do, but with assurance. She is a graceful child, slender, erect, and exquisitely boned. Her face is oval, and she has serious black eyes, black curls, and perfect teeth. Her skin is light brown.

"Did you get through with the piece?" her mother asked her.

"Oh, yes," Philippa said. "Half an hour ago. Look, Jody, do you remember that silly little riddle book I bought at the newsstand in the station at Cincinnati and never got a chance to look at?"

"Yes, I remember."

"Well, I've just been looking through it, and some of the riddles are funny. May I ask one, please?"

Mrs. Schuyler nodded, and Philippa asked, "What has four wheels and flies?"

We were silent a minute, and then Philippa said impatiently, "Give up, please, so I can tell you."

"We give up," Mrs. Schuyler said.

"A garbage wagon," Philippa said.

Mr. Schuyler groaned, and Philippa looked at him and burst out laughing.

"Was it that bad, George?" she asked. "Wait until you hear some of the others."

"Not now, Philippa," Mrs. Schuyler said, rather hastily. "Instead, maybe you'd like to play for us in your room."

"I'd like to very much," Philippa said.

. . . On top of Philippa's piano there was a Modern Library giant edition of Plutarch, a peach kernel, a mystery novel called "The Corpse with the Floating Foot," a copy of the New York *Post* opened to the comic-strip page, a teacup half full of raw green peas, a train made of adhesive-tape spools and cardboard, a Stravinsky sonata, a pack of playing cards, a photograph of Lily Pons clipped from a magazine, and an uninflated balloon. . . . I took one of the chairs and Philippa sat on the piano bench. Left alone with her, I felt ill at ease. I didn't know how to go about making small talk with a gifted child.

. . . I asked her if she had been reading the Plutarch on the piano.

"Yes," she said. "I've read most of it. I got it to read on trains."

"Don't you find it rather dry?"

"Not at all. I like biography. I particularly like the sections called the comparisons. Best of all I liked Theseus and Romulus, and Solon and Poplicola. Plutarch is anything but dry. I'm very interested in the Romans. I want to get 'The Decline and Fall' next. It's in the Modern Library, too."

"What are some other books you like?"

Philippa laughed. "Lately I've been reading a Sherlock Holmes omnibus and some mystery books by Ellery Queen."

"What book do you like best of all?"

"Oh, that's almost impossible to answer. You can't just pick out one book and say you like it better than all others. I bet you can't."

"I certainly can," I said. I was not bothered any longer by the difference in our ages, and had completely got over feeling ill at ease.

"What book?"

"Mark Twain's 'Life on the Mississippi,' " I said.

"Oh, I like Mark Twain," Philippa said, clapping her hands excitedly. "I like him very much. I guess you're right. I *can* say that there's one book I like best of all. That's the 'Arabian Nights.' George has an eight-volume set. It's an unexpurgated edition. I read it first when I was three, and at least four times since. I based my longest composition on it. I called it 'Arabian Nights Suite.' Oh, the stories in that book are absolutely wonderful!" She laughed. "Goodness!" she said. "I didn't mean to get so"—she paused and appeared to be searching for a word—"impassioned." . . .

. . . She turned to me, curtsied, and said, "Think about cockroaches while I'm playing this piece. It's 'The Cockroach Ballet.' This is the story: Some cockroaches are feasting on a kitchen floor. A human comes in and kills some of them. He thinks he has killed them all. But after he leaves, one little cockroach peeps out, then another, and another. They dance a sad little dance for their dead comrades. But they aren't very sad because they know that cockroaches will go on forever and ever. Unfortunately."

Mrs. Schuyler laughed. "Philippa took that piece to Mother Stevens at Sacred Heart the afternoon she wrote it," she said. "Mother Stevens is head of the music department. She asked Philippa why she didn't write about angels instead of cockroaches. 'But dear Mother,' Philippa said, 'I've never seen an angel, but I've seen many cockroaches.' "

Philippa curtsied again, sat down at the piano, and began playing. . . .

. . . After that came the "Caprice" she had finished that day. Then she played some pieces by other composers. They included Rimsky-Korsakoff's "Flight of the Bumble Bee" and Johann Sebastian Bach's "Two Part Invention No. 1." After she had played for at least half an hour without any sign of weariness, she said, "I'll play just one more, one I composed a long time ago, when I was four years old. It's 'The Goldfish.' A little goldfish thinks the sky is water. He tries to jump into it, only to fall upon the floor and die." . . .

We said good night to Philippa. Mrs. Schuyler went into the kitchen and Mr. Schuyler and I went into the living room. I asked him how many hours a day Philippa studies. He said that during school months she gets up at seven-thirty, has a bath and breakfast, and starts practicing on the piano at eight. She practices for two hours. Then for half an hour she plays anything she likes. At ten-thirty her music supervisor arrives. The supervisor, a young piano teacher named Pauline Apanowitz, is with her an hour and a half. Shortly before one, Philippa walks to Sacred Heart, eating green peas on the way. She spends two afternoon hours a day at the convent, attending history, geography, and English classes. She misses arithmetic, spelling, and reading, which are morning classes. However, her examination grades are always good in the subjects she skips. She is, of course, an honor student. "There wouldn't be much point in Philippa going to a spelling class," Mr. Schuyler said. "When she was twenty-nine months old she could spell five hundred and fifty words. She has an enormous vocabulary. She likes jawbreakers. At four, she discovered the scientific word for silicosis, which is pneumonoultramicroscopicsilicovolcanoniosis, and she spelled it morning and night. It fascinated her. We certainly got tired of that word." Once a week, Mr. Schuyler said, she goes to Antonia Brico's studio for lessons in score-reading and conducting; William Harms, an assistant of Josef Hofmann, also gives her a weekly piano lesson. Most afternoons she spends an hour in the convent playground; rope-skipping is her favorite exercise. . . .

Mrs. Schuyler came into the room, bringing several small books. "When Philippa was very little I kept a careful account of the stories and poems she wrote, the words she invented, the questions she asked, and such things," she said. "I wrote them down in the form of letters to her, letters for her to read when she becomes a young woman. The people at the gifted-child clinic saw the books and had the notations transcribed for their files. Perhaps you'd like to look through some of the books."

I opened one. . . . In it I found a poem Philippa wrote when she was five. She wrote it on Easter morning while sitting in the bathtub:

The sun is lifting his lid.
The sun is leaving his crib.
The sun is a waking baby
Who will bring the Spring maybe
Thump, thump, thump! out of the earth.

The poem was followed by this notation:

Tonight a red light flashed to green while we were walking across Fifth Avenue. The automobiles were whizzing by us. Suddenly you looked up and said, "Jody, will you please name for me all the diseases in the world?"

"Philippa must be difficult to deal with at times," I said.

"She is indeed," Mrs. Schuyler said. "People often tell me, 'You must not push her!' Their sympathy is misplaced. If there's any pushing to be done, she does it. We make it a rule to answer all her questions as simply and frankly as possible. If we ever answer the same question two ways we have trouble. Once, because I was dead tired, I refused to answer one of her questions. She kept on asking it. I kept account, and found that she asked it thirty-four times one way and six times another way." . . . (Mitchell, 1940, pp. 28–32)

This girl, who had charming nine-year-old interests alongside much more advanced concerns, went on to a dual creative career, as concert pianist and newspaper reporter. Her life came to an untimely, tragic end in 1967 in Vietnam. She had been giving concerts, mainly in schools and hospitals, and sending reports to a sponsoring newspaper back home. The helicopter in which she was traveling was shot down at Da Nang, and she was among those who died.

Lisa Skarp, a Precocious Mathematics Student

Since the early 1970s, Professor Julian Stanley and his colleagues at The Johns Hopkins University have been studying young pupils who show unusual aptitude for mathematics. Their project, the Study of Mathematically Precocious Youth (SMPY), combines thorough research into the early development of mathematical ability with imaginative designs for accelerated instruction.

The ablest girl they have discovered is Lisa Skarp,* who came to their notice when she was twelve years old and in the seventh grade. During succeeding years, the SMPY staff watched her carefully, suggesting appro-

---

*The name Lisa Skarp is a pseudonym. The brief biography given here was written by the author, based on files supplied by Professor Stanley. Ms. Skarp approved the use of these files, and she read, corrected, and finally approved the text used here.

priate mathematics classes and offering personal guidance. After eleventh grade—by which time she had earned a high-school diploma—Lisa entered a leading university to major in mathematics. She was of particular interest to the SMPY people because they were unable to find as many girls as boys with high aptitude for mathematics.

Lisa and her two sisters grew up in Baltimore and attended public schools there. Her father, a tax attorney, and her mother, a social worker and psychotherapist, had from the beginning taken a serious interest in their children's education. Lisa was a successful pupil from the time she started school, but she began to show a strong interest in mathematics in the second grade. "I was hooked on going to M.I.T. (my neighbor, a math 'genius,' went there). In fact, I even sent for a catalog" (Skarp, 1978). Throughout elementary school, Lisa ranked near the top among children her own age on nationally administered mathematics tests. When SMPY was in its early stages, she saw a bulletin about the program, applied, and was accepted.

One of the important features of SMPY is its close attention to the particular pattern of mathematical and other abilities demonstrated by each of its participating pupils. In order to construct the most appropriate programs, Stanley and his group try to find out as much as they can about their pupils' aptitudes, attainment, interests, motives, and general background. For example, when Lisa entered the program, she was at the very highest level for her age in mathematics aptitude. Her score was comparable to that of the top 5 to 15 percent of college sophomores. In verbal reasoning her scores were lower but still comparable to those of the upper 25 percent of college sophomores. (This slightly lower verbal score alerted the SMPY staff to the possibility of a certain bias in Lisa's abilities toward applied rather than pure mathematics. As we shall see, Lisa did in fact eventually choose to concentrate on applied mathematics.) She had congruent scores on tests of other domains: she could perceive three-dimensional patterns as well as some engineering students in college, her values were attuned to theoretical questions, and she had strong interests in research and investigative problems. On a stiff test of quantitative ability, she showed the capacity to reason well—at the average level of graduate students in education. In a letter interpreting the battery of tests she had taken, the SMPY staff wrote that "clearly you are oriented most strongly toward the theoretical—the search for truth, correctness . . . scientific or philosophical understanding."

The staff also asked Lisa about her personal interests and ambitions. She told them that she liked bowling, collecting stamps and other objects, chess, bicycling, photography, needlepoint, and sports. She also enjoyed mathematical puzzles, and in seventh grade had made up a sophisticated one that she submitted to an expert collector of mathematical games. As for possible career choices, she expressed an interest in a number of occupations, all of which were related to mathematics and science.

In seventh grade, Lisa had studied beginning algebra on her own. So in eighth grade, she was able to enter a special class that SMPY offered on Saturday mornings. In it a gifted teacher led Lisa and fifteen other pupils through second-year algebra and trigonometry. All the pupils had scored in the top 1 percent on tests of numerical aptitude. These Saturday sessions lasted two hours, and the pace was fast. There was a lot of homework, and they were expected to work hard. Arrangements at school excused them from regular mathematics classes. Results were excellent: on standardized tests of algebra and trigonometry, Lisa's scores were in the top 2 or 3 percent as compared to other eighth-graders, and in the top 10 percent as compared to high school and college students.

Toward the end of eighth grade, the SMPY staff discussed with Lisa and her parents what course of study would be most rewarding for Lisa. The staff believed that she could go directly into tenth grade, for she was "old in grade," having been born in February. But both Lisa and her parents were strongly opposed to skipping—they wanted her to get all she could out of each year in school. So Lisa entered ninth grade and enrolled in an honors geometry course. In tenth grade she took college algebra, where she quickly became bored with the repetition of her earlier work.

About that time, SMPY had been developing an unusual Advanced Placement course in calculus, in which Lisa was invited to participate when she was in eleventh grade. The class consisted of twenty-two pupils, mostly boys, from both the eleventh and twelfth grades. They were all able in mathematics, with some spread in verbal aptitude. The class met on Saturday mornings, went at a fast clip, and demanded a lot of sustained work for successful performance. During the year, Lisa had some ups and downs. When she studied hard, she did very well; when other interests occupied her, she slipped. The staff took note of this pattern and urged her to do her best all the time. This kind of urging, in fact, was a routine SMPY strategy: in the memoranda they often sent to their pupils, they would refer to themselves as "your friendly goaders and prodders." They repeatedly specified that one aim of the calculus course was to have its pupils earn fives, the highest score on the national examination given to all Advanced Placement candidates. Lisa smarted from what seemed to be hard criticism, but she responded to the prodding and earned not only a five (and the ten dollars promised to everyone who did so) but the highest score among the SMPY pupils who took the national test.

During this year, she was invited to represent SMPY pupils at a special symposium that Stanley and his colleagues organized to honor the memory of Lewis Terman, the pioneer American investigator of the gifted. Lisa participated on a panel that discussed accelerated mathematics programs. (Terman had been a strong proponent of acceleration.) The discussions aroused great interest in the Saturday-class format and in enlisting the skills of exceptionally able teachers. Stanley, referring to the good that can come from putting gifted pupils under the care of stimulating and demanding teachers, admitted that some people would consider this "spoiling." But, he countered, "all persons good in mathematics should be spoiled that way."

Also during this year, Lisa and her family decided that, after all, she should complete requirements for the high-school diploma a year early and then go on to a university. The SMPY group was helpful. They described various universities and colleges, ensured that forms and applications and other details were attended to in due time, and wrote in Lisa's behalf (especially about the unusual features of her participation in SMPY). She applied to five first-class institutions and was accepted by most of them.

At seventeen years of age, she entered the honors college of a leading university that has a very strong mathematics program. The SMPY staff got in touch with a professor of mathematics there who had shown interest in the SMPY project and arranged for him to advise Lisa after she arrived. Her first year was successful. She made new friends and looked at herself and her future from a new perspective. Some courses were more stimulating than others, but all were generally engrossing to her. Ironically, courses in the humanities—notably one about the Great Books—appealed to her more than some of her mathematics and science courses.

More and more, she came to accept the evaluation she had been given previously—that her main strength was in applied rather than pure mathematics. Perhaps her somewhat lower verbal aptitude put her at a mild disadvantage in speculative thinking. In any case, she shaped her vocational plans accordingly: systems engineering, actuarial analysis, computer specialist. She had entered the university determined to work hard, and she had confidence in herself and her abilities. At present, she is aiming for a doctorate in a field related to mathematics.

Lisa's experience demonstrates what sustained and intelligent support can do for a person with mathematical aptitude. Contrary to many stereotyped expectations, she was not generally lonely or isolated, taking comfort only in study. She says that there were some difficult times in high school, but that they were eased by her family and friends. But the new environment at the university made a great difference in her outlook. She felt herself to be more sociable, interested in a variety of things, and aware of herself and of others. She learned to get along with adults and to cultivate friends her own age. She was particularly fortunate to have been part of a program that maintained a close interest in her. She needed time to become fully independent, and she profited from the firm support and advice of those who helped her focus her efforts. The results have been gratifying to her and to the SMPY staff who were her mentors.

COMMON DIFFICULTIES

Most of the children presented in this chapter suffered occasionally from their brightness. Let us now look at a few children for whom such problems became stubborn hurdles. In England, Mia Kellmer Pringle has been working with over a hundred children she calls "able misfits." They have quick enough minds (IQ's from 120 to 200), but they haven't performed well. They were referred to her university child study department for a variety of school problems. Specialists tried to diagnose each child's difficulty, to plan with their families and teachers a program for improvement, and to check results.

The case studies that follow describe two gifted boys whose problems in adjusting to school may be traced to the most common sources of difficulty among the exceptionally bright: parents who expect too much and parents who do not expect enough.

Simon

First we shall look at Simon, who was eleven when referred. His tested IQ was 143, but there were serious doubts about his future schooling. Excerpts from the case report give details.

The Child

A tall, thin boy who seemed unusually self-contained for his age. While he cooperated well enough during the interview, success and praise made relatively little difference to his effort and he knew when a problem was beyond him. He made few spontaneous comments and showed a curiously detached, almost aloof attitude. Subsequently it emerged that this characterised his behavior both at home and at school.

According to his own judgment he was "rather a trial to my teacher because I am bored most of the time and don't try." Though he read well, he rarely did so for pleasure but mainly for information which he needed to follow his hobby of model-making and chemical experiments. "At present I do neither at school but I am told there will at least be some science when I go to a new school in the autumn."

Even when talking about his hobbies he grew only marginally more enthusiastic and would soon have dried up, had he not been encouraged to describe them at greater length. He had no "real friends" nor did he seem to feel the lack of them: "They rather get in your way when you want to press on with an experiment."

School

Having just failed to gain entry into a grammar school, the parents proposed to send Simon to a private school, since for social reasons they rejected both secondary modern and comprehensive schools. The present headmaster felt concerned, since in his view the boy's good ability was unlikely to receive the necessary stimulation in the establishment of the parents' choice; also, he wondered why Simon should have remained so unresponsive a pupil. Though always in an A class and never "any trouble," he rarely cared enough to make an effort; even in mathematics, his favorite subject, he did the minimum. The headmaster now regretted not having insisted on psychological advice earlier, but when he had suggested it the father would not hear of it.

Family Circumstances

The father, a professor of anthropology, had rather late in life married his much younger secretary. To begin with she had accompanied him on his field trips abroad but her enthusiasm had waned quickly. Since Simon's birth she no longer went with her husband but resented the long periods she was left by herself. Not being a particularly maternal woman, she was relieved when told she was unlikely to have more children; for the same reason she rejected the idea of adopting a child which her husband had thought would be company for Simon. He had himself been an only child and had always blamed this for his inability to make friendships in later life.

Parental Attitudes

The relationship between father and son remained a distant one, partly because he was away a good deal and partly because he considered young children tediously boring. He had hoped that his love of games would later on become a shared interest, but to his disappointment Simon proved to be physically timid and without any aptitude in this direction. Neither persuasion nor shock tactics were of any avail; in fact, having been thrown into a swimming pool by his father, the boy could not go near water without becoming sick. Otherwise, Simon conformed fairly readily to the strict discipline on which his father insisted but this, too, displeased the father as "showing a lack of spunk."

The mother had become a very dissatisfied woman. Once the glamor of marrying her boss and a don, had worn off, she was bored and lonely since she had found university wives to be standoffish and had felt obliged to discontinue her friendships with her previous office friends. Her disappointment in having a boy rather than a girl was made worse by his being a "very uncuddly baby." Eventually she acquired two toy poodles on which she lavished a great deal of time and affection. Her handling of Simon was a mixture of indulgence, inconsistency and baffled defeat: "He obeys his father instantly but I can never be sure how he'll behave; often he is as good as gold and you'd hardly know he is in the house; then he'll suddenly go all stubborn and there is nothing I can do about it."

To keep him occupied, Simon had always been showered with toys, but rarely had either parent played with him. When he developed his interest in model-making and in chemical experiments, the garden shed was fitted up with a work bench and from then on "he would potter about happily for hours."

The father's hope for an intellectual son whose guide and mentor he could become, had been dashed by what he called Simon's "practical, largely manipulative interests." These meant nothing to the father, a highly articulate, literate man, to whom a lack of verbal skills was a sure sign of limited intellectual ability. To the mother, Simon's lack of academic success meant that she felt again inferior in comparison with the many "university wives" who could boast one or more outstandingly able children. On the other hand, both parents spoke approvingly of Simon's self-sufficient, detached attitude and his capacity to keep himself amused. His lack of affection was ascribed to their "not being a demonstrative family."

Summary and Recommendations

Though home for Simon was an emotionally barren and intellectually unstimulating place, the likelihood of bringing about any real change within a reasonable time seemed remote: the father's age (58) and frequent absence from home, and the mother's relative lack of intelligence and maternal warmth, made modifying their attitudes and giving them some insight into the boy's needs a task hardly worth attempting.

Instead, the question of boarding school was explored and when Simon seemed quite keen on the idea, it was put to the parents. The school which was suggested catered primarily for normal children but was willing to accept a few who needed special help. It was coeducational, relatively small and organized along family lines, with married couples being responsible for groups of children. Though the atmosphere was not unduly competitive, the results achieved in art and science were quite outstanding.

After some initial hesitation—largely on grounds of finance—the parents took Simon to see the school and eventually agreed to his going there.

Subsequent Development

Simon's progress was followed for a period of seven years. Rather unexpectedly he enjoyed coming to pay a visit to our department during each of the school holidays, though gradually this tailed off to become a yearly call. The school sent reports regularly which showed that though he remained somewhat of a "lone wolf," Simon improved considerably over the years. He became very attached to his science master and to the headmaster's wife, and passed through a somewhat stormy period of being overdemanding and resentfully jealous of other pupils. During these periods of emotional crises his school work deteriorated, but during calmer times he made big strides forward. He became a good chess player, reasonably proficient at cricket and passionately fond of music.

While chess and cricket became something of a bond between father and son, the gulf between him and his mother grew steadily wider. Though he did well enough to have stood a good chance of getting into a university, Simon wanted to be economically independent at the earliest opportunity: his father was near retirement and had anyhow never let him forget that the need to pay fees had in the first place been due to his not exerting himself enough to win a free place at a grammar school. So he accepted a trainee post in the research department of a large industrial firm.

Prognosis
Reasonably good, though it looks doubtful whether he will ever use to the full his good intellectual abilities. One also wonders what kind of husband and father he will eventually make if he does not find some equilibrium between the detached self-sufficiency which he had acquired at an early age, and the jealous, overdemanding possessiveness which he developed during adolescence. (Kellmer Pringle, 1970, pp. 24–27)

Charles

Charles, also eleven when referred to Kellmer Pringle, had a tested IQ of 150 and a record of stealing and of "constantly being in trouble" at school.

The Child
An attractive, physically well-developed boy with a confident, charming manner. His reactions were quick to the point of being impulsive and many of his replies showed an imaginative and unusual mind. He made a quick, easy relationship and clearly enjoyed the opportunity to talk about himself. When he found out that I knew his school had referred him because of continuous disobedience and stealing, he seemed only momentarily taken aback. Not only did he recover quickly but he added "but do you know that they will probably expel me? This will be a record of a kind, anyhow."

School
Charles was one of the youngest boys who had succeeded in winning a place at this particular grammar school and became notorious within the first term. Previously he had attended a small private school where he had been suspected of being the ringleader behind many an escapade, but it had never been possible to prove his guilt. How hard the school tried is open to question, since it was realized that his outstanding ability and scholastic success would bring credit to the school. The only warning which had been passed on to the new school was that Charles was a "high spirited, unconventional boy."

That this was an understatement became clear within the first week. To begin with some doubt existed since he was clever in his misdeeds. When accused on suspicion, he coolly stared it out, even with the headmaster. It was many weeks before he was actually caught "in the act." By then a good deal of money had disappeared. All that was known until then was that on several occasions Charles had invited a number of boys to go into town with him instead of taking the school bus home (after giving them a treat in a cafe, he would see them all safely home by taxi); that he distributed sweets, fountain pens, and other desirable "goodies" on a lavish scale; that he began to sport an expensive waterproof, automatic watch; together with other signs of greater affluence than his home circumstances were likely to afford him.

The second galling aspect of the affair—not being able to catch him being the first—was that his school work remained excellent in a seemingly effortless, almost flaunting way. Reluctant to lose so promising a pupil the school hoped for a "quick enough psychological solution" to be able to keep him.

Family Circumstances

The parents looked old enough to be the boy's grandparents as in fact they could have been. The father, a civil service clerk, had been in the same job since his marriage and when Charles went to school the mother had taken up part-time clerical work to help with his fees. Both came from large families and had very much wanted to have children. On finding they were unable to have a family of their own, the parents decided to adopt a child. By that time they were well into their forties. They were not particularly choosey and Charles was in fact the first child they were offered. To their astonished delight they were told that he was the illegitimate son of an outstanding scientist but that nothing else about him could be revealed. In order "to give him the best of everything" they decided against further adoptions which they had previously had in mind.

Parental Attitudes

The parents, an ordinary warmhearted couple, felt a little overawed by the responsibility of bringing up what they thought of as a potential genius. They cherished him, indeed doted on him, not only because he was quite soon showing unusual promise and passed all his milestones extremely early; but also because they felt they had to make up to him for being adopted and hence deprived of all that his own parents, particularly his brilliant father, might have done for him. And so in their eyes, he could do no wrong. They dismissed the misgivings of his teachers in the private school as "old maids' imaginings" which was perhaps not unreasonable seeing they had never actually managed to prove anything against Charles. Though he was often disobedient and cheeky at home too, they excused this as being high-spirited. To some extent this was true since he reserved his most insolent behavior for his teachers. Indeed, there was a code of ethics to his misdeeds: he never stole from his parents, relatives, or friends but from those he knew to be better off than himself or those he regarded as his enemies; similarly, he was rarely cheeky to people he liked or respected but pompous and nagging teachers brought out the worst in him. Children were usually loyal to him—his charm, daring, and generosity aroused their admiration; and with his "enemies" he used a mixture of threats and bribery to good effect.

Even though the parents were shocked at what had happened, they felt convinced that there had been some miscarriage of justice or that he had been "framed" because others envied his great abilities and cleverness.

Summary and Recommendations

Charles seemed to be an almost classic case of the spoilt, indulged, and adored child of rather ineffectual, simple people whose sense of proportion had become distorted by what seemed to them a marvellous gift from heaven. They believed sincerely that there was no evil in Charles and in a sense they were right—he had grown up amoral and self-willed rather than immoral or vicious. It seemed highly unlikely that they could come to see the situation as it was and change their own handling of the boy quickly and radically enough for him to remain at home and attend his present school without further trouble. And further trouble could well mean an approved school order, were he to find himself before a Juvenile Court.

Therefore the parents were persuaded to agree to his going to a residential school for highly intelligent boys. Then in a number of preparatory talks the reasons for his being sent away were also discussed with Charles. Though he put up some resistance, saying he had learnt his lesson, one felt he half-welcomed the opportunity of help since quite spontaneously he admitted and described many of his previously undetected misdeeds.

Subsequent Developments

For several years Charles came to see us during his holidays. Despite settling well after a stormy first year, he went on each occasion through the ritual of discussing whether the time had not come for him to return home. After three years his previous school became very ready to take him back when they heard that there had been no serious incidents for some time past. However, it seemed inadvisable to take the risk of returning him, possibly too early, to an environment which was virtually unchanged. Educationally he did as well as one had hoped and eventually gained university entrance with ease.

Prognosis

Excellent academically and quite hopeful socially. (Kellmer Pringle, 1970, pp. 38–41)

Developing Tolerance

Finally, let us return to Leta Hollingworth (1942) for further examples of problems common to the gifted. She spent much of her energy urging bright children to be sensible and their teachers to be sensitive. The episodes that follow illustrate what moved her to place such emphasis on this counsel.

A lesson which many highly intelligent persons never learn as long as they live is that human beings in general are incorrigibly very different from themselves in thought, action, and desire. Many a reformer has died at the hands of a mob which he was trying to improve. The highly intelligent child must learn to suffer fools gladly—not sneeringly, not angrily, not despairingly, not weepingly—but *gladly,* if personal development is to proceed successfully in the world as it is. Failure to learn how to tolerate in a reasonable fashion the foolishness of others less gifted leads to bitterness, disillusionment, and misanthropy, which are the ruin of potential leaders.

Every day at school the opportunity presents itself to learn this lesson. Especially hard for these intelligent children to bear is the foolishness of accepted authority. For instance, our pupils found it stated in their encyclopedia that Mr. Orville Wright is dead. As is likely to be the case, a child in the group immediately identified error. "Mr. Orville Wright is as much alive as I am," declared this child. This was subsequently verified by the class as a whole. They wrote to Mr. Wright, fiercely protesting against the foolishness of the encyclopedia. They wanted to throw the false authority out at once.

The teacher discussed the incident on the basis of "glad suffering." I can't take time to describe the conversation that pivoted on this incident, but I can say that it was valuable as emotional education. The pupils still have the offending encyclopedia.

As a form of failure to suffer fools gladly, negativism may develop. The foolish teacher who hates to be corrected by a child is unsuited to these children. Too many children of IQ 170 are being taught by teachers of IQ 120. Into this important matter of the *selection of the teacher* we cannot enter, except to illustrate the difficulty from recent conversation with a ten-year-old boy of IQ 165. This boy was referred to us as a school problem: "Not interested in the school work. Very impudent. A liar." The following is a fragment of conversation with this boy:

What seems to be your *main* problem in school?
Several of them.
Name *one*.
Well, I will name the teachers. Oh, boy! It is bad enough when the *pupils* make mistakes, but when the *teachers* make mistakes, oh, boy!
Mention a few mistakes the teachers made.
For instance I was sitting in 5A and the teacher was teaching 5B. She was telling those children that the Germans discovered printing, that Gutenberg was the first discoverer of it, mind you. After a few minutes I couldn't stand it. I am not supposed to recite in that class, you see, but I got up. I said, "No; the Chinese *invented,* not discovered, printing, before the time of Gutenberg—while the Germans were still barbarians."
Then the teacher said, "Sit down. You are entirely too fresh." Later on she gave me a raking-over before the whole class. Oh, boy! What teaching!

It seemed to me that one should begin at once in this case the lesson about suffering fools gladly. So I said, "Ned, that teacher is foolish, but one of the very first things to learn in the world is to suffer fools *gladly."* The child was so filled with resentment that he heard only the word "suffer."
"Yes, that's it. That's what *I* say! Make 'em suffer. Roll a rock on 'em."
I quote this to suggest how negativistic rebels may seize on the wrong idea. Before we finished the conversation Ned was straightened out on the subject of who was to do the suffering. He agreed to do it himself.
I will cite another conversation, this time with a nine-year-old, of IQ 183.

What seems to be the *main* trouble with you at school?
The teacher can't pronounce.
Can't pronounce *what?*
Oh, lots of things. The teacher said "Magdalen College"—at Oxford, you know. I said, "In England they call it Môdlin College." The teacher wrote a note home to say I am rude and disorderly. She does not like me.

Just one more conversation, this time with an eight-year-old, of IQ 178, sent as a school problem:

What is your *main* trouble at school?
My really main trouble is *not* at school.
Where is it, then?
It is the *librarian*.
How is *that?*
Well, for instance, I go to the library to look for my books on mechanics. I am making a new way for engines to go into reverse gear. The librarian says, "Here, where are you going? You belong in the juvenile department." So I have to go where the children are all *supposed* to go. But I don't stay there long, because they don't have any real books there. Say, do you think you could get me a card to the other department? (Hollingworth, 1942, pp. 299–302)

We could go on to cite many other children, some famous, others little known. But there is no need to repeat what has already become apparent: most gifted children display early signs of a strong interest in ideas, a quick apprehension of what catches their attention, a capacity for sustained effort on many fronts, and often significant achievement in some demanding field. But in some ways, this collection of portraits is misleading, because so many of the children discussed have obviously come from well-to-do homes where education has been highly valued and have further profited from the kind of schooling that is unavailable in many communities.

Your own experience with the gifted may have led you to an entirely different conclusion about their attributes. You may, for example, have known them as unhappy individuals who suffered because they were skipped a year or two in school, who were unbearably snobbish about their talents, or who wasted their abilities in mere dabbling. Currently there is disenchantment with the psychometric methods that have so often equated "bright" or "gifted" with a certain IQ, thus diverting us from more inclusive descriptions and from other qualities of the mind, such as imagination, emotional sensitivity, and common sense.

The most immediate problem, then, is to find out how closely the collection of children in this chapter approaches a fair image of giftedness. Which traits or experiences do they share with most able children; which are their own personal property, not essential to precocity? The following chapter considers these questions by describing some systematic attempts undertaken in this century to develop an accurate description of the essential characteristics of giftedness.

2

Characteristics of the Gifted

Genius . . . means . . . the faculty of perceiving
in an unhabitual way.
William James

We have only in this century begun systematic inquiry into the characteristics of the gifted, as distinct from individual life histories of gifted persons. A major part of this inquiry has come from psychologists interested
in the scientific study of human behavior and its possible application to
social problems. Alfred Binet, a brilliant French experimenter, was one of
the earliest investigators. For years he sought a practical way to estimate
intellectual level—one that would not require prolonged observation. Because of his reputation as a psychologist, Binet was asked by the French
Minister of Public Instruction to serve on a committee to study the education of retarded children. One of the committee's tasks was to find out
how to recognize these children when they first entered school, so they
could be given the special help they would need. Binet collaborated with
a physician, Théodore Simon, on a special test of intelligence that they
published in 1905. The test attempted to measure the intellectual level of a
child by determining how many of thirty specially constructed problems
the child was able to answer correctly. With revisions in 1908 and 1911, the
Binet scales stimulated wide interest. From the start, they were used and
adapted for many purposes, including research on human intelligence and
decisions about pupil placement in schools.

Lewis Terman was primarily responsible for applying Binet's scales to
the bright rather than to the dull. He first learned of Binet as a young
undergraduate. Later, at Stanford University, he adapted Binet's scale to the
American setting, calling it the "Stanford-Binet" intelligence test. In the
early 1920s, Terman started what has become the best-known and most
comprehensive investigation we have into the characteristics of the gifted.
In a lecture he gave two years before his death, he told how he stumbled
onto his life work.

I have often been asked how I happened to become interested in mental tests and gifted children. My first introduction to the scientific problems posed by intellectual differences occurred well over a half-century ago when I was a senior in psychology at Indiana University and was asked to prepare two reports for a seminar, one on mental deficiency and one on genius. Up to that time, despite the fact that I had graduated from a normal college as a Bachelor of Pedagogy and had taught school for five years, I had never so much as heard of a mental test. The reading for those two reports opened up a new world to me, the world of Galton, Binet, and their contemporaries. The following year my M.A. thesis on leadership among children was based in part on tests used by Binet in his studies of suggestibility.

Then I entered Clark University, where I spent considerable time during the first year in reading on mental tests and precocious children. Child prodigies, I soon learned, were at that time in bad repute because of the prevailing belief that they were usually psychotic or otherwise abnormal and almost sure to burn themselves out quickly or to develop post-adolescent stupidity. "Early ripe, early rot" was a slogan frequently encountered. By the time I reached my last graduate year, I decided to find out for myself how precocious children differ from the mentally backward, and accordingly chose as my doctoral dissertation an experimental study of the intellectual processes of fourteen boys, seven of them picked as the brightest and seven as the dullest in a large city school. These subjects I put through a great variety of intelligence tests, some of them borrowed from Binet and others, many of them new. The tests were given individually and required a total of 40 or 50 hours for each subject. The experiment contributed little or nothing to science, but it contributed a lot to my future thinking. Besides "selling" me completely on the value of mental tests as a research method, it offered an ideal escape from the kinds of laboratory work which I disliked and in which I was more than ordinarily inept. . . .

However, it was not until I got to Stanford in 1910 that I was able to pick up with mental tests where I had left off at Clark University. By that time Binet's 1905 and 1908 scales had been published, and the first thing I undertook at Stanford was a tentative revision of his 1908 scale. This, after further revisions, was published in 1916. The standardization of the scale was based on tests of a thousand children whose IQs ranged from 60 to 145. The contrast in intellectual performance between the dullest and the brightest of a given age so intensified my earlier interest in the gifted that I decided to launch an ambitious study of such children at the earliest opportunity.

My dream was realized in the spring of 1921 when I obtained a generous grant from the Commonwealth Fund of New York City for the purpose of locating a thousand subjects of IQ 140 or higher. More than that number were selected by Stanford-Binet tests from the kindergarten through the eighth grade, and a group mental test given in 95 high schools provided nearly 400 additional subjects. The latter, plus those I had located before 1921, brought the number close to 1,500. The average IQ was approximately 150, and 80 were 170 or higher.

The twofold purpose of the project was, first of all, to find what traits characterize children of high IQ and, secondly, to follow them for as many years as possible to see what kind of adults they might become. . . . (Terman, 1954, pp. 222–23)

Research on the gifted in the first half of this century followed much the same path as Terman's investigation. It depended upon the IQ to indicate relative rate of development. It emphasized the sorts of behavior that the typical intelligence test covers, giving little attention to such things as imagination and motivation, which the tests do not judge. It focused largely on academic life, justifying the tests and defending their validity by demonstrating how well they predicted school success. Despite Binet's early influence, research on the gifted was heavily concentrated in the English-speaking countries. In fact, as Piaget is wont to say, concern for measuring brightness has been "the American question." In the second half of this century, as we shall see, the emphasis has switched from the measure of general intelligence, such as the IQ, to measures of more specific behavior, such as creativity.

In this chapter we shall become acquainted with Terman's findings. They are the landmark from which other and later approaches begin. We shall also look at some of the studies that have corroborated or extended Terman's. We shall then explore special talents and creativity, and some aspects of the individual that are difficult to assess in quantitative terms. Throughout the chapter it will be evident that we must remember what we saw in Chapter 1—that intellectual brightness exists at various levels of intensity. And we shall be reminded of conditions that affect giftedness, such as family background, opportunity for schooling, and the various nonintellectual sides of the personality.

INCIDENCE OF GIFTEDNESS

"Gifted," "bright," "talented"—we use different words to refer to children who offer unusual promise. They all imply a high rank. But exactly what proportion of the child population do we mean when we refer to "the highest"? Binet had thought only of successive levels of accomplishment in his tests, from dull to bright. In 1912 William Stern, a German pioneer in differential psychology, first used the term *intelligence quotient* (IQ) to tie the developmental level in Binet's tests to a child's chronological age. Terman and most others adopted this simple formula, and it has entered the language of everyday use, though not always with precision.

The IQ is the ratio between *mental age* (MA) and *chronological age* (CA), between how well a child does on the test and how long it has taken the child to reach that level. Thus, if Chris answers, say, forty questions correctly, and a score of 40 is the average for eight-year-olds, Chris is assigned a "mental age" of eight. If Chris were eight years old, then the ratio of MA to CA would be even. But he is only four. So by already reaching the level of eight-year-olds, he is classed as gifted. Arithmetically it works out this way (with the ratio multiplied by 100 in order to be rid of decimals):

$$\frac{MA}{CA} \times 100 = IQ$$

$$\frac{8}{4} \times 100 = 200$$

We may say that Chris's IQ of 200 means he is developing, according to the test, at 200 percent of the normal rate, or twice as fast. If instead his IQ were 160, he would be developing at 1.6 times (or 160 percent) the usual rate. Conversely, children who are "retarded" move more slowly than normal: IQ 40 would mean 40 percent of the normal rate.

Most surveys that use standardized intelligence tests and report IQs find that the results, from dull to bright, follow the familiar bell-shaped curve of "normal" distribution: most children are in the middle range, with fewer and fewer children located toward the extremes. The gifted, out at the high-scoring end, would theoretically show the frequencies noted in Table 1 if the curve we ordinarily use were exactly mirrored.

To the extent that people have used Stern's convenient IQ metric, they have emphasized the *rate* of children's mental development. It is still an open question whether precocity is in large or small part a response to stimulation—a question we shall take up in detail later. But it has been obvious from the earliest studies that there is some relation between IQ and home background, since surveys nearly always find that children with high scores come disproportionately from homes that have some accepted economic or cultural advantage.

James Gallagher (1959) gave representative percentages of bright pupils for what he called "average" and "superior" communities, using American data from the 1950s and earlier (see Table 2). He based the "average" and "superior" ratings on the general economic and social status of a community, much as another writer might say "blue collar" and "white collar." Note that the percentages in Gallagher's "average" column resemble those given in Table 1, except that he expressed them as ranges. Thus, where Table 1 listed 17.4 percent of children as theoretically having

---

TABLE 1   PREDICTED PERCENTAGES AND FREQUENCY OF HIGH
           INTELLIGENCE

Stanford–Binet IQ	Percentage of random school population	Approximate frequency
115+	17.4	1 in 6
120+	10.6	1 in 9
125+	5.9	1 in 17
130+	3.1	1 in 32
140+	0.6	1 in 167
150+	0.1	1 in 1,000
165+	0.003	1 in 33,300
180+	0.00003	1 in 3,330,000

(Adapted from Dunlap (1967), p. 147)

TABLE 2   APPROXIMATE PERCENTAGES OF VERY INTELLIGENT
PUPILS IN COMMUNITIES AT TWO SOCIOECONOMIC LEVELS

IQ	Percentage of pupils	
	in an average community	in a superior community
115+	16–20	45–60
120+	10–12	30–40
125+	5–7	15–20
130+	2–4	6–12
140+	5–1	2–3

Adapted from Gallagher, (1959, p. 11)

IQs of 115 and higher, Gallagher listed 16 to 20 percent. The range is useful because it reminds us that communities are not exactly alike, but vary somewhat from one to the other. Note also that, in general, the superior community has roughly three times as many gifted children as the average community. For the total number of children (those above IQ 115), the average community has up to 20 percent, the superior community up to 60 percent. At successive IQ levels, the ratio remains about three to one.

In 1963 Cyril Burt pointed out that we may have been mistaken all along in using the classic normal curve as the expected pattern for gifted children's IQs. He analyzed the data Terman had used in devising his original Stanford-Binet test and concluded that the more appropriate curve was a less familiar one, known to statisticians as the "Pearson type IV." This curve has a greater number of cases at both ends than the classic bell-shaped curve. For the gifted, Burt said, this implies about twice as many children at IQ 145 and above as the bell-shaped curve would suggest, and over twenty times as many at IQ 175 and above. Burt's interpretation makes it easier to understand why Terman and Hollingworth found so many children in the range from IQ 170 to 200 (Vernon, Adamson, & Vernon, 1977).

Thus, for various reasons, we answer the question, "How many gifted children are there?" by countering, "At what level do you mean?" The working range accepted for research and school programs is from about IQ 115 to well over IQ 150. Research has often used relatively strict definitions: Hollingworth paid primary attention to those at 180 and above, like E. School districts may offer a variety of special programs to pupils whose IQs go down to 115 or even farther. Sometimes one hears of a hierarchy, using a vocabulary from "gifted" or "genius" at the top (180 and above) down to "above average" (115 and sometimes lower). "Superior" and "bright" are other words used, often interchangeably. In this book we shall refer chiefly to the upper reaches of this hierarchy, above IQ 125 or 130. We shall mainly use the terms "gifted" and "bright," without meaning to imply a strict difference between them.

The terms "gifted" and "bright" refer to *general intelligence*, a faculty that, in its most powerful manifestations, organizes and manipulates problems in a broad range of subjects. As we shall see, intelligence also shows itself in special abilities or in very particular activities. We have met Lisa Skarp, a precocious mathematician, and Philippa Schuyler, a musical prodigy. We could also cite children who have exhibited marked artistic talent, an ability for mechanical invention, or remarkable powers of imagination. How many of these children are there?

If we want to know how many people have already produced work that shows exceptional talent, we have but to count documented cases of precocity. But if we wish to estimate how many children have some latent artistic, mechanical, or creative potential that could be stimulated, the answer becomes more elusive. One of the reasons is that definitions of imagination or aesthetic sensitivity differ. Another is that the available tests of special talents tend to be complicated, time-consuming, and unreliable. They involve asking children to judge the relative merit of pictures, or to answer a range of questions involving musical judgment, or to show on demand how imaginative they can be. The most serious difficulty with these tests has to do with determining the extent of the overlap between general intelligence and special talent or creativity. We shall discuss this problem in more detail later, but here we wish to point out that our inability to gauge this overlap makes the question of how many gifted and talented children there are a complicated one. Some of these children will have all-round abilities, some will have specific talents, some will have highly creative imaginations. But many will have them all.

If we aren't sure how separate all these mental abilities are, counting can be ambiguous. But if we want to offer help, say, in school, we should have a pretty good idea of how many children to plan for and of what kinds of abilities they possess. To be safe—that is, to catch as many individual children as we can in our net—we must find some process that is both powerful and economical. Philip Vernon, a British psychologist with rich experience, has suggested a strategy (Vernon et al., 1977). First pick children with overall IQs above a certain point, and then pick children who appear talented or creative and who also have IQs above a somewhat lower point. For example, use IQ 130 and above to find the children in the top 3 percent of those tested for general intelligence; then apply measures of specific talents to the children of IQ 120 and above. According to Vernon, by using this approach we would be able to thus assemble a dependable group falling within the top 5 percent of gifted and talented children.

TERMAN'S STUDIES

The major source of our systematic knowledge of the bright is the monumental work of Terman and his colleagues. It deserves close study. For his investigation, Terman chose a cut-off point reached by only about 1 in 200 school-age children. He sought originally 1000 pupils who had the highest IQs in a school population of a quarter million in California. To reach that many children, he set as a minimum an IQ of 140 on the original (1916) version of the Stanford-Binet test. Starting in the early 1920s, Terman followed his subjects (who came to be known affectionately as "termites") until his death in 1956. Furthermore, he arranged for his program to continue during his subjects' lives until about the year 2000. He (and after his death, his colleagues) published extensive reports (in 1930, 1947, 1959, and 1977) describing his subjects when they had reached average ages of about twenty, thirty-five, and so on. Let us look at the important details.

Aim

Terman wanted to reach a significant number of highly intelligent children; he planned to follow them to see if they would fulfill their early promise and to compare them to children of normal intelligence. Originally, he also wanted to undertake a parallel investigation of children with exceptional talents in music, art, and mechanical inventiveness. But he abandoned the second study, partly because the means to measure these talents were unreliable and—much more significantly—because he had found that nearly all the children nominated for special talent also qualified for his high-IQ group. Recently, research has returned to this problem, as attempts are being made to discover how similar creative children really are to high-IQ children. We shall go into this research in Chapter 3.

Selection

In all, Terman finally selected 1528 children: 857 males and 671 females. The ratio of males to females in elementary school was 116 to 100; in high school it was much higher: 160 to 100. Selection was strict but somewhat varied. Initial nomination was by teachers. They were asked to name the children they thought were the brightest or (because bright children were often skipped into higher grades) the youngest children in their classes. Elementary-school pupils nominated by their teachers took group intelligence tests as a further screen and, finally, the individually administered Stanford-Binet (the test that Terman and his associates had developed during the previous decade). High-school pupils nominated by their teachers were screened by group tests, chiefly the Terman Group Test (an offshoot of the Stanford-Binet). Of the 1528 total, the closest attention went to a "main experimental group" of 643 children (352 male, 291 female), who were between two and thirteen years of age when chosen.

After analysis, Terman concluded that this selection identified nearly 90 percent of all those who could have qualified as having IQs of 140 or higher. This percentage encouraged him to believe that his group was representative, that the same attempt elsewhere would have found a similar group of children. The IQs he used for selection were arbitrary, but were those he believed would aim at the top 1 percent or higher.

Information Gathered

In the beginning, Terman's assistants supplemented intelligence test scores with the following information: a long questionnaire that parents filled out about the home; a somewhat briefer one that teachers answered about schoolwork; a medical examination on over half the children; a three-hour standardized test battery covering school subjects given to 550 of the elementary-age children; standard anthropometric measures (height, weight, body proportions, etc.); an inventory of personal interests given to all who could read and write; a record of books read by 550 of the children during the preceding two months; a survey of information about and attitude toward play (to determine traits of masculinity/femininity and sociability, among other things); and a set of seven "character" inventories that gauged temptation to cheat, emotional stability, and certain related interests and attitudes. Comparable information in most of these categories was also gathered on randomly chosen children who would serve as a control group for comparing gifted and average children.

Over the next decades, Terman's staff continued to collect this sort of information. They did so by thorough correspondence with parents and teachers—and later the subjects themselves—and by a series of careful interviews at extended intervals. One of the most impressive aspects of the enterprise has been the extent of mutual cooperation throughout all these years. Even in the major follow-up studies, when the subjects were in middle age, the investigators were able to reach over 90 percent of the original group. By then, the research staff was also looking systematically at offspring, suggesting to some observers that the project might go on forever.

Background

Terman wanted a representative group of children who could get very high scores on his intelligence tests. His children came from Latin American (mostly Mexican), Oriental, and black families—the chief minority groups in California then—as well as from white backgrounds. They came from the full range of socioeconomic and occupational categories, from various religions, and from the several regions of California. But despite Terman's efforts to avoid bias, the distributions were skewed. Overrepresented in the group were children with professional, well-educated, white parents who had settled in the cities. More than 10 percent were of Jewish ancestry, twice the statewide incidence at the time. A number of families contributed more than one child, including two families in which five children qualified.

Critics point out that Terman did not give the attention to these biases that would be *de rigeur* now. He noted them, without exhaustive analysis. His laconic comment at the end of a brief recapitulation of family background in the 1959 follow-up is typical. After briefly alluding to families from which several siblings had been selected for the study, he said he thought that common ancestry or common environment—or more likely both—accounted for so many families having two or more children in his study (Terman & Oden, 1959). He was content to say that his children generally came from homes with above-average advantages, whether of heredity or opportunity. To go further would have required a different research design, using close comparison of matched children (as opposed to group averages), as well as more extensive study of relationships among the significant features of his children's backgrounds.

Physical Development

The most persistent of the myths about the bright is the conviction that they are spindly bookworms. Terman dealt this myth a major blow. His children were bigger, healthier, and more vigorous than average. They were not "undersized, sickly, hollow-chested, stoop-shouldered, clumsy, nervously tense, and bespectacled" (Terman & Oden, 1959, p. 8). Rather, they were larger at birth, walked sooner, went through puberty earlier, had fewer diseases or operations, and reported less nervousness than we would expect from average persons. The entire picture was one of physical superiority.

Now this superiority was not comparable to their intellectual prowess: they were not one and one-half to two times as big or as healthy. But the trend was reliable, and it probably played no small part in permitting these children to employ their mental gifts with energy and élan. Nor does this physical superiority necessarily imply hereditary origin. Florence Goodenough, one of Terman's original research assistants, frequently pointed out that the physical health and vigor typical of Terman's children may have been the result of the relatively higher standards of diet and medical care in their homes. One study took her hint and made physical measurements on siblings with widely different intelligence test scores (Laycock & Caylor, 1964). These siblings were not significantly different in physique; instead, they were about as similar as we would expect siblings to be. A physician working with Terman had also seen this possibility; he believed the physical superiority of the gifted group was related to the higher average of nutrition in their homes. It is still an undisputed fact that Terman's group had above-average physique and vitality. But we are not sure why.

Schooling

This group started school early. Nearly half of them could read before kindergarten (6 percent before they turned four years old). One in five skipped part or all of first grade. They passed through school ahead of schedule, on the average about 14 percent faster than normal. On standardized tests of academic attainment they consistently did very well, averaging about 40 percent ahead of their age-mates. They were usually furthest ahead in reading, arithmetic reasoning, and general information; least advanced in arithmetic computation and spelling. They were not typically narrow or one-sided in their achievement. Close inspection of their records showed that there were about as many children with lopsided achievement as among normal pupils.

Terman was a missionary about the implications of this pattern, especially the tilt between achievement and placement. He recited over and over again the fact mentioned above—that the typical gifted child was 40 percent above average in academic achievement but only 14 percent above average in grade placement at school (Terman, 1925). He was, that is, an advocate of much greater acceleration than was common in California schools, something we shall discuss later.

These children maintained good academic records, though few skipped school grades after age twelve. In high school they averaged in the top 10 percent on tests of achievement. Marks were mostly A, even though the group was younger than its classmates. Over 10 percent were graduated from high school before age sixteen (that is, about two years early), and over 33 percent before age seventeen. Most went on to college directly (87 percent of the men, 83 percent of the women), and most graduated (70 percent of the men, 67 percent of the women). The figures for women are striking when we recall that many of them went to college during the economic depression of the 1930s, when the proportion of women graduates generally was much smaller (about 40 percent).

The real proof of staying power came after the bachelor's degree. Two thirds of the men and almost three fifths of the women earned one or more higher degrees. The 1959 report listed 97 doctorates (10 percent of those who had graduated from college), 54 medical degrees (6 percent), and 92 legal degrees (10 percent). These figures are three to five times those for college graduates as a whole. The undergraduate and graduate programs were spread across the curriculum, with the heaviest concentration of majors in the social sciences.

Terman's subjects liked school. As they reminisced in maturity, the majority said they were satisfied with their schooling and had received as much as they wanted. It was no doubt crucial that they were encouraged along the way by their parents and teachers. There was a firm relation between the parents' education and the stress they put on schooling for their children. Over one third of the fathers and one sixth of the mothers had graduated from college. Terman contrasted the education of the parents of his subjects with the radically lower college attendance for the general population in the same generation, in which fewer than 2 percent of the people of college age were graduated from college (Terman & Oden, 1959). The preponderantly favorable attitude toward school that these children remember may have been colored by rationalization or later experience, but it was surely related to the parents' education.

In spite of his group's general educational success, Terman himself was less than completely satisfied. Even among his children were some who could have done better. He made a practice of noting how many of his "potentially superior college material" did not even start college (10 to 15 percent) and how many did not finish or go beyond college (30 percent and more). The reasons he suspected: money, motivation, and encouragement. He held the schools accountable for a great deal, especially when they did not interest his pupils or sustain their efforts. He was intensely proud of what his "termites" did and deeply disturbed by unnecessary failure.

Careers

The story of employment is like that of schooling, since so many of Terman's group entered occupations for which advanced education is prerequisite. The 1959 and later reports described the adult years, when general patterns were set. Here the male/female distinction was sharp and very likely indicative of social expectations: over half the women were housewives with no steady outside employment. Of the women who held full-time jobs, the largest group was in teaching, the next largest in business. Among them were some women with very distinguished careers in science, education, art, writing, and business; a few had multiple careers. Terman pointed to the number of women who coordinated part-time careers with homemaking and childrearing as well as to the high number of women involved in community service.

However, career involvement was mainly for the men. Their record is remarkable. Nearly 90 percent were in professional or managerial positions, the remainder in retailing, agriculture, or semiskilled occupations. Fewer than 3 percent were unemployed, half of them because they had independent means or had retired. Terman liked to read off the list of accomplishments: by age forty, they had written 67 books, more than 1400 professional and scientific articles, over 400 short stories and plays, and miscellaneous articles. This record, he proudly said, was ten to thirty times as large as that for 800 randomly chosen men of the same age (Terman, 1954).

Interests

Terman's staff kept track of the group's interests and activities throughout the growing years and into adulthood. In general, abstract rather than rote or manual activities stood out. For instance, the children were enthusiastic about making up stories but they disliked penmanship. Sewing, cooking, and manual training were unpopular. Reading was a consistent childhood favorite: when seven years old, the average child in the group read more books than a fifteen-year-old classmate of ordinary intelligence. Furthermore, the books they read were more serious: biographies, science, history, travel, poetry, drama, and informational fiction. They kept on reading as adults, enjoying fiction, biography, history, travel, and specialized matter for professional or avocational reasons.

While children, they played games that were above their years, often quiet games requiring reasoning and judgment. Sex differences in choice resembled those of ordinary children. They generally engaged in a variety of games. They had great stores of information about rules, records, and the like, and they were adept at revising games or making up new ones.

Personal-Social Development

Teachers and parents were asked to rate the children in many ways: for popularity, emotional maturity, aesthetic sensitivity, moral judgment, and willpower. The children generally came off well, being cited as above average in everything but mechanical ingenuity and getting especially high ratings for such volitional and emotional traits as perseverance, self-confidence, sense of humor, and steadiness of mood.

As they matured, these children kept up their satisfactory, all-round development. They had often been leaders among their classmates, and they took disproportionately large responsibilities in academic affairs, business enterprises, and community activities. Fewer became alcoholics, psychotics, or suicides than is true for the general population. They reported their marriages to be somewhat happier than average; they were divorced about as often as is normal. Even those in the highest level of IQ 170 and above (73 persons) reported themselves to be well enough adjusted emotionally.

In one of the most penetrating analyses, Terman and his staff rated 150 of the men as "most successful" in their careers and another 150 as "least successful." They then compared the two groups. The first, whom Terman called the A group, had a greater drive to achieve and came from families with significantly higher education. They were said to have a greater "integration toward goals," and stronger perseverance and self-confidence. By contrast, the other group, C (Terman didn't choose a B group), received less encouragement at home, perhaps because their parents had had fewer years of schooling. They scored lower on the indications of motivation that distinguished the A group. Terman thought this comparison revealing and discouraging, for he kept insisting that the entire group, A's and C's included, had enormous potential. He was disappointed that any significant number of them should fall short. In recent years, this A–C contrast has become important, because attention is now being given to nonintellectual supports, like motivation, that are required for full development of the personality.

Adult Intellectual Development

Terman had started by picking children for their high test scores in an examination of general intelligence. It is feasible to construct such an examination for the young, because sufficient items in the "top," or most difficult range, may be included to challenge even the brightest. But what of their mental powers after the early years? How could Terman find out if they had kept their superior mental capacity? There were no tests hard enough to meet his group's capacities, so Terman and his associates developed a "Concept Mastery Test" intended to "reach into the stratosphere of intelligence" (Terman, 1954, p. 222). It had two parts: one using synonyms and antonyms and the other using analogies. It was a short but very difficult test, usually taking half an hour. Items were from many fields and were designed to test one's ability to handle complex abstractions. However, the test had no time limit—the purpose was to test the power of the mind rather than the speed of the mind. Analysis showed that there seemed to be no bias in favor of those who had had more years of formal education. Two forms of the test were used, one in the 1947 follow-up, the other in the 1959 follow-up. In both testings, Terman's group kept to a high level. Attempts to compare average scores with the earlier Stanford-Binet IQs showed a modest drop (from 152 to about 135); Terman and McNemar interpreted this drop as no greater than would be expected from statistical regression over a period of twenty-five years, and they did not think it was a dependable indication of real decline (Terman & Oden, 1959). When the 1947 and 1959 administrations of the new test are compared, there is, in fact, a consistent rise in score among both men and women in the several occupational groups, and across the various levels of final education. Terman thus disposed of another myth, that of "early ripe, early rot."

Latest Follow-ups

Terman's 1959 report, *The Gifted Group at Mid-life,* was finished after his death in 1956 by his colleague, Melitta Oden. It was the last full book to come out of the Terman project, and it was based on questionnaires and other information gathered when the average age in the group was in the forties. Later reports have been less sweeping and have appeared in articles and monographs. In 1968 Oden published an analysis of the 1959 follow-up. She found that, in general, earlier trends continued: superior vocational achievement; satisfaction with home life; low incidence of death, disease, and disorder; and sustained intellectual vigor. She also further analyzed the *A-C* comparison between highly successful and less successful men. She found that the gap between the two had widened—especially in accomplishment—and attributed this to the greater motivation and emotional stability of those in group *A*.

The most recent reports are a pair of articles on the career and life satisfaction of the Terman men (Robert Sears, 1977) and women (Pauline Sears & Ann Barbee, 1977). Both are based on questionnaires sent out in 1972, when the participants' average age was sixty-two. Nearly 500 men and over 400 women responded with detailed information and commentary on themselves.

The questions for men centered on their jobs, their family lives, and their plans for retirement, because these seemed to be the aspects of one's life most significant to persons in late middle age. Sears found that, when laid alongside the voluminous data assembled during these persons' earlier years, there was considerable continuity. Over the decades from ages thirty to sixty, attitudes toward "work, health, and self-worth" were very consistent, so that one could (as Sears did) go back to the earlier files and predict later behavior. Prediction about family life was less successful, perhaps because, according to Sears, gifted men "have capacities that permit them a high degree of autonomy in the control of occupational activity. . . . In their family life, however, they are as much dependent, for satisfaction, on . . . the other family members as are any other men . . ." (Sears, 1977, p. 128). Nonetheless, these men, despite their generally very great occupational success, put greater emphasis on a satisfying family life, and "they believed they had found it."

In the parallel study of the Terman women, Pauline Sears and Ann Barbee questioned them as to how satisfying they had found their lives. Most of the women (57 percent) were homemakers, currently married and living with their husbands. A large number (43 percent) held jobs, with average earnings markedly higher than those reported for all working women in the 1970 census. The jobs were more often full-time and professional than was generally true of the majority of the women in the census. Most of the women (75 percent) had children. In assessing satisfaction, Sears and Barbee looked at the women's backgrounds, their sense of worth and identity, and the salient facts about their marriages and careers. In general, happiness was related to earlier experiences: women who had warm and loving parents in a stable marriage tended to report that their own marriages were happy. Childless and single women also reported general satisfaction with their lives. In fact, 89 percent of the single, childless women were overwhelmingly satisfied with their adult lives. This particular finding surprised the authors, who had predicted a closer tie between happiness and motherhood. They decided that their original hunch had been naive, or more exactly, that it had been rooted in the expectations of an earlier day. They found that women who had been self-confident and ambitious in youth said their adult careers and personal lives were more satisfying. As a general conclusion, Sears and Barbee commented, "What does stand out is that happiness . . . depends on our earlier experiences. . . . The degree of satisfaction . . . is part . . . of a total developing personality. The life style which brings happiness to one woman with one kind of life experience does not necessarily bring it to another woman with a different . . . background" (1977, p. 60). For these bright women, however, background and schooling allowed them to take greater advantage of opportunities. Sears and Barbee also suggested that the high level of general intelligence these women possess may have been in part responsible for the flexible manner in which they have coped with life's changing demands.

Further analysis can be expected from the rich store of information the Terman study has amassed over half a century. Robert Sears and Lee Cronbach, who are serving as guardians of the data and prime movers toward further research, expect the next investigations to deal with specific questions, including career changes in later life, motivation, and the special experiences of women in the group (Fincher, 1973). We can hope the search will continue, for the Terman project is unique. Such extended longitudinal research is rare. As Cronbach put it, "The trouble with these cradle-to-grave studies is that the investigator is always in his grave before the subjects are" (cited in Fincher, 1973, p. 14).

Criticism

We have given a large amount of space to the Terman study. This attention is justified if only by the deference the study has earned throughout the community of scholars concerned with the gifted. There is no other research comparable in scope and detail, following its subjects through more than fifty years. It is no disservice to recognize, however, that the study has its significant limits. Terman and his staff followed the latest canons of the day in their investigation. But they could not foresee all possibilities, and we would be wise to note some caveats.

First, and most critical, is the way Terman selected his tests and his children. The Stanford-Binet is now known mainly as a school-related test. It is a powerful indicator of school performance, but it does not (and was not expected to) measure other aspects of development that reflect upon intellectual endeavor, such as motivation and imagination. It is not fair to damn a test because it doesn't do what it wasn't intended to do. But it is naive to accept its results across a broader domain than is warranted. The clearest signs of superiority in Terman's children as they grew up were in the fields most closely tied to schooling. Selection on broader grounds might have tapped a greater variety of gifted children by including more who failed to win a place on test scores alone but whose later development would have justified selection. As for the children themselves, they were drawn disproportionately from favored homes, and Terman's design did not provide for fully understanding why.

Second, comparisons between his children and more normal ones were group-to-group, using averages. Critics now prefer to have person-to-person matches, with each pair rated according to the same tests and other measures. Such a design would have permitted more sophisticated comparisons and given us more confidence in his results. Note, however, that this criticism must not be overdrawn. What Terman did is very important: he avoided exclusive reliance on large-group, cross-sectional data in favor of expensive longitudinal study of individual children over several decades. Such longitudinal follow-up shows what actually happened to the children over the years and is not pieced together from soundings taken all at once on different persons of varying ages. But the comparisons with normal children would have been that much more powerful and convincing if matching had been more intimate.

Third, and perhaps less important, is the fear that so large an enterprise, requiring the services of so many people, must have had some effect upon the children while they were being studied. Certainly we know of children labeled bright who have resisted the label and reacted against it. No doubt some of Terman's children did, too. However, there is no convincing evidence that this possible difficulty seriously flawed the study. It would be hard to tease apart membership in the study from membership in family or school—hard to know how much further families or schools encouraged children beyond what they would have done without the stimulus of Terman's research. It is not so much that the children were pushed to extreme heights by the constant awareness of their participation in a major research. Rather, as studies in psychology and business suggest, they may have been more likely to reach their peak because of sustained attention and subtle help. Current practice has sensitized us to the problem of so-called reactive measures, and we must read Terman's data with suitable caution. But this caution should not blunt the impact of the work. In his foreword to Terman and Oden's 1959 report, Robert Sears wrote:

> And so we reach the end of one stage in this extraordinary research enterprise. When Professor Terman came to Stanford in 1910, as an assistant professor of education, the scientific study of the intellect had scarcely begun. In Paris Alfred Binet had constructed an ingenious test for measuring academic ability in school children; at Columbia University's Teachers College E. L. Thorndike had begun work on the measurement of school achievement. But it remained for Lewis Terman to conceive the development of a rigorous intelligence test that could select the ablest children and thus allow society to focus its full educative power on developing their potential. . . . What has started now remains to be finished. . . . We can be grateful for the courage and vision of the man who finally broke the barrier of the limited lifetime allotted to any one researcher, and got under way a study of man that will encompass the span of the *subjects'* lives, not just those of the researchers. . . . On actuarial grounds, there is considerable likelihood that the last of Terman's Gifted Children will not have yielded his last report to the files before the year 2010! (pp. viii–ix)

OTHER IQ STUDIES

Nobody has duplicated Terman's research, but others have responded to the dream of discovering what the gifted are like. The closest to a parallel, but in reverse, was an unusual investigation done by one of Terman's co-workers, Catherine Cox. She traced the childhoods of certain known geniuses to see if they had shown promise of their future achievements when they were young. Terman had started this venture into "historiometry" with a study of Galton, which appeared in a psychological journal in 1917. Cox proposed to follow his lead by analyzing biographical material on a large number of eminent men. It was a big job, but the plan was simple, and the result is a fat volume that appeared in 1926. Cox started with a list that James McK. Cattell had published in 1906 of 1000 famous men. She arbitrarily eliminated over half: those with insufficient childhood information, those whose eminence was not of their own making (such as those from the hereditary aristocracy), and those born before 1450. There remained 301 men dating from 1450 to 1850. Cox examined material on their childhoods to approximate information of the sort the Stanford-Binet would have provided. She wanted to derive an IQ for each person, based on historical records rather than actual test protocols. Three psychologists, including Terman, read over the documentary evidence and estimated an IQ rating for each case; the average of these three ratings was the IQ assigned to each case.

> It is easy to scoff at these post-mortem IQs [Terman later admitted] but . . . I think the author's main conclusion is fully warranted: namely, that "the genius who achieves highest eminence is one whom intelligence tests would have identified as gifted in childhood." (Terman, 1954, p. 225)

Cox's 1926 volume is fascinating to read. She presents her analysis and conclusions in the first 219 pages and then devotes most of the remaining 600 pages to compact biographies that summarize childhood traits and later achievements. One appendix gives Schiller's history in full; the other includes excerpts from the writings of many of those studied.

The estimated IQs in Cox's collection range from the low 100s to 200. Mill, our opening case in Chapter 1, is in the very top group, along with Pascal, Bentham, Goethe, Leibnitz, Macaulay, and Grotius. IQs for all 301 men averaged between 155 and 165. There was a pattern in which philosophers were highest, followed in order by writers, statesmen, scientists, musicians, artists, and military leaders. A subgroup of 100 men on whom Cox had the fullest records was studied for evidence of character, home background, emotional life, and other personality traits that might bear on their development. This group was generally superior in all traits, especially persistence, depth of understanding, and originality—the same pattern Terman found in his own study.

Many other less ambitious surveys have also verified Terman's assertions. Paul Witty (1940) followed fifty youngsters from 1924 to 1940 in the Chicago region. Like Terman's group, these children had IQs of 140 or higher; unlike his, they were individually paired with control children ranging from IQ 90 to 110 and matched for race, sex, and age. Witty found essentially the same pattern as Terman for the childhood years, and the same persistence in mental ability and accomplishment in later years.

Leta Hollingworth (1942) compiled extensive records of a small number of the very brightest children she could find, one of whom was *E* in Chapter 1. She called attention through them to what she saw as their special problem: so far removed from the average, they often had difficulty adapting to other people. They tended to be solitary, to read enormously, and to develop rich imaginary lives. This study led Hollingworth to believe that it is valuable to subdivide the term "gifted." She thought the lower range of IQ, from perhaps 125 to 150, was the optimal base for social leadership and personal fulfillment. She found that children at this level can win respect for their abilities and get experience leading others. They can manage their own affairs competently and find enough persons like themselves for companionship. Children above about IQ 170 are "too intelligent to be understood by the general run of persons, . . . have to contend with loneliness and with personal isolation" (p. 265). Hollingworth emphasized that the very brightest, her IQ 180+ children, have a unique value for society. However, if they do not have satisfying human contact, society may lose some or all of their potential contributions.

In New Zealand, G. W. Parkyn (1948) studied fifty children (mostly boys) above IQ 120 who were roughly comparable to Terman's children, with scores in the top 5 percent on the 1937 Stanford-Binet. Most of these children were age twelve at the time of selection. Parkyn gathered information, as Terman had, about their school performance and home background, and their personal and social traits. In the main, his children resembled Terman's in the pattern of their intellectual and other development.

Much earlier, before Terman began his research, Cyril Burt began to study English schoolchildren. Burt's study was part of a plan originally proposed by Galton, which could not be continued intact during World War I. Nevertheless, in 1915 Burt, then a psychologist to the London schools, began collecting information on the brightest 3 percent of children—a level fairly comparable to a Stanford-Binet IQ of 128. Burt studied their school careers, homes, recreation, and other interests. He kept track of his pupils—nearly 300 of them—until they had finished school, paying special attention to those who either failed the scholarship test for a free place in secondary school (roughly equivalent to high school in the U.S.) or passed but then did not do well in secondary school. Burt (1962a) found that these children had many of the characteristics Terman reported, but he warned that social and home conditions were very different from those of a later era and that therefore his data might no longer be typical.

In a study done in England about the time that Terman started his research, James Duff (1929) looked at the lives of some English children as they faced the transition from elementary to secondary school. He picked sixty-four boys and girls who had group IQs of 136 or higher (most of them between 136 and 140) and twenty-eight controls with IQs between 95 and 105. Duff wanted to know if one group test score on a child would predict later school performance. He was especially curious about how the score would relate to attending and completing secondary school, which was then in England a very competitive level of education to which only a few children gained access. Most of his brighter children entered secondary school; few of his controls did. Duff's children resembled those of Terman's gifted and normal children, although there were very few who were comparable to Terman's highest scorers. Duff's bright children were readers, did well in school, and had broad interests. Their plans for the future—in an agricultural and coal-mining area in northeastern England that had few resources of culture or industry—were much more ambitious than those of the control children, whose plans were limited by their meager opportunities. Few of the brighter children came from homes of any distinction, but there were many more control children whose fathers were unemployed or unskilled laborers. After pointing to the importance of character and intelligence as influences upon school and career, Duff emphasized that environment appears to have a powerful influence on how far a child will dream of going.

Much later, in France, G. Heuyer and Henri Piéron (1950) studied a large number of children who had been identified in 1944 as gifted. They compared children from the top 10 percent with children from the middle range of intelligence. After seven years, some of these pupils were still in elementary school, some had gone on to technical or secondary school, and some had left to take jobs. By that time, the groups ranged in age from thirteen to eighteen. Heuyer and Piéron examined their school progress and the kinds of work they had chosen, and looked at scholastic marks, tests, and diplomas and at problems they encountered that handicapped them. In general, the results were what we should expect. Three quarters of the bright group had stayed in school beyond the usual exit age (age fourteen), while fewer than half of the controls had. In school, teachers (who knew nothing about the research or about the pupils' test scores) rated most of the bright as excellent to average pupils, the controls as average to poor. The difference in academic achievement between the two groups was noticeable in both elementary and secondary school, but it was less pronounced in the latter, probably as a result of selection and attrition. Heuyer and Piéron believed that those bright pupils who did not prosper in secondary school were those who suffered from illness or family problems, who were not motivated, or who were geographically isolated. Half of the bright stayed in school after age eighteen, with most (two thirds) entering *lycées* or other competitive upper-level schools; fewer than a third of the controls continued.

All these studies corroborate Terman's findings that bright children stay on the academic track longer if they come from homes that encourage schooling. These may be professional homes where the pattern of extended education has already been set, where children learn early how important the parents think it is to study hard and do well. They may also be, as Duff showed, homes where the parents have not themselves entered professions, but where clever children are pushed to do better than their predecessors. These home patterns are probably most important in countries such as England and France, where academic competition is very strong and where it makes itself felt early in a child's school life.

CHILDREN WITH SPECIAL TALENTS

Many a child shows extraordinary talent for a specific activity—often from a very early age. Let us examine now the child who may or may not possess broad intelligence, but who certainly shows remarkable skill in a particular field. This skill may be in music or mathematics, science, poetry, or drawing, but whatever it is, the child not only does well but often seems to be impelled by some inner drive. In the most impressive cases, the combination of talent and drive produces remarkable progress.

Underlying Factors

It happens that psychologists have not settled the primary question about how closely general intelligence is related to a specific talent, especially whether one must first have a wide base of intelligence in order to develop the particular skill. But even without a definitive picture of this relationship, we have some clues about specific talents.

First, there is the matter of basic perception and thinking. Does a young musician hear more acutely or a young artist see more vividly? Does the mathematician have an unusual sense of spatial relations, or the linguist a facile memory? According to research on the senses (notably hearing, vision, and touch), superiority in one sense does not necessarily imply superiority in the others—especially as the basis for organizing complex abilities (Horn, 1976). A precocious musician has acute hearing, or an artist a special sensitivity to color, and perhaps no more. Verbal thinking (as in solving problems) seems to be a specific gift, differentiated from general intelligence: children who score high in one do not always score high in the other (Kogan & Pankove, 1972). Furthermore, there are apparently some persistent sex differences. Boys seem to have a better visual sense and to be more skillful at noting visual patterns that have been clouded by camouflage. This male superiority has even been suspected to have a recessive, sex-linked character (Bock & Kolakowski, 1973). On the other hand, girls show significant superiority in verbal thinking, and perhaps in imaginative activity expressed in words (Horn, 1976). All of these characteristics (sensory and verbal) occur in patterns that are relatively independent of general intelligence.

Then there is the matter of stimulation. Whether a child with talent has some very specific skill or a general ability that has seized upon just one activity for expression, progress is dependent on motivation. Most talented children are unusually enthusiastic. They concentrate on what they do far more intently and often for much longer periods than most children—or adults—do.

Nearly all gifted children are good at organizing ideas and sensing relationships. They readily perceive the core meaning common to various experiences that otherwise appear diverse. They show more spontaneity and abandon in trying solutions or perfecting techniques. So if certain children center all their efforts upon something specific—like writing poems or mastering algebra—they may bring to it an awesome combination: particular sensory or perceptual superiority, high interest in how the activity is organized, and great staying power. No wonder that they so often move rapidly through their music lessons or algebra assignments, or that they tax their teachers with tough questions, or that they even invent their own techniques of fingering or painting or calculating. But although some children can persevere against social disdain or school rigidity, many others need sensitive handling and steady encouragement. As a consequence, some experts are less persuaded by the possibility of specific or independent underlying talents in music or mathematics than by the importance of interest, opportunity, and support.

Characteristics of Children with Special Talents

Leaving aside now the puzzling question of how specific talents arise, what are the children like who develop them? If we brought together a sizable group of talented children, what would they have in common? The best recent answers come from Julian Stanley's ongoing Study of Mathematically Precocious Youth (let us refer to it simply as SMPY) at The Johns Hopkins University in Maryland. The children in this study (Lisa Skarp in the opening chapter is one) all displayed unusual mathematical skill by the time they were in late elementary school. It was, in fact, this skill that attracted notice in the first place. But these several hundred boys and girls have some other salient traits. They are bright by the standards of general intelligence tests (but, as Stanley sternly emphasizes, their recorded IQs did not usually prompt their schools to recognize or nourish the remarkable talents they had).

The group has been mainly boys, especially at the highest level of tested mathematical achievement. In the 1972 screening test, the highest girl's score on the mathematical part of the Scholastic Aptitude Test was 600; quite a few boys scored up to 790 out of about 800—and these were all junior high-school pupils taking a test designed for high-school seniors. This sex difference is consistent. Citing just one typical statistic, in 1969, fewer than 10 percent of the Ph.D.'s awarded in mathematics went to women, and fewer than 20 percent in science (Bisconti & Astin, 1973). Part of the explanation is surely that women in Western society have traditionally had little opportunity or support to develop mathematical talent. In school and elsewhere, girls have learned early that it would be "unfeminine" to show much interest in numbers or science. But the SMPY does not show that social factors *alone* account for the sex differences they have been finding (Fox, 1976). Certain cognitive differences between boys and girls (especially those in spatial perception) may be partly responsible. Certainly, however, SMPY supports the judgment that some differences between the sexes, at least at the higher levels, begin in the social patterns boys and girls learn as they grow up (Keating, 1976).

In some ways, these mathematically precocious youngsters show the variety we find in any group of people. Some of them are very gregarious, others rather solitary. Some study more diligently and more regularly than others. Some like school; others don't. They vary in mechanical comprehension and spatial perception, and in knowledge of science. But in general they are superior to most children their age. All this variety is to be expected, since they were chosen as a group primarily for a specific, focused trait—mathematical skill.

Nonetheless, these youths are mainly creative, socially mature, and achievement oriented. Two of their traits seem to work together: verbal skill and desire to learn mathematics (Keating, 1974). Most of these pupils had learned much by themselves, by going through mathematics books or puzzles or games, by asking adults questions, or by intuitively setting and solving their own mathematical problems. Self-instruction like this requires a good verbal base to cope with the materials one must use, as well as the discipline to keep at a task without formal direction (Anastasi, 1974).

In a complementary study of another group of Maryland youth, some of Stanley's colleagues have sought out pupils with very marked verbal precocity (McGinn, 1976). These pupils, too, are socially mature, achievement oriented, and—as expected—highly verbal. They tend to be very interested either in creative writing or in the social sciences. The boys are analytic, theoretical, pragmatic, and mildly withdrawn. The girls are more imaginative, intuitive, and socially inclined. As with the mathematical group, these youngsters come mainly from well-educated homes with small families. The research team continues to look for information that would more sharply describe verbal precocity and its origins. So far it is tantalizingly difficult to assess some of the critical aspects, especially those dealing with originality, tolerance for ambiguity, and reflective thought. As Martin Covington (1970) wrote, it is just these traits that may be necessary for a child to learn how to formulate good questions and figure out how to answer them.

For both verbal and mathematical precocity, the research of Stanley and his colleagues demonstrates the importance of parental influence. Homework, school attendance, and intellectual stimulation depend heavily on the attitudes prevalent in the home. In the SMPY, the children whose parents get involved make the most progress (Keating, 1976). The same is true of children who show musical prowess, who persevere in the rigors of ballet, or who show an early bent for science or poetry. Sustained progress usually depends on providing lessons and other opportunities for instruction, as well as independent trial and error. It is the parents—and ideally the schools—who must help guide a child's experiences toward high accomplishment.

We return to the underlying question of how important general ability and special talent are. Whichever is the more potent, there is the same necessity to develop skill through regular practice and careful guidance. From a practical point of view, as SMPY shows, it is very effective to single out a skill and look for the children who have it. They may be broadly intelligent as well, but the pedagogical problems involved are centered on the skill itself. Stanley's group is convinced that the place to start is the search for mathematical precocity rather than for overall intelligence. More theoretically, we need to be aware that skill is an amalgam of interest and ability. Which is the determining factor—the interest or some underlying aptitude—is a question still to be answered. Some years ago Florence Goodenough (1956) decided that the relation between talent and interest is probably circular. She herself believed in the great powers of general intelligence to succeed in whatever specific enterprises a person might choose. But she also pointed to the crucial characteristics that talented children show when they put their minds to a project: intense interest and a great "zest for living and doing." Stanley's most recent research has reinforced Goodenough's picture of effort, interest, and enthusiasm.

CREATIVITY

Recently we have been developing a broader definition of "gifted." Most of the surveys in the Terman tradition have depended upon standardized tests of general intelligence on which a specified score would qualify a child as gifted. Many of these tests provide only a single score, usually an IQ. Some also offer subscores to reflect varying degrees of refinement: quantitative aptitudes, nonverbal skills, and so on. However, they do not indicate how imaginative a child is. In the last few years, this quality of imagination has been systematically studied, and tests have been produced in an attempt to measure it. Ideally, we should know how many very creative children there are and what kinds of backgrounds and personalities they have. But we don't know. Brightness and creativity are not distinct enough traits to allow us to distinguish children as one or the other. Rather, there is considerable overlap. So questions must be put more carefully. To what extent should we give particular attention to creativity? How far can we expect children who show it to be bright in the more conventional sense, and vice versa? The evidence so far is incomplete and sometimes contradictory.

One reason for the confusion is the diversity of approaches researchers have used in defining and studying creativity. Brewster Ghiselin (1952) relied on collected life histories to illustrate how creative adults work. John Dewey (1933) set out the steps inherent in problem-solving—from stating the problem to verifying a clever solution. Others have looked for the subskills that, taken together, support imaginative activity: flexibility, perceptual discrimination, and confidence in taking risks. Anne Roe (1953) and Donald MacKinnon (1962), among others, observed practicing scientists, architects, artists, and professionals who had a reputation for creative production. Paul Torrance (1966) and J. P. Guilford (1959) developed tests designed to detect and measure creativity. It is not surprising that among so many approaches there is no dominant theme or conclusion.

Donald MacKinnon's 1962 study of creative persons from many different fields gives us a start. He found them to be, in the main, skeptical, nonconforming, and independent—seeing things their own way and making up their own minds. They were curious and highly energetic, and yet introverted and reflective. They enjoyed solving problems and depended heavily on intuition—prizing the large pattern more than its details. Raymond Cattell (1971), who observed artists and writers, noted their intelligence, fluency, flexibility, and emotional sensitivity.

They drove single-mindedly toward their goals, often brushing aside conventionality. They appeared confident, self-sufficient, and tenacious. Viktor Lowenfeld (1957) concluded that creativity in the arts is similar in many ways to creativity in the sciences, as measured by J. P. Guilford and his followers.

How close is the relation between brightness and creativity? The question is made difficult by disagreement over definitions, and any answer is complicated by conflicting and ambiguous data. On the one hand, there is a fairly long tradition that brightness and creativity coexist within tolerable limits. We have mentioned that Terman found that nearly all of the pupils nominated as creative also qualified as gifted. Roy Simpson and Ruth Martinson (1961), in a smaller California study, found that children who were picked for high scores on intelligence tests had varied talents and showed versatile imaginations. Most other studies that start by seeking high-IQ scorers discover their children are also above average in creativity. Going in the opposite direction, recent interest in children's imagination has shown, sometimes only obliquely, that most creative children are also bright in the traditional sense. Of the pupils who went through the Ohio State University High School during an experimental period in the 1930s, those who were most creative were also brightest by orthodox standards (Willis, 1961).

On the other hand, much attention has been drawn to research that suggests that brightness and creativity may tend to be somewhat separate and to concentrate in different children. The best-known work, by Jacob Getzels and Philip Jackson (1962), studied children at the University of Chicago Laboratory Schools. The authors picked out four groups of pupils: high-IQ and low-IQ, high-creative and low-creative. The creativity they sought was what Guilford had called "divergent thinking," that is, being able to think or do the unusual rather than the conventional—to maintain an open-ended approach to a problem rather than to seek the one solution for it. The high-creative children avoided stereotyped answers, sought activities outside the prescribed syllabus, and were nonconformers. The high-IQ children were more or less the opposite, preferring "convergent" over "divergent" situations, and problems that required "right" answers.

As a result of the Getzels-Jackson study and other similar efforts, we now hear a familiar litany: that high-IQ children are conformists, that IQ tests reward stereotyped thinking, and that the tests are insensitive to creative children who may score low. This last criticism is telling, if in looking for bright children we regularly miss creative ones. Much of this criticism is not well founded. Readers should note that Getzels and Jackson were working in a school where all the pupils were bright by the conventional code—the student body was attending an academic "hothouse" widely respected for its high standards. The high-IQs *and* the high-creatives both had very high academic achievement. The authors themselves did not exaggerate, but many of their readers have. All the authors did was pick out pupils who were relatively higher in either IQ or creativity. They eliminated from their study pupils who were high in both categories. A number of statistical quirks can be introduced with this method, however. If the full spread of ability is restricted by cutting out the lower end (as a selective school usually does) or if the measures of creativity have a narrow range, then the correlations between intelligence and creativity may be depressed.

Gertrude Hildreth (1966) took a middle course that seems to follow the bulk of the evidence. She said that high intelligence is a sure element in truly creative thinking, but it does not itself guarantee high creativity. Consequently, it is reasonable to expect highly creative children to be bright. But we should also expect them to show pronounced traits of independence and flexibility—even to push hard against what they find unwise. We should, above all, be cautioned against assuming that high-scoring children must necessarily be rigid and unimaginative or that creative children will be rather stupid in mundane intellectual activities.

SUMMARY OF CHARACTERISTICS OF THE GIFTED

Let us briefly summarize what systematic studies of the gifted have shown to be their salient characteristics.

Intellectual: superior at reasoning and difficult mental tasks; learns quickly; shows intellectual curiosity; has wide interests; reads well; works independently; shows originality; impatient with routine and drill; may show unevenness of ability and interest in academic subjects.

Physical: tends toward bigger build, better health, fewer nervous disorders, earlier maturity.

Social and emotional: superior in desirable traits (courtesy, cooperation, sense of humor), self-critical, resists cheating, less boastful, social leader (especially in middle range of brightness), has play interests and friends some years older, prefers complicated and often quieter games.

To the extent that Terman's work has sifted into popular thinking, this list will sound familiar. Indeed, it may sound like common sense. It is in contrast, however, to the stereotype of the gifted as thin, nervous, brash, snobbish, difficult to tolerate, and concerned only with books, ideas, and self. Whatever our personal experience with individual bright children, we have an overwhelming body of systematic evidence that converges on the traits above. To put it another way, if we are looking for bright children, or if we wonder about a child we have just met, the prudent course is to use such a list as a guide. Exceptions will be just that—exceptions.

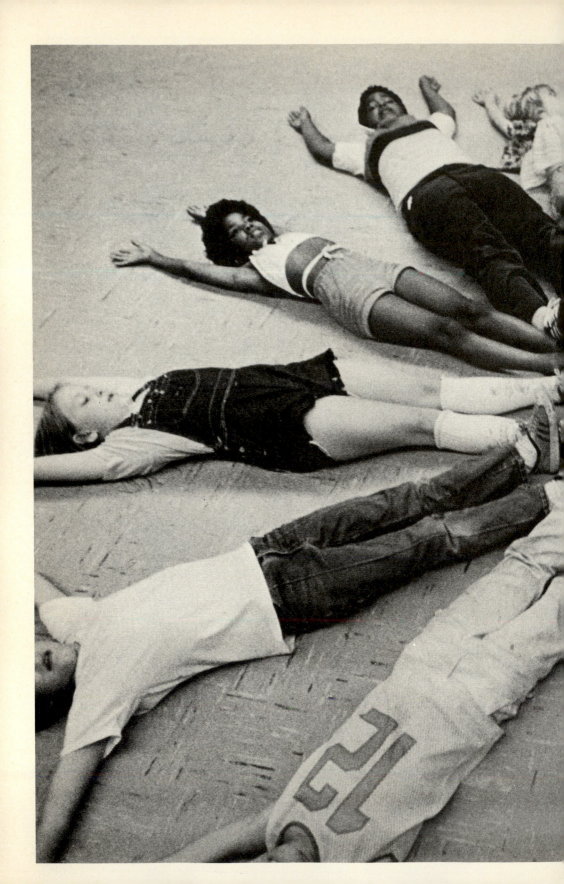

3

Intelligence, Specific
Abilities, and Creativity

The gifts of nature are infinite in their variety,
and mind differs from mind almost as much as
body from body.
Quintilian

In Chapter 1 we presented several biographical sketches of gifted persons, and in Chapter 2 we described characteristics most gifted persons have in common. In this chapter we shall take a closer look at giftedness itself— examining the various approaches investigators have taken to discover how it arises and how it relates to intelligence. We shall soon see that attempts to explain giftedness depend on the definition of intelligence we choose: in some definitions intelligence is a broad and underlying power; in others it is a variety of specific abilities. It makes a difference which definition we use, because we set our expectations accordingly. We may believe that gifted children have broad superiority, or we may look for them to have narrower, more specialized talents. As we consider special school programs or develop community support, we lay our plans and check our progress against the definition that seems best.

GIFTEDNESS AS ABNORMALITY, MOTIVATION, OR SUPERIORITY

Let us start by reviewing some influential explanations of giftedness. Anne Anastasi (1958), an American investigator noted for her research in the measurement of psychological differences among people, classified the theories of genius according to whether they emphasized pathological or abnormal conditions, psychoanalytic or motivational sources, qualitative superiority, or quantitative superiority.

Abnormality

Extremely bright persons are not just unusual: their aberration is often taken to be a sign of sickness. Seneca claimed that there is no great genius without some touch of madness—although some scholars believe that the word Seneca used should be translated as "divine inspiration," not "madness." People have suspected a link between high intelligence and vulnerability to psychosis since classical times. This belief flowered in the nineteenth century. More recently, in this century, Lange-Eichbaum (1932) noted that, among hundreds of geniuses, he found few who were free of mental abnormalities. The connection, he thought, was that a genius' greater mental ability brings greater emotional responsiveness and sensitivity, richer fantasy, and, perhaps, feelings of inferiority—precursors of magnificent achievement but also of emotional illness. Anastasi, like most modern scholars, suggested that Lange-Eichbaum based his argument upon unevenly selected cases rather than upon a systematic series of biographies. She also suggested that where genius and psychosis do coincide, the link between them may be only indirect. Intense mental life does not in itself bring on illness. Rather, it may alienate the genius from the social group, and this alienation and its attendant unhappiness could conceivably provoke insanity. Extending this argument to most geniuses, of course, does not stand up under the weight of evidence that the gifted are generally well adjusted and productive. Cases do exist of gifted children who later became psychotic, and they are often striking. But they are the exception.

This is not to suggest that the extremely bright are not confronted with special problems as a result of their exceptional capabilities. But vulnerability and maladjustment are not the same things as psychosis. Leta Hollingworth's study of the extremely bright (those above 180 IQ) led her to conclude that there are "special perplexities in the life of a gifted child" and that "the more intelligent the child, the more likely he or she is to become involved in these puzzling difficulties" (1942, p. 255). As children, they have few, if any, friends who can really converse with them. Daily they face routines at school that they believe are a waste of their time. They may be taunted by bullies or isolated by their own superior achievement. The wonder is that they do *not* grow into emotional cripples. It may be, as Hollingworth suspected, that the optimal IQ range stops short of 180, especially when we consider personal and social adjustment. But the unique contributions of the most intelligent do not necessarily doom them all to psychotic personalities and ineffective lives. Lange-Eichbaum's syndrome of genius and insanity does develop in some gifted persons, but it is not inevitable or typical. As we shall see in a later chapter, we must realize this *possible* outcome in an extremely bright child, and then try to arrange home and school affairs to prevent it. There is nothing, however, that preordains it.

Motivation

Sigmund Freud and other followers of psychoanalysis believed that strong motivational forces, rather than intellectual forces, were the real determinants of giftedness. They reasoned that mechanisms such as sublimation and compensation push some individuals toward high achievement—even those with seemingly ordinary minds and talents. The intuitive leaps of the creative artist would thus spring from great interest and desire more than from superior mentality. In the classical Freudian system, it is sexual drive that is sublimated, emerging in great music and poetry that testify to the inexorable power of the sublimated drive.

Physical infirmities or inferiority feelings do prod some persons to work hard enough to develop great skill and to make important contributions, but this is not the usual case. Now that we are getting over our protracted affair with psychoanalysis, we often find its competing schools confusing, their arguments forced, and their evidence unconvincing. The Freudian legacy remains, however, especially in current debates over creativity. But its assumptions and its dicta are no longer axiomatic. We grant motivation a broader, less doctrinaire place. It is, in fact, one of the major centers of current attention, particularly as it relates to the question of why bright children with the same test scores vary so in their educational and professional activities. We watch for the way motivation and other forces act upon basic intelligence, but without reliance upon psychoanalytic definitions and terminology.

Qualitative Superiority

Since earliest times, genius has been considered such an extraordinary thing that it has often been attributed to some superhuman power: divine inspiration, demonic intervention, witchcraft, or mystical experience. Sometimes this interpretation seems to reflect the observer more than the genius—it is difficult for ordinary minds to follow giant strides of the spirit. Or, when a genius confronts us with a proposal that conflicts with long-held beliefs and traditions, we may become defensive and cast out the unwanted, seeing the devil's hand. But whatever our reaction, when we find a quick and inventive mind outstripping us, we can easily conclude that it is operating on an entirely different plane. So, as Anastasi and many others have pointed out, it is tempting to put a special label on gifted minds—to decide that they must use peculiar strategies and have unique experiences. But is it *necessary* to consign the gifted to a different world? The next section offers another explanation, one that is currently the dominant view.

Quantitative Superiority

We must not minimize the impressive difference between Johnny Jones and Albert Einstein. But we need not assume that they are basically different kinds of human beings or that their minds deploy radically different resources. It is no insult to geniuses to assert that their achievements come from awesome combinations of ordinary mental operations, rather than from unique endowments. Anastasi pointed out that the social effects of a genius' thinking may carry so far as to produce something truly new in the world. But this qualitatively distinct result does not necessarily spring from a sharply distinct and separate form of mental life. It is a signal contribution of differential psychologists to have shown that average and gifted persons are actually at different points along the same line.* What the gifted have in abundance, the rest of us have to a limited extent: sensitivity to experience, ability to solve problems, capacity to learn abstractions, and so on. In fact, the evidence is compelling that as one goes out from the central mass of people toward the lonely genius, there is a finely graded increase in mental powers. The contrast between Johnny Jones and Albert Einstein is there, but between the two is not a gulf but a steady march of gradually more intelligent people.

DEFINITIONS OF INTELLIGENCE

In the eighteenth century, before there were professional psychologists or IQ tests, Samuel Johnson (1779) hit upon a definition of intelligence that has a remarkably prophetic ring: "The true Genius is a mind of large general powers, accidentally determined to some particular direction" (p. 2). In the twentieth century, systematic inquiries have tried to establish just what general and particular powers the mind has. These inquiries have concentrated upon intelligence itself, and only later or coincidentally upon the special case of the gifted.

Alfred Binet's reputation as a psychologist was built upon his imaginative and dedicated study of many human activities, among them intelligence. At the request of the Paris school authorities, he agreed to examine young children as they entered school, in order to pick out the ones who were retarded enough to need special attention. The tests that Binet and his colleagues developed came to the notice of Lewis Terman in the United States. Terman revised the tests and then used them to find children with high intelligence, so that he might follow a large group of the gifted over many years.

Binet and Terman illustrate the typical sequence of research: ideas that originate with specialists in intelligence are applied to studies of brightness. The reverse sequence—when research on the gifted alters theoretical models of the mind—is less common. In some ways, this asymmetry resembles that in the field of psychology as a whole. For example, child psychology has tended to use the theories and techniques of general psychology, adapting them from the animal laboratory to the clinic or the classroom. Apparently it takes time for a specialized application to mature, to develop an independent tradition.

Therefore, the broadest perspective on giftedness comes from research into intelligence itself. Even Terman's towering work has not yet brought to the study of the bright the autonomy and authority of its own

---

*Terman's massive study of gifted children, discussed in detail in Chapter 2, identified children who were very superior in the abilities that ordinary children also have. For a general discussion of how broadly individual differences among people are distributed, see Anastasi (1958), especially pp. 23 *ff.*

theory, its own discipline. The reason is probably that in approaching the bright, most people have focused on testing and on social service, leaving insufficient motive or support for considering brightness from a strictly theoretical perspective.

Intelligence tests were borrowed for application to the gifted, and the rough-and-ready explanations of intelligence built into the tests came with them intact. In general, the tests fall into two groups: those that try to plot intelligence as a single underlying, energizing force; and those that look mainly for a variety of separate talents or abilities. The first type of test may derive a comprehensive score (most often an IQ) by simply combining a child's answers to questions that "sink shafts" (as Galton put it) into various activities of the mind. Or it may try to order the answers into a pattern, from broad to specific. The second type of test, the multiple-manifestation type, may appraise several related but distinguishable mental operations, such as perceptual speed, reasoning, or memory. Or it may assess a host of talents that are only in the loosest way connected with "intelligence"—for instance, a battery of tests of musical aptitude, mechanical comprehension, artistic sensitivity, mathematical skill, and so forth.

At a superficial level, these two classes of tests produce quite distinct reports: the first yields a single score, the second yields several. At a more sophisticated level, the distinction between them is important but blurred. We are not agreed whether we should consider intelligence to be a single power underlying a variety of demanding mental tasks, or whether we have to see it as inevitably split. Stephen Wiseman (1967) noted that the British tend to see the structure of the mind as a hierarchy, in which general ability (*g*) oversees subsidiary groups and subgroups of particular abilities. American investigators, on the other hand, tend to view the mind as a composite of "primary abilities," without postulating an overall or commanding intellectual power. Wiseman, who has studied both approaches to intelligence, pointed out that they do not contradict each other. He noted that when Americans explain the complex relationships among primary abilities by positing intermediate factors, they are actually implying a hierarchy.

Wiseman's conclusion that there is such a hierarchy in all explanations of intellect may well reflect his British training. It is appealing, nonetheless, to see both unitary and diversified approaches to intelligence converging to form a more complete picture of cognition.

Let us now look at a series of excerpts from researchers' attempts to define intelligence. The dates given are those of the particular texts chosen; in some cases, notably those of Terman and Cattell, the definitions were influential much earlier. These statements represent—although not exhaustively—the concepts of intelligence that have been applied to the study of the gifted.

The first group has approached intelligence as something basically unitary. Some definitions (Binet and Simon's, and Wechsler's, for example) include particular ways in which the underlying intelligence expresses itself. Others (Spearman's, Burt's, and Vernon's) place mental operations in a definite order of complexity, with the general factor playing the guiding role. Hebb, more explicitly than the others, considers the underlying potential to be innate, depending upon experience to stimulate its development.

The second group either avoids assuming that a single power underlies intellectual activity, or treats the notion as a wispy ideal that defies demonstration. The definitions focus on particular kinds of intellectual activity, each of which is considered sufficiently distinct from the others to warrant specific attention. Over a number of years, two persons in this group have had a strong influence upon the study of intelligence: Thurstone and Guilford. They analyzed a large number of intelligence tests and devised many themselves, in order to identify the significant components to intelligence. Thurstone's work led to published tests of intelligence that give separate measures of seven kinds of intellectual activity (his "primary mental abilities"). Guilford's research has yielded a large number of tests, based on a model of intelligence from which he hopes eventually to yield tests of 120 components. Thorndike's three-part definition of intelligence led to his "CAVD" test (so-called because its four sections are Completion, Arithmetic, Vocabulary, and Directions). His work in the 1920s was the precursor of the later, more sophisticated tests of specific intellectual aptitudes. In recent years, Cattell's broad classification into fluid and crystallized intelligence has attracted attention because it emphasizes the difference between pure, abstract cognitive activity and highly specific mental operations that depend on instruction and experience.

The definitions of intelligence offered by Jean Piaget stand apart from all the others because they are not associated with the ordinary kind of standardized test or with the approach to quantitative discrimination among levels of intelligence that underlies most tests. His concern has been to see how a child's mind grows, how it learns to grapple with problems, how the body's nervous system relates to the universe of substance and experience.

Intelligence as a Unitary Structure

Alfred Binet and Théodore Simon (1905–11)*

Thinking, in our opinion, consists of three distinct parts: purpose, adaptation, and correction.

First, purpose. To perform consciously and confidently . . . it is necessary to know "what is to be done." . . . There is not only direction to thought, there is development . . . [in] the successive states of mind we go through. This development . . . has often been called choice; . . . it consists in choosing continually among several states, several ideas, several methods. . . . Thinking . . . moves toward decision; it starts with chaos . . . and ends with a conception whose definite outline conforms to reality. Adaptation does not occur decisively, at the first attempt, but by exploring, . . . by successive trials; we are like a locksmith, called to open a locked door, who searches through his . . . keys and tries

---

*Binet and Simon quotes are author's translations.

several: . . . his attempts are not blind, but guided, chosen. The last part of the mental mechanism that we are trying to take apart is an apparatus for correction. It has been given different names: critical sense, . . . judgment, . . . self-correction. . . . Before pulling the trigger a marksman makes sure his weapon is correctly aimed. Likewise [in thinking] control intervenes to see that a method will work. . . . Without this careful selection, no adaptation would succeed. (Binet & Simon, 1909, p. 128)

Understanding, imagination, purpose, and correction, intelligence is summed up in these four words. (Binet, 1911a, p. 117)

Intelligence, it seems to us, has a fundamental activity: . . . judgment, otherwise called wisdom, common sense, initiative, adaptability. To judge well, to understand well, to reason well—these are the mainsprings of intelligence. A person can be a moron . . . . if he lacks judgment; with good judgment, never. Everything else in the psychology of intelligence seems hardly to matter alongside judgment. (Binet & Simon, 1905, pp. 196 *ff.*)

Charles E. Spearman (1927)

[The continued] success of the same person throughout all variations of both form and subject matter—that is to say, throughout all conscious aspects of cognition whatever—appears only explicable by some factor lying deeper than the phenomena of consciousness. And thus there emerges the concept of a hypothetical *general* and purely *quantitative* factor underlying all cognitive performances . . . g . . . taken to consist in something of the nature of an "energy" or "power."

. . . Each different operation must necessarily be further served by some *specific* factor peculiar to it. (p. 5)

. . . Cognitive events . . . admit . . . of being reduced to a small number of definitely formulatable principles[:] *Apprehension of Experience.* . . . Any lived experience tends to evoke immediately a knowing of its direct attributes and its experiencer. *Eduction of Relations.* . . . The presenting of any two or more characters tends to evoke immediately a knowing or relation between them. . . . *Eduction of Correlates.* . . . The presenting of any character together with a relation tends to evoke immediately a knowing of the correlative character. For example, if the idea of "good" and that of "opposite to" are presented, there can out of these be obtained the correlative idea of "bad." (pp. 341–43)

Lewis M. Terman (1954)

Granting that both interest patterns and special aptitudes play important roles in the making of a gifted scientist, mathematician, mechanic, artist, poet, or musical composer, I am convinced that to achieve greatly in almost any field, the special talents have to be backed up by a lot of Spearman's g, by which is meant the kind of general intelligence that requires ability to form many sharply defined concepts, to manipulate them, and to perceive subtle relationships between them; in other words, the ability to engage in abstract thinking. (p. 224)

Cyril Burt (1949)

My own view was that the structure of the mind is essentially hierarchical. Mental processes and mental capacities appear to consist of systems within systems.

According to their relative complexity, the various components seem assignable to one or other of four or five distinguishable levels. . . . Elementary sensory impressions or . . . elementary motor reactions . . . constitute the lowest mental level. The next includes the more complex processes of perception with equally complex reactions on the motor side. The third is the level of mechanical association—of memory and of habit. The fourth and highest of all involves the apprehension and application of relations. "Intelligence" as the "integrative function of the mind," is involved at every level; and its manifestations therefore differ not only in degree, but also in their qualitative nature. (pp. 110-11)

Philip E. Vernon (1961)

. . . a feature which appears to be highly characteristic of mental structure [is] hierarchy. After the removal of *g*, tests tend to fall into two main groups: the verbal-numerical-educational on the one hand (referred to as *v:ed* factor), and the practical-mechanical-spatial-physical on the other hand (referred to as *k:m* factor). If the analysis is sufficiently detailed, . . . these types themselves subdivide. The *v:ed* factor gives minor *v* and *n* (number) group factors. In other analyses, *k:m* splits similarly into mechanical information, spatial and manual subfactors. Thus a first approximation to mental structure is provided by the hierarchical diagram of [the figure], resembling a genealogical tree. (pp. 22-23)

Donald O. Hebb (1949)

. . . it appears that the word "intelligence" has *two* valuable meanings. One is (*A*) an *innate potential*, the capacity for development, a fully innate property that amounts to the possession of a good brain and a good neural metabolism. The second is (*B*) the functioning of a brain in which development has gone on, determining an *average level of performance or comprehension* by the partly grown or mature person. Neither, of course, is observed directly; but *intelligence B*, a hypothetical level of development in brain function, is a much more direct inference from behavior than *intelligence A*, the original potential. (p. 294)

(Note: To Hebb's two kinds of intelligence, Vernon later added *intelligence C*, that aspect of mental ability that is actually measured by a particular test, since no one test draws upon the entire domain of mental abilities.)

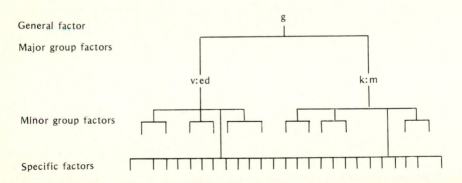

General factor

Major group factors

Minor group factors

Specific factors

David Wechsler (1958)

Intelligence is the aggregate or global capacity of the individual to act purposefully, think rationally, and deal effectively with his environment. (p. 7)

Intelligence as a Composite of Abilities

Edward L. Thorndike (1927, 1940)

We have learned to think of intellect as the ability to succeed with intellectual tasks, and to measure it by making an inventory of a fair sampling from these tasks, arranging these in levels of intellectual difficulty, and observing how many the intellect in question suceeds with at each level (and, if we wish, how long a time each success takes). (1927, p. 412)

. . . [There are three kinds of intelligence:] 1) *abstract* (verbal intelligence or ability with ideas, as in language and mathematics, and much of science and affairs); 2) *mechanical* intelligence (ability to understand things, as in skilled trades and much of science); 3) *social* intelligence (ability to understand persons and other animals). (1940, p. 57)

Louis L. Thurstone (1938)

Intelligence, according to Thurstone, is made up of these "primary mental abilities" (Cronbach, 1970):

V (verbal), as in a vocabulary test;

N (number), as in simple computation;

S (spatial), as in reasoning about visual forms when moved about or transformed;

M (memory), as in rote learning;

R (reasoning), as in logical inferences, for example, the Binet water-jar problems;

W (word-fluency), as in supplying words rapidly, for example, giving as many words as possible that start with a certain letter;

P (perceptual speed), as in clerical tasks comparing pictures and symbols rapidly.

Joy P. Guilford (1959)

The factors [making up the structure of intellect] . . . can be classified . . . in certain ways. One basis of classification is according to the basic kind of *process* or operation performed. This kind of classification gives us five major groups of intellectual abilities: factors of cognition, memory, convergent thinking, divergent thinking, and evaluation. . . .

A second way of classifying the intellectual factors is according to the kind of material or *content* involved . . . : figural, symbolic, semantic. . . . When a certain operation is applied to a certain kind of content, as many as six general kinds of *products* may be involved . . . : units, classes, relations, systems, transformations, and implications. . . .

The three kinds of classifications of the factors of intellect can be represented by means of a single solid model . . . , which we call the "structure of intellect"[:] (pp. 470–71)

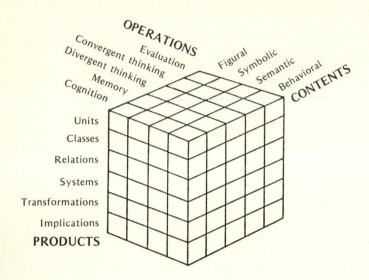

On this cubical model we see each category shown as it relates to the others: content (the subject of a problem, for example), operation (how the problem is attacked), and product (what kind of answer the problem has). Note that there are four contents on this cube, whereas in the quotation above, Guilford listed only three: figural, symbolic, and semantic. Later on in the same quotation, he discussed the fourth content, behavioral, to refer to social intelligence. Altogether there are 120 possible combinations (four contents × five processes × six products), each defining a unique mental operation. Guilford has systematically devised tests for most of these individual operations, the best known of which have to do with the operation of divergent thinking.

Raymond B. Cattell (1971)

Crystallized general mental capacity shows itself heavily in such primary abilities as verbal, . . . numerical, . . . reasoning, . . . mechanical information and skills, . . . and experiential judgment (in social and other fields). Fluid ability appears in series, classifications, analogies, topology, and other well-known intelligence tests, when couched in shapes which are neither verbal nor pictorial, but such as would be equally accessible to a person of any background. . . .

. . . [C]rystallized ability . . . operate[s] in areas where the judgments have been taught systematically or experienced before. The differences between the words, say "aplomb" and "savoir faire," or between "definite" and "definitive," in a synonyms test, or, in a mechanical knowledge . . . test, between using an ordinary wrench or a box spanner on part of one's automobile, requires intelligence for the initial perception and learning of the discrimination (wherefore some never will learn it). But thereafter it becomes a crystallized skill, relatively automatically applied. . . .

Fluid ability, by contrast, appears to operate whenever the sheer perception of complex relations is involved. It thus shows up in tests where borrowing from stored, crystallized, judgmental skills brings no advantage. . . . In short, fluid intelligence is an expression of the level of complexity of relationships which an individual can perceive and act upon when he does not have recourse to answers to such complex issues already stored in memory. (pp. 98-99)

Jean Piaget (1950, 1952)
Finally, let us consider the different approach of Jean Piaget, who stands somewhat apart from the measurement tradition behind the other definitions.

... Intelligence is a particular instance of biological adaptation. (1952, pp. 3-4)

[Intelligence] is the form of equilibrium toward which all the [cognitive] structures . . . tend. (1950, p. 6)

[Intelligence] is essentially a system of living and acting operations. (1950, p. 7)

These three statements emphasize the special interest Piaget has in children's mental activity. He is not much concerned with measuring their levels of "pure intelligence," or comparing one child to another. Rather he would find out how a child—of any age, in any culture—goes about discovering and understanding reality. For Piaget, this is a continuing process of interpreting and reinterpreting experience, of actively coping in more and more sophisticated ways with increasingly complicated perceptions of the world.

APPLYING THE DEFINITIONS

The definitions above make a bewildering series. Clearly no succinct statement would be acceptable to all investigators. The differences in the definitions are not merely semantic; they are fundamental. However, some order is feasible, for a common concern has informed most large-scale and systematic surveys of the gifted: the need for a system by which children can be placed along some continuum of brightness that enables both educators and researchers to group the brightest together. For example, a clinician typically administers an intelligence test and then writes a lengthy report telling in some detail how the child's mind seemed to work in solving the various problems the test presented. But when asked if the child qualifies as gifted, the tester usually bases a nomination to a considerable extent upon a single shorthand label, say the IQ. No matter that some subscores are also available, such as those for verbal versus quantitative abilities. The gifted children assembled for study would first of all have been picked according to a single, summary score.

It is this pragmatic challenge—to find some feasible basis for grouping children as gifted—that helps us understand how the definitions of intelligence given above relate to the study of gifted children. Let us now look more closely at the dominant definitions, those emphasizing general intelligence and those emphasizing specific abilities.

General Intelligence

The unitary view of intelligence has been the commonest basis for grouping gifted children. It goes back to Binet: the capacity to make judgments, to adapt to demands, to maintain a direction, to be self-critical. A series of questions or problems would probe how a child judges, checks, perseveres. These "shafts" would be added together into a total performance without assuming any systematic relation among the different shafts (a hierarchy, for instance, or clusters of similar types of questions). Neither would a child's personal and perhaps idiosyncratic kinds of mental performance be recognized in the eventual score. Terman was not concerned with *how* a child figures out the answer to a question (as Piaget was learning to do in about the same era). Terman's focus was upon how correct the child's answer would be. According to the task set, "correct" would mean accurate (as in arithmetic problems), or efficient (as in searching for something), or quick (as in naming things), or even arbitrarily approaching a norm (as in questions about social customs). Sometimes the quality of the answer would dictate partial or full credit. But always the tester and the child would understand that the "questions" have "answers." To put it another way, these tests are based on the assumption that the bright child can reason more powerfully than the average child: more completely, more sophisticatedly, more accurately, and more spontaneously. The opposite inference is always there: the "dull" child doesn't know the answers, misunderstands the questions, or gives wrong answers, or can't really come round quickly enough to a proper strategy. The bright child's intelligence, then, is defined as quick development, accumulation of compendious information, or clever strategies or astute observations—some of them or all of them, depending on the test and the tester. The test samples brightness in such a way that the total impression the child makes can be identified with a certain level or percentile of ability (as with Binet) or in a score like the IQ (as with Terman and most later specialists).

Spearman accepted the unit-score rationale and the successive levels of accomplishment applicable to all children. His main concern was for *g*, whether as an actual test score or as the mathematically derived abstraction of features common to various tests. He was uncomfortable with a grab bag of individual contributions from mental operations, each treated as equal to any other. He preferred tracking down mental operations to their source, trying to keep separate the specific manifestations (his *s*'s) that are quite particular and often small scale from *g*, the more important central stimulus to them all. His view was that the bright are simply those whose underlying mental force (*g*) is great, and who can be expected to produce a greater variety and higher quality of particular products than those with a weaker *g*. The difference in approach, then, is between the pragmatic acceptance of any number of manifestations of intelligence, major and minor alike, and an elegant arrangement that pushes the commanding element into the foreground.

Burt and Vernon, like Spearman, emphasized a hierarchy of intellectual activity. They insisted that the series of increasingly particular mental operations we see as we go from *g* to *s*, from general to specific, makes up a beautifully arranged whole. Individual mental acts, however narrow, derive from the overall, commanding source of intellectual behavior. For Hebb, the distinction between Intelligence *A* and Intelligence *B* is also hierarchical, with *A* taking the prior, even hereditary position, supplying the potential which *B* is to develop. Wechsler made explicit the integrative nature of intelligence, its unifying capacity to coordinate body and experience, abstract and specific.

However, all these distinctions were more interesting to students of intelligence than to students of brightness. It was mainly scholars studying intelligence, not those studying brightness, who confronted the problem that arose when the general public became accustomed to the term "IQ" and improperly used it as a synonym for intelligence. Hebb and Vernon were the most persuasive explicators of the distinction between an underlying entity presumed and abstractly described ("intelligence," "mind," "mental function," "*g*") and a child's performance on a particular test (the "IQ").

Research workers have always respected this subtlety, but only recently has it become recognized in public debate. This has usually occurred in a situation where a test score is questioned because a given child's background seems at odds with knowledge and abilities demanded in the test—a question referring to things the child could not have learned in the home or neighborhood, or problems couched in unfamilar terms. We shall look into these issues in the next chapter on social policy and educational planning. Here it is enough to say that, until recently, the working definition of gifted has referred to an individual's ability to score well on the line of intelligence tests coming from Binet and Terman, and to emphasize the significant fact that these men chose certain children when they standardized their tests.

Terman sent his associates out to give his new test to hundreds of children (whose scores would then become the norms against which to judge any child to whom a tester would later give the finished test). He explicitly ordered that the children were to be "representative" of the whole population of American children. That meant, of course, that they should come from all over the country and from various economic levels (Terman's plan very carefully matched his children's backgrounds against the census data available). But he was even more specific: the children must have had "average opportunity to learn." Only then could differences in their test performance be properly credited to their mental ability. Terman defined "average opportunity to learn" to include all of the following: Caucasian racial stock, English as the preferred language at home, attendance at public (not private) school, and freedom from chronic illness or handicap. This is not the time to enlarge on this specification. But note that a test with these assumptions will be most properly used with children who have *all* four traits. Children of foreign or nonwhite origins, or physical frailty, or intermittent schooling make a demand on the test that it was not designed to meet. Low scores might be ambiguous (do they indicate low intelligence or insufficient opportunity?) and high scores might be depressed (how much higher would they be if the children came from a different background?).

Specific Abilities

So far, we have been discussing intelligence as a single, basic entity, something that can usefully be estimated in a score or a rating. Brief labels have been a decided convenience to persons who look for gifted children, because they simplify identification and grouping. Indeed, for years, typical programs for bright children have depended upon terse labels to compare children's intellectual levels. There have been arguments about which definition of intelligence to heed, which test to use, which span of scores to include. But the effort to choose children for gifted programs has biased the search in favor of simple methods. So "gifted" has often meant "high IQ," or excellent performance on some narrow estimate of all-round intelligence.

Group factors

But look again at the series of definitions of intelligence cited earlier. They do not converge on a single dominant trait, such as problem-solving or skill with abstractions. Nor have tests of intelligence always provided a single score, as with the Stanford-Binet. During much of the twentieth century, in fact, there has been serious disagreement about whether intellectual behavior, as complex as it is, should be reduced to a simple level or score. This disagreement eventually affected social programs for the gifted, which used to consider only high IQ as a criterion for selection but which now employ numerous methods for discovering mental prowess.

British psychologists have kept consistently to the notion of a hierarchy, the idea that an overall intellectual force is made up of related but less comprehensive parts. At first, Spearman found two levels of behavior significant: the highly idiosyncratic specific factors in particular test items, which he called *s*'s; and something that all the *s*'s shared to one degree or another, the "general factor," or *g*. Later he was persuaded to add an intermediate level of behavior when data seemed to show dependable associations among *s*'s well short of the overall *g*. These associations he attributed to "group factors."

Spearman's successors have followed this main outline, as can be seen in Vernon's pyramid. At the bottom of the pyramid is a great array of *s*'s, very specific and often minute, the skills required for mental labor: an arithmetic combination, a definition of a word, a projection of a series by one more step, a paraphrase of a proverb. Covering as they do a wide domain, these *s*'s group themselves in various ways. Major group factors common to many *s*'s might be, in Vernon's scheme, *v:ed* (ability to deal with tasks requiring verbal and mathematical aptitude) and *k:m* (relatively nonverbal ability, such as understanding spatial relations or solving problems that do not depend on the formal languages of arithmetic or prose). Minor group factors are subdivisions of the major factors. For example, understanding proverbs and knowing certain word definitions are different skills, but they both share a common basis of language facility. At the top of the pyramid, arising from everything underneath, is *g*, the comprehensive, general factor. H. J. Butcher has made a persuasive case for this *g*-dominated pyramid, saying that intelligence is "the broadest and most pervasive cognitive trait, and is conceived of as being involved in virtually every kind of intellectual skill" (1968, p. 24). He added an important qualification: while intelligence as a unitary trait will always serve in an integrating manner, the hierarchies it manipulates will vary in content and complexity according to the individual. Thus, while the British view gives the prime role to underlying, unifying intelligence, it gives a very high place to separate, specific abilities, because they are the raw materials upon which intelligence works.

In the United States, a somewhat different attitude prevails. American investigators tend to view group factors as the broadest aspect of intelligence that can be demonstrated. Anything more inclusive, such as *g*, is considered no more than a statistical abstraction—something that either has not been tested directly as such or has not been equated with specific behavior. Thorndike, an early investigator, settled on certain specific aspects of intelligence that he thought of prime importance in understanding how pupils learn. As we noted above, he used his three-part definition of intelligence to build his so-called CAVD test.

After Thorndike came two major figures, Thurstone and Guilford, who set the basic American strategy for analyzing intelligence, which has been the same as in Britain—factor analysis. Thurstone, in his pioneering work, developed statistical means for detecting discrete groups of abilities from among the answers that persons give to the many questions on a test. Each grouping so located would be attributed to a particular intellectual factor that is relatively independent. Thurstone isolated seven such factors and developed tests to measure them in children. Guilford has carried Thurstone's logic further, to the point of postulating 120 theoretically separate components to intelligence.

Cattell has preferred to avoid minute analysis, looking instead for very broad components, which he calls "fluid" and "crystallized" intelligence. He had been a student of Spearman, and these two aspects of intelligence come out of the British tradition. *Fluid intelligence* is akin to Vernon's *k:m*, and refers to reasoning, especially reasoning that does not demand school-learned vocabulary or tactics. This reasoning is concentrated in test questions that ask a person to detect a design that is part of ("imbedded in") a larger pattern whose own dominant characteristics obscure or camouflage the part to be sought. *Crystallized intelligence*, like Vernon's *v:ed*, may reflect experience and direct teaching, as in test questions that require computation or factual knowledge. Cattell believes that fluid intelligence is the more basic, giving rise as a child grows to the crystallized forms and strategies that can vary so from child to child and from culture to culture.

Erness Brody and Nathan Brody (1976) noted in these two kinds of intelligence the contributions of biology and environment. Like Cattell, they assigned prior importance to fluid intelligence. All three Americans—

Thurstone, Guilford, and Cattell—have concentrated on identifying components of intelligence, denying the necessity or existence of any general power. Current discussions, however, are returning attention to general, overall intelligence. Thurstone's Primary Abilities Test, for example, which derived from analysis of several separate mental operations, routinely provides an IQ that is a summary, numerical statement determined by the contributions of the various "primary mental abilities." Cattell has offered what may be a synthesis of the traditions: he does not deny the central importance of Spearman's g, but he thinks that any general factor is best approached by first identifying components and then interpreting what they have in common as the g (Butcher, 1968).

Once we take the theoretical, central-versus-component argument and try to apply it to the schools, we encounter difficulties. While the proponents of g have elaborated an attractive model of the mind, they have been unable to produce a satisfactory test of it. The single-score tests presently used to identify bright children ask a variety of questions that are thrown together without a truly systematic method of relating them all to underlying capacity. The typical IQ is not a direct measure of g, then, but a score based on diverse intellectual tasks—none of which is given priority in evaluation. Citing an IQ as a direct measure of intelligence is, therefore, distressingly inexact. On the other hand, attempts to tease apart intelligence into factors have been more successful statistically than they have been empirically. This is especially true of Guilford's work. While the many facets of intelligence he has delineated show up in factor analysis, they do not yet adequately correspond to the actual kinds of activities children display. And Brody and Brody pointed out that even though a statistical average may well show a general factor underlying the questions on a test, an individual child may have a discrete and personal set of techniques that would be lost in the group averages. Butcher (1968), speaking of the tendency to seek more and more specific factors, noted that what we gain in rigor we may lose in richness and reality. Vernon (1977) has been more blunt; for him, the largest number of component factors that has practical value is three or four—verbal, mathematical, spatial, and inductive.

Levels of intellectual development

The hierarchical view of intelligence and the search for its specific components have both depended on the statistical analysis of tests. Another major line of investigation has only slowly made its way into the mainstream. It is the search for how intelligence—whether unitary or multiple—changes as children grow up. The towering figure in this endeavor is Jean Piaget, the Swiss psychologist, who views intelligence as a biologist and who attends as much to *how* children go about solving problems as he does to checking their final answers. His theory assumes a constant interplay between the stimuli that experience offers children and the children's growing ability to cope with experience. Piaget sees successive steps in the strategy of coping. These steps start with raw sensations and motor reactions in infancy, go through considerable refinement in ways of imposing order on concrete experiences during childhood, and finally reach abstract thinking in adolescence. We should not construe these steps as separate special abilities, but rather as increasingly sophisticated manifestations of a child's growing ability to cope with the environment. To this extent, Piaget stands somewhat apart from the group of investigators we are here considering, who look for different and separate components to intelligence.

A major effect of Piaget's research has been a growing awareness that children's thinking is different from adult thinking—not merely a cruder or sloppier form of it. Instead, as Piaget has shown in marvelous detail, children become more and more adept at finding their own order in experience. When confronted with a problem, they employ the shrewdest solution available to them at their level of understanding. A basic demand throughout their intellectual maturation is dealing with the increasingly complex contradictions in their experience. Piaget assumes that each intellectual stage is a prerequisite to the next, culminating in the stage of abstract reasoning, which usually occurs in adolescence and enables the individual to understand and resolve many contradictions that were puzzling in childhood—the "triumph of logic over the senses." Klaus Riegel (1973) has suggested a further stage, where adults need not always insist on resolving all contradictions in concrete experience. At this point, fully mature reasoning may accept some stubborn contradictions as givens, while working to resolve others.

Essential to Piaget's theory is the notion that a child must reorganize earlier strategies of problem-solving before moving on to more sophisticated forms. Gifted children (who happen to interest Piaget very little) might pass through the several stages more quickly than other children, but the stages would all have to come in their proper order to ensure adequate reorganization. Critics have attacked this position. They admit that Piaget has demonstrated different levels of intellectual activity, which tend to get more demanding as age increases. But, as John Horn (1976) has pointed out, children's increasing ability to solve more difficult problems does not prove that they have reorganized their actual mode of thinking. It may indicate no more than the fact that they have learned how to solve problems that happen to be more difficult. Just how reformulation goes on, what prompts it, and how long such a process takes in different children are still important questions to ask about Piaget's interpretation of mental growth. Already his theory has had a strong impact on the direction of current research into intelligence and specific abilities. Several persons have been developing standardized tests based on his clinical method of exploring problems with individual children. These tests and the parent literature by Piaget and his colleagues show that as children grow, they employ changing mixtures of sensation, perception, motor coordination, concrete experience, and abstract reasoning in their mental processes.

Both traditional psychologists and Piaget have also shown that children develop more and more specific ways of analyzing their experience. Anastasi (1970) has found reliable evidence that the higher a child's performance is in a particular cognitive area, the larger the number of discrete intellectual factors developed in that area. Therefore, tests that aim at broad, general intelligence would be more suitable for elementary children than for adolescents. J. McVicker Hunt (1961) has recommended that we avoid seeking even the major group factors (mathematical or verbal aptitude, for instance) in children, and wait instead until secondary school to measure them. Some data support this recommendation: with the young, global IQs predict later progress; with older children, more sensitive differential scores are useful.

Very recent longitudinal investigations have also given further information about Cattell's distinction between fluid and crystallized intelligence. In the past, cross-sectional studies (which measure people of many ages all at about the same time) have suggested that there is a decline in basic intelligence during adulthood. But longitudinal studies (which follow individual persons as they get older, retesting them from time to time) have not shown such a steady decline. This is especially true when attention is paid to the point at which senility begins to occur. Decline comes as death approaches, whether in the forties or in the eighties. In Cattell's categories, fluid intelligence is more likely to be what deteriorates, while crystallized intelligence tends to remain intact. That is, age brings increasing trouble with organizing, finding relationships, making hypotheses, and changing tasks. It does not erode already organized behavior or habitual skills. Presumably, gifted adults resist decline in both categories, although we do not have enough empirical information to be certain.

Special talents

Programs for the gifted have rarely been developed in order to make distinctions such as that between fluid and crystallized intelligence. We shall examine later how Guilford's divergent thinking tests have stimulated interest in creativity, but first let us look at some other specific intellectual abilities that have traditionally received more attention in the schools. We must remember, of course, that the overwhelming majority of systematic efforts to help the gifted have proceeded on the assumption that they possess a general, overall intellectual superiority. Terman's credo has been pervasive: a high score on a general intelligence test identifies a child who has the broad capacity to develop particular interests and skills. That is, general intelligence is related to specific manifestations. But some people have asked why we don't look directly for specific, concrete talent, rather than approaching it indirectly through general intelligence tests.

The most impressive contemporary example of direct intervention in the area of special talents has come in the field of mathematics. There is a long tradition to suggest that some children show an early and marked ability for the manipulation of figures and a remarkable insight into abstract mathematical concepts. Julian Stanley and his associates at The Johns Hopkins University have, since 1971, been studying just this sort of mathematical precocity, focusing on how to recognize it and how to develop it. In Chapter 7, we shall look in detail at the variety of changes Stanley's group has stimulated in school procedures. Here we shall review what they have found to be the underlying features of mathematical precocity.

Stanley's boys and girls are generally high scorers on traditional intelligence tests, but he has found that more exacting and difficult tests of mathematical skill are needed to identify and help the truly precocious (Stanley, Keating, & Fox, 1974). Difficult high-school and college tests given to elementary and junior high school pupils each year aid in identifying a significant number of children who have already learned—usually on their own—far more than their classmates. These pupils show strong interest in mathematics, and they respond well to radically accelerated instruction and independent study. Some do well in individual college-level mathematics courses when they are only thirteen or fourteen years old, and some undertake full-time college study several years early.

Stanley's research is unique in that it not only focuses on the search for the characteristics accompanying mathematical skill, but carefully promotes and assesses pedagogic tactics for fostering this skill. For example, like others, he has found more boys than girls with precocious mathematical talent. But he is also exploring the social sources of this difference and trying to develop specific school curricula to stimulate girls. Stanley is already convinced that we can identify children who have strong ability in mathematics early, directly, and reliably. We can thus begin sooner to give them the proper attention and instruction.

So encouraging have the results been that a parallel strategy is under way at Johns Hopkins to locate and help children with demonstrated verbal skill. Early results make it appear that there may be fewer children who show verbal precocity than quantitative precocity (Keating, 1976). The reason for this is not clear, but Daniel Keating suggested that at least part of the explanation may be that while mathematics is a more "closed," inner system of thought, verbal facility depends to a larger extent on life experience and is therefore more "open." We are reminded of earlier work by Harvey Lehman (1953), who showed that people make major contributions to mathematics and science at a much earlier age than their peers do in the social sciences. The explanation is similar: mathematics (with the sciences that draw upon it) is a self-contained discipline. Social thought, on the other hand, requires broad (and often lengthy) experience before clever minds can make novel contributions.

In both the language and mathematics programs at Johns Hopkins, the nature of the testing process is such that promising students are chosen on the basis of abilities they have already cultivated. But Stanley believes a larger number of potentially high achievers could be located if *both* a general-purpose intelligence test and a demanding measure of demonstrated achievement were employed in the schools—a general intelligence test alone is not responsive enough to the highest levels of mathematical talent.

Educators face a similar situation when they seek children with musical talent. This talent, an awesome mixture of aesthetic sensibility, abstract thought, and (for performers) motor dexterity, often emerges, like mathematical ability, at an early age. While tests have been produced to locate children with unusual sensitivity in this area, they have not been widely successful. Traditionally, children stand out as precocious musicians precisely because they are already capable of remarkable musical performance—most of them having received early training.

But Shinichi Suzuki (1969) has challenged the common assumption that only a few children have musical aptitude. He has pointed out that a phenomenon most of us take for granted—a child's ability to learn the native tongue and speak it fluently—displays remarkable use of talent. If the same approach were used with music as with language acquisition, Suzuki believes children would display equally remarkable abilities in that sphere. Therefore, he urges exposure to music from infancy, with mother and child learning together, if possible. As he said in a 1964 interview, "if a child hears good music from the day of his birth, and learns to play it himself, he develops sensitivity, discipline, and endurance. He gets a beautiful heart" (p. 73). Some of Suzuki's pupils (about 5 percent) have become professional musicians. But his major aim is to develop musical ability in all children.

There are still other talents that seem to be relatively independent of general intelligence, and which have traditionally been encouraged separately. Anastasi (1958) reported low correlations between tests of general intelligence and tests of artistic (including musical) talent and mechanical invention. Vernon et al. (1977) also cited the low correlations between general intelligence and scientific, mathematical, and writing aptitudes. It is still an open question, whether or not we should consider these several talents as outlets for intelligence or as separate activities that depend little upon any common, underlying source of productive energy. Vernon likened this question to the one concerning the root of intelligence—the heredity-environment controversy.

A major obstacle to determining the link between talent and intelligence is that we simply do not have enough concrete data about separate talents: how many children have which kind, how old they are when they display talent, and how many will also score well on more general measures of intelligence. Given this uncertainty, educators should probably cast a wide net in the hope of catching as many talented children as possible. Such a selection program would include children scoring in the top 10 percent of general intelligence test scores (about IQ 120 and above) and other children scoring in the top 10 percent on tests of special aptitudes. Vernon considers this total of 20 percent too high, because the most talented in either group would probably get inadequate attention. He recommends instead including the top 2 to 3 percent on intelligence tests (IQ 130 and up) and as many promising children as can be selected by tests of special talent or achievement.

Creativity

Of all the components of intelligence that have been analyzed in the mid-twentieth century, the one most often isolated for study in connection with brightness is variously called "creativity," "imagination," or—following Guilford—"divergent thinking." As with special talents, people frequently ask how much overlap there is between the domains of high intelligence and highly developed imagination. At one extreme are those who answer that at the very least there must be a minimal—and fairly comfortable—level of brightness for a child to be really creative. At the end of his career, Terman was convinced that great achievers in almost every field rely heavily on the use of their general intelligence (Spearman's g) in order to develop and work with specific concepts and to recognize the many relations between them.

At the other extreme are those who would make of imagination a special talent, whether broadly potent or specific to particular activities such as music or mechanics. The Getzels and Jackson report in 1962 (which contrasted high-creatives and high-scorers) is frequently cited to support separate attention to creativity and to supplement traditional intelligence tests with instruments that will uncover imaginative youngsters who might otherwise be missed.

What is creativity? Current interest in it is largely American, stemming from the same shift in educational policy that led to the renewed study of giftedness in the 1950s and 1960s. Investigators have observed imaginative children and adults across a broad range of activity: painting, poetry, architecture, and science. Most of the systematic study has been heavily influenced by Guilford's research during and after World War II into traits associated with novel thinking. He developed and analyzed tests of routine and innovative modes of thought, eventually synthesizing his results in a model for all mental activity—the well-known cubical diagram shown on page 68. Persons interested in creativity took their cue from Guilford's extended work on one part of the cube—that devoted to the process of divergent thinking. But another facet of the cube, dealing with the associated products of thinking, also includes elements closely related to the creative process. Guilford particularly stressed the importance of transformation—the mind's ability to consider change and process. Examples of transformation might be: reinterpreting a concept or a poem, following the path of a trajectory through space, or using objects and ideas in new and unusual ways. Guilford thinks that the two necessarily go together and that divergent-productive operations and transformations are equally essential components of creative thinking. The actual creative production is, of course, determined by the area in which the creative individual works: art, mathematics, and so on.

But no single definition or easy explanation of creativity has yet emerged. Liam Hudson (1966) has irreverently and persuasively damned both the idea of a constant called creativity and the claim that this constant differs from so-called general intelligence. He pointed out that tests of divergence don't correlate well with each other or with standard intelligence tests, citing the findings of Getzels and Jackson, who quoted correlations between open-ended tests at 0.3 to 0.4 and correlations between open-ended tests and a standard intelligence test at 0.2 to 0.3. These are low correlations and, as Burt (1962b) pointed out in a critical notice regarding the Getzels and Jackson report, they display about as much similarity (or dissimilarity) among themselves as they display dissimilarity (or similarity) with intelligence. Burt went on to remind us that British psychologists agree that general intelligence is the most important factor in creative activity and that it is what actually makes creativity meaningful. He cited Galton, pointing out that creativity divorced from guiding and underlying intelligence would be worthless. And as for the correlations Hudson thought so little of—Burt believed a single general factor accounts for them nicely. In fact, since creativity measures are more strongly correlated to general intelligence than they are to each other, he maintained that they should be used as corroborative measures for the usual battery of general intelligence tests. Finally, Gallagher found the Getzels and Jackson investigation a "deceptively easy study," difficult to interpret confidently (1975, p. 55).

Similarly, the rigorous comparison of creative and intelligent youngsters undertaken by Michael Wallach and Nathan Kogan (1965) did not settle definitively the question about overlap between intelligence and creativity. Their investigation allowed children the latitude to perform highly creative activities and to use unusual approaches to problems during the creativity-measurement segment of the tests. After examining the results of the tests, Wallach and Kogan found that the two aspects of mental life *did* have distinctive characteristics, but they rejected the notion that they were mutually exclusive. The important differences they found between high-scoring and creative children already presupposed that all were within "the upper part of the intellective range."

The current trend, then, is to accept a distinction between high intelligence and inventiveness, while also recognizing that they are not completely separate. We may need to use different tools to discover or assess them, and they probably do not show up in the same children to the same extent, but it appears that they coexist comfortably. In studying bright children, we may therefore expect them to be creative to varying degrees.

SUMMARY

As we look back on this chapter, what are the chief points? First, giftedness has called up a number of explanations, from the mystical to the prosaic. The dominant explanation is more a description: gifted children show intellectual powers far superior to those of ordinary children. Second, modern-day research has been more occupied with exploring what these powers are than in studying what it is that makes some children so superior. Third, these explorations of intelligence have tended to emphasize either a unitary characteristic—"intelligence"—or the several and varying activities that together may be thought of as intellectual. This difference in emphasis should not be exaggerated, for one may concentrate upon a unifying pattern while still examining its parts, just as one may focus on identifying separate activities that happen to have some connection with each other. Fourth, certain specific activities often receive separate consideration, notably aptitudes for fields like music and art and the broad category of imagination or creativity. The relation between these activities and a more general and perhaps underlying force is still being explored.

Until recently, most programs for gifted children have depended upon inclusive scores, like the IQ, that assume a very general intelligence. We are now giving greater attention to specific gifts, although we are far from abandoning either the idea of general intelligence or the practice of identifying gifted children—at least in part—according to their standing on some broad test of intelligence. We shall return to consider this question of definition in Chapter 5, when we look at the many ways in which gifted children are chosen. But before we discuss these procedures, let us try in the next chapter to answer the more fundamental question of why we should give special attention to the bright.

4

Society and the Gifted

We must dream of an aristocracy of
achievement arising out of a democracy of
opportunity.
Attributed to Thomas Jefferson

Long ago Plato described an ideal society. In *The Republic* he wrote of a plan by which citizens should be assigned roles according to their abilities. Those who would hold the greatest responsibilities would need long and careful training, so it was important to find the most promising children and start their education in good time. In the parable of the metals, Plato counseled the authorities to seek these "children of gold." Socrates is speaking to Glaucon:

> All of you in the city are certainly brothers, . . . but the god, in fashioning those of you who are competent to rule, mixed gold in at their birth; this is why they are most honored; in auxiliaries, silver; and iron and bronze in the farmers and other craftsmen. . . . It sometimes happens that a silver child is born from a golden parent, a golden child from a silver parent, and similarly all the others from each other. Hence the god commands the rulers first and foremost to be of nothing such good guardians and to keep over nothing so careful a watch as the children, seeing which of these metals is mixed in their souls. . . . If . . . one should naturally grow who has an admixture of gold or silver, they will honor such ones and lead them up, some to the guardian group, others to the auxiliary, believing that there is an oracle that the city will be destroyed when an iron or bronze man is its guardian. (Book 3, Section 415)

We need not adopt Plato's social order, giving supreme political power to the gifted when they have grown up. But Plato's vivid metaphor still has validity. We should look carefully at children to sense their traits, in order to recognize those who have promise and give them proper guidance.

If people took Plato's advice, there would be no need to catalog reasons for making special provisions for the gifted. But people don't. Let us take a recent example from the United States. A special report on the gifted (Marland, 1972) analyzed the federal government's 1971 distribution of school funds for exceptional children. Taking as "gifted and talented youth" the top 8 percent of the school population, the report showed that for every dollar spent on them, twenty-eight dollars went to "educationally deprived" pupils and forty-three dollars to handicapped pupils. In the United States, the federal government is not the major source of financial support to public schools, but a similar imbalance in allotment of funds occurs at all levels of government, in philanthropic contributions, in research support, and in teacher training. It is, without doubt, easier to attract sympathy to the handicapped than to children who combine the gifts of wit and vigor and grace. "They, above all, can take care of themselves," most people would say, and funds are dispensed accordingly. Once in a while, the pattern shifts, as in 1956, when the first Sputnik shocked America, and brought about an upsurge of interest in rigorous and accelerated education for the gifted. But the Sputnik effect faded away as the crisis died down. Today it seems to be shifting again.

How can the cause of the gifted be defended, in good times or bad, with or without crisis? Should it be? Is it really true that if we treat the gifted like everybody else, their native gifts will carry them along? Or would they and society alike suffer? There is a strong case for special attention to bright children, and great benefit would accrue to society and to the children themselves if we heed it. Let us summarize the case and then look at some of the arguments and problems that complicate the issue.

REASONS FOR ATTENDING TO THE GIFTED

Society's Needs

Plato's scheme was utopian, but in other eras there have been examples of practical programs in which the brightest children were educated for service to the state. In the next chapter we shall discuss various methods of choosing the bright. Here we shall focus on the reasons for choosing them.

Historical paradigms
A historic pattern that is not well known to the West developed from the fifteenth to the nineteenth centuries in the Ottoman Empire. The Palace School in Constantinople was its center. Each year the rulers assembled hundreds of boys from all over the empire. They were the handsomest, most intelligent and promising youths of their age in all the empire. The very cleverest among them would attend the Palace School for twelve to fourteen years. Those who finished successfully would go on to the highest posts in the imperial government.

In one way this recruiting was unusual: none of the boys could come from Turkish families, that is, from the commanding stratum in Ottoman society. Instead, they were deliberately drawn from subject peoples. They were, in fact, slaves. The rulers feared the political threat that a self-perpetuating bureaucratic caste might pose, so they ensured a constant turnover of fresh and capable young men from the outreaches of the empire. According to Barnette Miller (1941), the education offered in the Palace

School so effectively molded these young men to the Turkish norm that they rarely rebelled. He assessed the school as one of the main reasons for the remarkable success of the Ottoman Empire.

We have few examples of so thoroughgoing a commitment by a government to educating the brightest of its children for major service at every level: not education of the ruler's children or of his vassals' children, but education of the brightest from *without* the establishment in order that they might become its leaders. We do not endorse such slavery now; we recognize that excluding native Turks retarded cultural development; we know that the empire eventually fell prey to corruption and destruction. But during its high period, a cornerstone of its policy was recognition and training of the brightest youth.

Better known to the West is the much older and longer Chinese tradition of systematic examinations for the imperial civil service. As early as the Han dynasty in the second century B.C., a sort of imperial university was created to train promising young men for government service. Admission to the university, and later to government positions, depended on passing tough examinations. "The land, though won by the sword, could be governed only by the writing brush—that is, with the aid of men of education" (Reischauer & Fairbank, 1958, p. 107). It was a civil service system based on merit, almost 2000 years before the West developed such a system. And it lasted, with permutations, until the fall of the Manchu dynasty in 1912. Confucius was the spirit behind the examinations; in the *Analects* he said that there could be no good government unless the rulers followed this dictum: "Get the words right." Governing a vast empire demanded efficient communication, so the mandarinate had to write well: this included both officials in the provinces who communicated with the central government and ministers at the capital who received these communications and who wrote and revised the Emperor's decrees. The examinations, therefore, stressed writing skill, including poetry and calligraphy, as well as knowledge of basic Confucian writings. The mandarins were literate as few ruling classes have been, and to reach their posts they had to show early signs of verbal ability. In the high periods, hundreds of prospective candidates would complete their schooling and take the examinations each year. For thirteen centuries, most of the political leaders in China were products of this system, which aimed to instill ethical principles and respect for the proper rituals and behavior. Reischauer and Fairbank called this system of searching out talent "one of the world's greatest political inventions and a major reason for the extraordinary strength and stability of the Chinese Empire since T'ang times" (p. 166).

Early in our own era, Thomas Jefferson's restless mind turned to many problems that faced the infant United States. He believed that the new government would demand talent and that talent must be carefully sought. His "Bill for the More General Diffusion of Knowledge" (1779) opened with this pronouncement:

Experience hath shewn, that even under the best forms [of government], those entrusted with power have, in time, and by slow operations, perverted it into tyranny; and it is believed that the most effectual means of preventing this would be, to illuminate, as far as practicable, the minds of the people at large, . . . that . . . they may be enabled to know ambition under all its shapes, and prompt to exert their natural powers to defeat its purposes; and whereas . . . people will be happiest whose laws are best . . . administered, and that . . . laws will be . . . honestly administered, in proportion as those who form and administer them are wise and honest; whence it becomes expedient for promoting the publick happiness that those persons, whom nature hath endowed with genius and virtue, should be rendered by liberal education worthy to receive, and able to guard the sacred deposit of the rights and liberties of their fellow citizens, and that they should be called to that charge without regard to wealth, birth or other accidental condition or circumstance.

Democracy requires enlightened citizen-leaders. Jefferson proposed an elaborate scheme for the schools of Virginia, all based upon merit "without regard to wealth, birth or other accidental condition." Why? Because government is subject to tyranny and other abuse, and only the vigilance of a well-educated populace could preserve the new democracy in America.

In various cultures this argument endures: the body politic must have competent leaders and servants, whether the ultimate seat of authority is a tight oligarchy or a mass citizenry. Therefore, generation after generation, competence must be nurtured else the regime will fall. A corollary to this proposition is that the reservoir of talent is limited. Even in a political system where everybody is potentially eligible to take important social responsibility, there are levels of competence, with few who show the highest level.

Modern perspectives

In our day, the argument that society needs its talented children is most often couched in the jargon of world labor specialists. At a conference in Kungälv, Sweden, organized by the Organization for Economic Cooperation and Development (O.E.C.D.), the general theme was that modern societies need highly trained persons at every stage of economic and political complexity (Halsey, 1961). Delegates analyzed the problem from several vantage points. Dael Wolfle discussed how the "talent pool" in a country is determined. Jean Ferrez and Jean Floud demonstrated how geographic and class barriers may account for the uneven distribution of opportunity. Torsten Husén summarized the ways in which school organization affects development of talent. Attention also went to what looks like the opposite problem, that is, the threat posed by an oversupply of trained graduates in some countries (e.g., India). But the whole conference agreed with Pieter De Wolff and Kjell Härnqvist that on ethical as well as economic grounds, persons responsible for education must know better than they now do what their reserves of ability are. Only then will these countries be able to use them fully.

That same year John Gardner, in a discussion on excellence and social responsibility, said that high morale and drive are necessary for a free society to meet the challenge of the times—that prosperity would bring apathy unless the people had goals that would win commitment and inspire respect. Gardner's excellence is not exclusively academic or political, either:

> An excellent plumber is infinitely more admirable than an incompetent philosopher. The society which scorns excellence in plumbing because plumbing is a humble activity and tolerates shoddiness in philosophy because it is an exalted activity will have neither good plumbing nor good philosophy. Neither its pipes nor its theories will hold water. (1961, p. 86)

One major reason advanced to encourage the bright, then, is that society must have their contributions. It needs them, whether for sheer survival or for cultural enrichment, in countries that are struggling to industrialize and in countries that are struggling with the effects of industrialization. The institution of a rash of school reform plans in Europe after World War II was prompted by a critical need for trained, intelligent individuals who could help war-torn nations maximize resources, revive prosperity, and return to sane living. Those who planned the reforms based them on hard data about trained-labor reserves, unmet quotas, and cost-benefit ratios. Or they argued for the fundamental cultural benefits that accrue to the entire society when its talented young take up music and poetry.

Individual Development

Society's needs are not the only reason for giving special attention to gifted children. There is a powerful complementary argument: in a society committed to the development of the individual, each person has the right to an education that will lead to his or her fullest growth. This growth is not limited to finding a place in a technological society and doing a competent job there. Michael Wallach (1971) pleaded for greater attention to the more personal side of development. We should, he maintained, show

> greater concern for those neglected and inherently meaningful aspects of human functioning implicated in art, music, drama, literature, dance, and other endeavors to which . . . imagination, creativity, and expressiveness have some applicability. (p. 3)

But a thoroughly balanced view would expand Wallach's concern—encouraging creativity and sensitivity in the areas of science and industry as well. It would require individuals well-trained in these disciplines to redirect technological capabilities to remedy the harmful results of unchecked expansion and chart the course for future development—to guard, in short, against the tyranny of unchecked technology.

In the pure form, the argument for personal development has an ethical imperative, unsullied by profit to the body politic. Comenius, the great Moravian reformer of the seventeenth century, said, "All who are born as human beings need education because they are destined to be real men, not wild beasts, dull animals, and clumps of wood" (cited in Ulich, 1950, p. 342). Comenius was speaking of education for every child, in a day when only the very privileged got any. Today, with basic education for all widely accepted, even enforced, we face a parallel question: How can we serve each child with the most suitable education? Both mass education and special education are intended to ensure that children have the opportunity to realize their potentials. For the gifted this is not the huckster's admonition to nurture the bright because they will pay so much back on the investment. It is a majestic insistence that the human condition presupposes a high degree of sensitivity—sensitivity that will deaden if neglected. It is an injunction that children become full persons. If we believe that school should fit the child and develop potential to the utmost, then the gifted require their own special support.

The core of Jean Piaget's work shows that children's perceptual development depends on opportunities to experiment. Unless their environment provides such opportunities, perceptual development and thus conceptual thinking are retarded. In the same line (albeit with rats and dogs), Donald Hebb has shown that rearing in a restricted environment cuts down skill at problem solving and the ability to learn new things. What sort of surroundings will allow for the healthy intellectual growth of a very bright child who asks questions, who senses relations, who tries novel strategies, who wants to do many different things? If Piaget and Hebb are right, we may be stunting development if we do not give stimulation that is tuned to their capacity to respond.

But we cannot give all our attention to the gifted. If we do, George Bereday (1961) said bluntly that we shall paradoxically lose what we seek:

> There is no doubt that talented people render great services to the enrichment of our civilization. . . . But such talent will not be elicited if we fail to provide the spontaneous *total* upgrading through which the many intangible, immeasurable, and unsuspected human talents can find true fulfillment. How many Mozarts can we hope to find if six-tenths of the children of the world have never seen or heard a piano? Where is the much needed Miltiades to come from in the hour of need, if six out of ten children are illiterate or rachitic? If eliciting of high talent is to be the goal of education, its achievement . . . depends upon an advanced schooling for all. . . . It is the mass that creates the market for the talented. . . . No one is trained for a position of leader in a true democracy. All are trained to exercise qualities of leadership. (p. 365)

To say that it is a moral imperative to help the bright fulfill their promise—on their terms—implies the same imperative for the less bright, whose needs for fulfillment and accomplishment are just as compelling.

With these reservations in mind, we can summarize the two major arguments for helping the bright: society needs their talents, and they deserve to develop them. The two are often advanced separately, perhaps by different sorts of people, as Denis McMahon (1962) said in a lecture on the uses of talent:

> Basically, I suppose, . . . disagreement . . . reflects philosophically different standpoints, views on the relationship between the individual and society. Those

who come down on the side of "the needs of society"—a besetting though hidden temptation of the occupational psychologist—favor having the whole thing planned, parcelled and controlled. Those who come down on the side of the individual—essentially a liberal, democratic tropism (and according to Pastor Niemöller, . . . a litmus of Christianity)—try to keep things fluid, flexible, open.

Whichever appeals to influential planners, neither has yet secured to all bright children the stimulation and support they should get. Let us turn to some of the reasons why.

SOCIAL PROBLEMS AND IMPEDIMENTS

Elitism

A common objection to giving special attention to gifted children is that it favors a few unfairly and leads to the creation of an elite. Sometimes this complaint comes from disgruntled parents whose child wasn't chosen for a special class—and sometimes these parents are right. Test scores and evaluations can be inaccurate, so that deserving children are passed over. More often than not, however, these complaints arise from a "sour grapes" mentality rather than reasoned judgment. But sometimes the charge is more fundamental, made by someone who is committed to social equality, and this charge must be examined.

Partial rebuttal comes from a closer look at the meaning of "social equality." In their classic study of unequal opportunities in education, Lloyd Warner, Robert Havighurst, and Martin Loeb (1944) pointed out the difference between legal and civic equality and biological equality. They stressed that equal opportunity is not the same as identical opportunity. By the time children are five or six years old, they show such a diversity of ability, personality, and temperament that treating them all alike would be like "putting little chicks, ducklings, baby swans, puppies, kittens, and bear cubs all in a pond together and waiting to see how they respond to this 'equal opportunity' " (p. 149).

If children were really alike by school age, an identical curriculum might be sensible and just for all of them. But given the wide differences among them, the just school takes them as they come and treats each in the best way possible. There is a tradition that says crippled or deaf or retarded children require special teaching methods or classes—at least part of the time—because treating them as if they were normal would be asking them to learn under impossible conditions. They would be denied the same opportunity to learn that the regular curriculum offers to most pupils.

The same logic applies to the bright. Regular treatment is just as unfair. They, too, deserve to develop their potential, and this usually requires extensive schooling. Of course, such schooling gives them an advantage later for higher pay and larger responsibility. And it is this advantage that can look to the egalitarian like the grooming of a few for undeserved prestige and power. A quotation attributed to Thomas Jefferson answers this concern directly and succinctly: "We must dream of an aristocracy of achievement arising out of a democracy of opportunity." If all children are to have their fair opportunity, then specialized attention that fits individual gifts or handicaps is not only defensible but mandatory.

Another way to avoid elitism is to improve the lot of *all* children. We can't escape the diversity of endowments that children have, and we may not eliminate corresponding differences in income, status, and influence. What we can do is guarantee children equal opportunities during their formative years, so that the differences that emerge by adulthood have not come as a result of penalizing some persons or unfairly rewarding others. As we demand appropriate treatment for bright children in a general campaign to improve services for *all* children, the charge of elitism will probably die down. The charge expresses outrage at unfairness. We can counter by pointing out how unfair it is to treat brilliant children as though they were ordinary. We should mitigate the charge by working to see that average and exceptional children alike get appropriate attention.

The Reservoir of Talent

It is one thing to debate about elites, quite another to hear that there really isn't any problem. Principled belief in social equality guarantees a stiff and spirited argument, but apathy makes for no real discussion at all. In order to show that there is cause for concern, demographic data often sound more urgent than philosophical claims. Consider these twin questions: How many bright people are there? and How many do we need? If the supply is more than ample, perhaps we can afford to let the bright work out their lives as best they can. However, if the supply is short, the issue affects us all. The data are unambiguous: the bright are a small minority, and we aren't training enough of them for present or future needs. These data do not permit apathy.

Dael Wolfle has looked at this problem for many years, especially at the higher levels of American education and employment. In a major address in 1960 he pointed out that earlier in its history, America needed individuals who could help push back the frontier, introduce agriculture to the land, and build cities. Then the need shifted to those who could expand financial capital and develop industry. But in postindustrial America, the greatest need is for "men and women who can teach, who can roll back the boundaries of ignorance, who can perform demanding tasks upon which the further development of a free industrial society depends" (Wolfle, 1960, p. 535).

Since Wolfle's call for action, social conditions have changed in the United States. Many more young people have gone on to college and advanced training, to the point where an economic recession has now made it hard for some of them to find desirable employment. But there is no serious observer who would assert that the problems facing the United States and other countries, in recessions or in affluence, can be solved without calling upon more of our talented people than we do.

Regional, Class, and Racial Factors

Although details vary from country to country, there are some social forces that put certain bright children at a great disadvantage. The number of bright pupils identified and the encouragement given to realize their potential are artificially depressed.

Surveys of school attendance show pockets of concentration where large numbers of pupils quit school early. Typical is a series of tabulations in France (Ferrez, 1961) that showed that, except for the Paris region, school attendance and holding power are better in the south than in the north. Especially in industrial areas in the north, employment has greater attraction than education, and children take jobs as soon as they can. In the south there is a tradition in Provence and Aquitaine that puts high value on education and culture. There is also the need to leave the home area for economic advancement. Both these forces keep children in school longer.

In most countries, city ghettos and rural or isolated areas do not offer students the programs or broad social support found in prosperous towns and suburbs. The test of a school system's ability to retain students qualified for a university education occurs in the secondary school. Recognizing this, Sweden's massive school reform program concentrated on providing enrichment and encouragement to youth in isolated and rural regions. As a result, the proportion of such students who remained in secondary school increased by as much as twentyfold. These improvements have particular importance for the brightest pupils because they are the ones who need sustained schooling the most.

Social-class status is another potent determiner of support. Jean Floud (1961) studied this pattern in Britain after World War II. She pointed out that social-class structure promotes artificial inequality in education—an inequality that does not reflect real differences in ability. She charted a general trend:

> Until 1945, roughly speaking, the problem of social class in education was seen, by social investigators and policy makers alike, primarily as a *barrier to opportunity*. The problem was . . . to secure equality of access for children of comparable ability, regardless of their social origins, to institutions of secondary and higher education designed for, and still used in the main by, the offspring of the superior social classes. . . . Only in the postwar period has the continuing attempt to democratize secondary and higher education in unfamiliar conditions of full employment and wide-spread prosperity confronted us with the need to formulate the problem more subtly and to see social class as a profound influence on the *educability* of children.
>
> Here we are not concerned with snobbery in education—with invidious social differences in school or overt social bias in selection procedures—but with the existence of fundamental differences as between the social classes in ways of life, values, attitudes and aspirations, as well as in material circumstances. (1961, p. 95)

Nevertheless, the working class in both France and England *has* been taking advantage of the increased accessibility of traditionally middle-class grammar schools and lycées as a result of postwar educational reforms in these countries. From the grammar schools, these students are now entering the universities, the professions, and the higher levels of industry.

A similar trend has been apparent in American education over a longer period of time. High schools, which in the nineteenth century enrolled only a fraction of the eligible population, have steadily increased their enrollment. For example, between 1910 and 1970, the number of pupils in elementary and secondary school more than doubled. But the percentage of pupils who stayed on into high school increased over six times. Among the newcomers have been gifted children who, in former days, might have left sooner in order to start making a living. The most significant change, however, has been the expansion of state universities and the rise of junior colleges. Charging lower fees than private colleges, they have attracted bright but needy students. Very recently, "open admission" policies have relaxed university admission requirements. For certain students—notably those from minority backgrounds where standard preparation for college is uncommon—these policies offer the chance to catch up. The result of all these changes is a much broader constituency of students, one that gives more nearly equal opportunity regardless of social or economic handicap.

Yet, with all these opportunities, why do some students respond while others remain unaffected? In France, the coined phrase, *"la famille éducogène,"* refers to the most important single factor. It is a small family where the parents have an education beyond the compulsory minimum and where attitudes toward school are supportive. Floud (1961) suggested that the correlation between socioeconomic status and school performance may arise from the distribution of *"familles éducogènes."* At each step up the social scale, there are more of these families. She added that the subtle relation between home and school determines how educable the children will be.

We have considered regional and social-class problems that affect how well we serve all gifted children. Now we come to a stubborn imponderable: race. The best-documented examples of the relation between race and schooling come from work with blacks in the United States. Two facts stand out: performance by black children on intelligence tests is lower (averaging about 15 IQ points); the range of their scores is wide, including black children who score above 160 IQ (see Brody & Brody, 1976, pp. 168 *ff.*).

The first fact is very complicated and is not the main subject to discuss here. Briefly, most informed opinion attributes the lower average scores to cultural conditions rather than to strictly racial, inherited, or biological traits. Arthur Jensen's controversial article in 1969 includes an exhaustive compilation of data describing various manifestations of this average performance. His attribution to blacks of a racially biased difference in learning style (notably a lower capacity for abstract thinking and perceptual development) cannot be verified until researchers can find and study children who have not undergone the racial prejudice that exists in the United States. The difficulty in finding such a group of subjects, coupled with the sort of strong resistance from the scientific community that Jensen met, illustrates the major obstacles such a project would meet.

The second fact is more important: the wide range of intellectual ability in blacks includes very high levels. There are few systematic studies available, but the ones we have show the same general pattern as with other gifted children. What Martin Jenkins reported after World War II is typical:

> I have assembled from various sources the case records of 18 Negro children who test above IQ 160 on the Stanford-Binet examination. Seven of these cases test above IQ 170, four above IQ 180, and one at IQ 200. . . . Analysis of the case records indicates that these children . . . manifest the same characteristics as do other very high IQ children: originality of expression, creative ability, and surpassing performance in school subjects. . . . It is of some significance that all these children were found in Northern or border-state cities. . . . No Southern Negro child, so far as I have been able to ascertain, has been identified as testing at or above Binet IQ 160. (1948, p. 400)

Later surveys have identified other high-scoring black children, but they usually conclude that blacks are underrepresented.

Jenkins, like others, ruminated on the fact that fewer black than white children test at the highest levels, attributing the difference largely to a difference in environmental stimulation. Clearly, as long as society maintains a prejudicial attitude toward blacks, they will suffer detrimental restrictions in education and work that do not affect whites. Jenkins wrote before the massive American civil rights movement of the 1950s and 1960s, during which time opportunities for blacks improved dramatically. But the effects of prejudice still haunt and hamper bright black children.

SOME RESERVATIONS

This discussion has implied that bright children ought to be found and encouraged for their own and for society's good. Let us recognize, however, that certain cogent reservations must be kept in mind. We must, first of all, recognize and avoid the urge to play God. In 1961, Wolfle pointed out,

> If one nation can bring 8 or 10 or 12 percent of its youth into the university, another nation cannot claim that only 3 or 4 or 6 percent of its youth is intellectually qualified for that level. (cited in Halsey, 1961, p. 26)

Wolfle's assertion needs qualification. Perhaps some nations or races do have a higher percentage of gifted children than others. And some countries may need more farmers and coal miners right now than they need Ph.D.'s. Enrollments may be smaller for still another kind of reason. As Ralf Dahrendorf of Tübingen University in Germany said:

> A man or woman has the right *not* to be educated and certainly the right not to be trained for a job and career according to the passing requirements of the national economy. (cited in Halsey, 1961, p. 20)

As Lloyd Lovell (1977) put it, "I see no reason why Somalia should aspire to send 40 percent of its youth to college because the U.S. has demonstrated that it can do so." But neither qualification robs Wolfle's argument of its implied challenge: before settling for a relatively small number of university students, examine carefully the reasons for doing so.

There are indeed some poignant problems that may result when children who extend their education are carried far from their family roots. Parents may have scrimped to send their children to college only to find them inexplicably alienated. And some of the children, in turn, may feel torn and guilty that they cannot continue in the attitudes and activities they had once shared with their families. Fortunately, many children sense the problem and modify its impact. They may study in some depth their religious or racial or cultural heritage and share their growing awareness with their families. They may help the family as their careers advance. One would expect a gifted person to be particularly able to find a healthy resolution to generation tensions.

But the most serious cases of alienation result from exploitation. Lovell has pointed out that a talented person (athlete, scholar, musician) may be trained and pushed for the benefit of others, often with high salary as the bait. But too little notice is taken of the personal cost this policy may exact from the child and the family. Exploitation, of course, is not inherent or inevitable. The wise advocate for the gifted realizes that it may occur and keeps watch against it.

There is a reservation beyond the possible negative effects on the gifted themselves. There are those who fear the dangerous impact that exceptionally able individuals who have been given outstanding educations and large responsibilities might have upon society. Particularly when we widen the definition of giftedness to include creativity, we must face this question: What if we nurture imaginative children only to have them attack society? A. H. Halsey described this possibility as the release of

> the energies of those who will disturb the existing social structure whereas the traditional function of education . . . has been to give an adaptive schooling to those who must fit into a social structure. (1961, p. 21)

This fear is common to the reactionary bureaucrat, who sees a revolutionary in every college or university student. But it can also be a rational consideration, one to ponder whenever we would make education an agent of social change. But the risk must be taken if society is to keep renewing itself, if it is to avoid stagnation and collapse. The chief source of new ideas will continue to be the brightest and most imaginative of citizens, and they will inevitably push at the limits. Now, as many countries are entering a period where their economic growth is no longer explosive, the imaginations of the young will be drawn increasingly to problems of leisure, social welfare, and other concerns that have been obscured by the push for industrial production and distribution. Perhaps the persons who can solve these new problems will have somewhat different patterns of ability than those who worked out the old technological problems. Certainly we shall fare badly if we resist change and suppress those who have the ingenuity to understand and direct it.

With this in mind, the broadest search for giftedness should include not only special talents and creativity, but various personal qualities like sensitivity to others and the capacity for strong leadership. This broad view recognizes more children as gifted, to their benefit and society's. It also gives proper weight to the great variety of situations that gifted children will face when they have grown up. A narrow, exclusively IQ-based definition is useful in strictly academic settings: the top scorers will do best in meeting academic, bookish demands. It does not apply directly to many personal and occupational activities of adulthood. There is truth in the cliché that one needs high scores and marks these days to get into medical school, but many other qualities make up a wise and effective physician.

SUMMARY

Let us summarize. There are two major reasons for giving special attention to bright children—concern for individual development and community self-interest. Of the two, the first is the more basic. Once a society decides that it owes to each child an education suited to optimal development, then a common pattern of schooling for all will be grotesquely ill-matched to uncommon children. It has been fairly easy to make this case for blind or crippled youngsters who can't learn as well as normal children without changes in pedagogy. In fact, we have gone so far toward "special education" for the handicapped that we are now concerned with bringing them back into the mainstream. But while this argument is equally valid for the bright, it has had little impact. After all, in ordinary schools they seem to get on at least as well as average children. To do more for them looks like undue favoritism. That it is not requires us to recognize just how much, how fast, and how imaginatively gifted children learn when they are stimulated to the level of their abilities. On grounds of IQ alone there is as much difference between a moron (IQ 50) and an average child (IQ 100) as there is between that same average child and many of Terman's children (IQ 150). Like Terman, we should be eager to see that gifted children fulfill their promise as well as average or handicapped children do theirs. Otherwise we mock our commitment to individual development.

The fact that gifted children who develop their potential make unique returns to society is a marvelous bonus. But by itself, this is not a marvelous argument. Especially when funds are scarce, it pits one special interest group against another. Who will be Solomon, to decide whether funds go to the gifted or the retarded—or the blind or the disturbed? To prisons or to psychiatric clinics? Replying that the gifted will return more to us all in discoveries and leadership and progress is to state a fact but not to make a full case. Better to draw the whole picture. If our society's obligation to individual fulfillment—for *all* persons—is in the foreground, then the contributions of all will take their proper and persuasive place.

5

Selecting the Gifted

An "intelligence quotient" may be of
provisional value as a first crude
approximation when the mental level of an
individual is sought; but whoever imagines
that in determining this quantity he has
summed up "the" intelligence of an individual
once and for all . . . leaves off where
psychology should begin.
William Stern (1938, p. 6)

As we have seen, there are different definitions of *gifted* and different purposes for choosing them. Historically, the common denominator of the definitions has been the goal of training apt people for major social responsibility. The purpose of such training has varied. As Plato said, "What is honored in a country will be cultivated there." Military prowess, diplomatic finesse, artistic sensitivity, mercantile shrewdness, pioneering drive—times change and with them the demand for excellence. But, however different the goals, somehow societies identify their talented children. Most often the school does the job. In fact, taking the long view, schools have existed mainly to train the elect few whose station it would be to rule. Educating the masses has a short and spotty history.

Given this variety, how have the brightest been chosen? First let us look again at two of the most durable past traditions—those of the Palace School in Ottoman times and of the imperial civil service in China. Then we shall examine certain influential patterns in recent decades in Europe and America. Throughout we shall see that a society's current demands have determined how many persons to select, from what groups, and with what methods. It is the same within a country, especially one with considerable local autonomy (as is true of the schools today in the United States and Britain). The kinds of children sought are the ones the local community is concerned about, and the techniques used to choose them are the ones the community approves.

THE LONG TRADITIONS OF OTTOMAN AND CHINESE EXAMINATIONS

The Palace School

For more than three hundred years, from the fourteenth to the sixteenth centuries, the Ottoman Empire was despotic, with its ministers drawn deliberately from a slave class. As late as the eighteenth century, when the empire was in decline, a French observer noted that the sultan did not consider either the pedigree or fortune of prospective ministers, but chose exclusively from those indebted to him for their welfare and education (cited in Miller, 1941). The source of talent was the whole empire, scoured each year for the most promising boys. The number of slaves brought into training for government service fluctuated from several hundred a year to thousands. The choicest of them were sought for the Palace School when they were ten to fourteen years of age (sometimes as young as eight or as old as twenty).

Barnette Miller (1941) told how these candidates were carefully screened by an examining board, which asked questions resembling those in modern intelligence tests. This board also considered physique and dexterity, and reserved the strongest and handsomest physical specimens for the Janissary corps. The boys who went into palace service were divided into two groups: the cleverest became student pages, the others became apprentices for manual service as gardeners or artisans in one of the royal palaces. The student pages were further examined, and the most intelligent were sent to the Palace School. Referring to this last elite group, an eighteenth-century ambassador from Europe made a revealing comparison between European and Turkish priorities:

> The Turks rejoice greatly when they find an exceptional man as though they had acquired a precious object, and they spare no labor or effort in cultivating him; especially if they discern that he is fit for war. Our plan [in Western Europe] is very different; for if we find a good dog, hawk, or horse, we are greatly delighted, and we spare nothing to bring it to the greatest perfection of its kind. But if a man happens to possess an extraordinary disposition, we do not take like pains; . . . the Turks [receive] much more [pleasure] from a well-educated man . . . in proportion as the nature of a man is more admirable and more excellent than that of the other animals. (cited in Miller, 1941, p. 99)

Training at the Palace School was unrelenting. Mentors watched for particular talents. The system of merit in the school paralleled that in the government: regular promotion according to demonstrated achievement, with no attention to a page's origin or friends. The entire course was subsidized, with stipends and scholarships as additional incentives for the most successful. A broad intellect was required, because the curriculum spanned a very wide range: several languages (Turkish, Arabic, Persian) and their literatures, including special competence with the Koran; calligraphy, jurisprudence, philosophy, logic, theology, mathematics, science, and music were also emphasized. In addition, there was constant physical exercise, with special attention paid to horsemanship. Each page also learned a useful craft so that he could make a living if times were bad. After fourteen years—the average duration of the curriculum—pages entered a regular government service. They had survived a rigorous selection process and a very demanding education.

The Chinese Imperial Civil Service

Imperial China never had a tradition of hereditary, aristocratic rule. Philip DuBois, in a paper presented at the 1964 Invitational Conference on Testing Problems, described in detail the Chinese system of selection. To enter the official ranks, it was necessary to pass a series of increasingly severe tests. Except when the Mongol emperors suppressed it, this system of examinations over a period of hundreds of years was only occasionally and temporarily suspended. There was a kind of proficiency testing as early as 2200 B.C., and the emperor promoted and dismissed his officials according to their performance on these tests. For centuries before Confucius, there were job-sample tests requiring skill in music, archery, horsemanship, writing, arithmetic, and the various rites and ceremonies of public life.

From the second century B.C., imperial examinations for government positions were based on the Confucian classics, which emphasized just government by worthy men. In the early centuries A.D., the tests covered these classics, plus empire geography, law, military affairs, agriculture, and taxes. By the seventh century, the examinations were systematic, open, and competitive. From the late fourteenth century, there was a three-step sequence that endured until the early twentieth century.

In 1870, a Westerner described this tripartite process of selection at some length. The first step was an examination given in the chief city of each district. In the nineteenth century, this examination would typically attract about two thousand competitors who would range in age from the early teens to old age. Each person had a night and a day in which to produce a poem and one or two essays on assigned topics. About one out of every one hundred would be honored with the degree of *Sui-t'sai*, or Budding Genius, the lowest level of mandarin. The second step came every three years, when Budding Geniuses would go to their provincial capitals to compete for the degree, *Chu-jin*, Promoted Scholar. In three sessions lasting nearly three days each, as many as ten thousand competitors would be examined by special officials sent from Peking. Prose and verse were required, and themes were predetermined to test depth of scholarship. Here again, one out of every one hundred candidates would be granted the second degree. Neither Budding Geniuses nor Promoted Scholars received either employment or prize money.

The third step brought Promoted Scholars from every province to Peking for the final examinations. Winners were designated *Tsin-shi*, Ready for Office. This degree was one to be coveted, for it meant employment in the government and the possibility of eventually sitting in the highest councils of state. Each group of winners drew lots for their entering assignments to the civil service. A select few had a further chance to take a special examination set by the Emperor himself, to choose persons for the Imperial Academy. From them, the Emperor designated one person for the highest honor of all, *Chuang-yuen*, Model Scholar. This winner, his family, and his home city received elaborate recognition, in ceremonies rivaling coronations.

The Chinese depended on this system to keep a far-flung empire from falling apart into contending states with different languages and customs. An important effect of the examinations was to promote the written language, itself a powerful tool for unity. Throughout the empire several versions of Chinese were spoken, and persons knowing one dialect could not understand persons speaking another. But the Chinese developed a single writing system based on meaning rather than sound. Literate people, therefore, always understood this common written language, regardless of the dialects they spoke.

In early times the Confucian classics were guides to conduct and to government administration. Generations of leaders not only revered but practiced the Confucian way. But in time, students came to study the classics more by rote. Because the examinations continued to be based on Confucian classics, students kept on memorizing them, but much of their vitality was lost. Consequently, pressures grew to change the examinations. During the eleventh century—a time of political upheaval—Wang An-shih, an official to Emperor Jen-tsung, sent a "memorial" to the emperor. Wang was reform minded and urged that the examinations be directed more at practical problems of administration and less at literary matters. In his memorial, Wang noted that the examinations were designed to select men with excellent memories and an impressive familiarity with literature, but that they provided practically no indication of the candidates' leadership abilities or their knowledge of the principles of philosophy and government. Wang went on to criticize the tremendous waste of time and effort expended in the students' preparation for selection. He insisted that it would be far more logical and expedient for them to direct their energies toward absorbing knowledge and experience directly related to government work than toward "rhyming couplets" and memorizing poetry (De-Bary, Chan, & Watson, 1960).

The examinations were eventually expanded to include non-Confucian cultural materials and practical issues in statecraft and administration. Proposals were also made to broaden the system of selection to include other methods than the examinations alone. The most systematic and concise critique, according to DeBary et al., came from the seventeenth-century scholar Huang Tsung-hsi. His "Plan for the Prince" suggested several major changes in the selection process for officials. For example, while retaining the regular examinations, Huang sought to give special consideration to applicants with recommendations, graduates of the imperial academy, sons of high officials, and junior officials who would attain eligibility through a merit system. Recognition would also be given to those who had displayed exceptional scholarship or who presented outstanding memorials.

Throughout the centuries, the examination system successfully chose able officials while remaining relatively immune to patronage or prestige. To a singular extent it emphasized scholarship, particularly in literature, in its search for the "wise, virtuous, square, and upright." Its record is secure—it was one of the greatest achievements of Chinese civilization, producing most of its great political leaders over a period of thirteen centuries.

From a twentieth-century view, the Chinese imperial examinations were remarkably modern, employing a broadly based group of candidates, a definition of the human traits sought, systematically administered testing sessions, scrupulous attention to anonymity in scoring, and revisions to suit changing times. We shall refer later to some problems, especially the difficulty (despite efforts to avoid it) of ensuring that *all* persons have an equal chance regardless of family circumstances. But despite the problems, we have nothing on record to approach the comprehensiveness and continuity of this Chinese examination system.

RECENT TRENDS

In modern times traditions are briefer. We shall discuss selection programs from several countries. In considering these examples, we must take note of how they have been affected by the growing demand for universal education. In meeting this demand, the selection of the brightest has become both easier and harder. It is easier because we can more nearly draw upon the entire population of children as a reservoir, but harder because the numbers of children and the definitions for selection have multiplied. Clearly, however, we have abandoned the assumption in the West that education beyond mere literacy goes automatically and only to those whose families can afford it.

As this new idea has spread, it has required that education encompass the wide variety of children who go to school. In Western countries this problem has appeared most insistently in secondary schools, the places where pupils have historically prepared for the universities. Equalizing opportunities now means, not so much mass education at the primary school, as access to secondary and higher education. Access to higher education has become easier throughout the twentieth century, until now in various countries it is taken for granted, much like primary education in earlier generations.

England's Eleven-Plus Examinations

One of the best-documented modern examples of a large-scale effort to equalize opportunities comes from England. Looking toward a better world for postwar Britain, the Education Act of 1944 stipulated that every pupil should have an appropriate kind of secondary education. Up to that time, secondary schools had been available only to a small percentage of pupils, with the rest continuing primary school until they were old enough to leave for work. After 1944 secondary education was to be standard for all, and the specific type of secondary school attended would be decided by the eleven-plus examinations taken by pupils eleven years old. Ironically, what started as a way to democratize secondary education by making it available to everybody became a competition for places in grammar schools, just one type of secondary school. These were the schools that had traditionally prepared their pupils for the university, and in class-conscious Britain they therefore had high prestige. The 1944 Act prescribed "parity of esteem" among all kinds of secondary schools, but this parity never really developed in the public mind. So to many a family the eleven-plus examinations appeared to be tense contests for coveted places in grammar schools.

Let us see how selection for grammar schools worked, as summarized by Philip Vernon (1957). Each February, eleven-year-olds took three standardized objective tests of intelligence, English, and arithmetic. Their teachers gave and marked the tests and then sent them on to local school headquarters. There the marking was checked for accuracy, and the total of each pupil's three scores was converted to a standard score or quotient, for comparable meaning among pupils. These total scores were then arranged in rank order for all pupils in a district.

The final responsibility to match the list of scores to the number of grammar school places available fell to a district examining board (which often invited experts from outside the district to participate). There were never places enough for all—nor, as the Act envisioned it, was it expected that every pupil would profit from a grammar school education. The top-scoring pupils automatically gained places while those at the bottom were dropped from the list. Of the remaining "border-zone children," about half eventually got places after the board sought additional evidence about them: reports from their primary schools, earlier essays and tests, information from visits and interviews at their schools, and special examinations to supplement the eleven-plus. After some weeks, the board made up the final list of grammar school entrants, and sent out notification.

Over the entire country, about a quarter of the children would win places in grammar schools (20 percent in England, over 30 percent in Wales). The range was extensive, from 10 percent in some areas to over 60 percent in others. Local districts varied substantially, too, because the only uniformity imposed upon them by the central government was that they provide schools suited in number and facilities to the different ages and aptitudes of their pupils. How they allocated the children to the several kinds of secondary schools was a local decision. Increasingly, districts bought published tests, and within a decade after the Education Act of 1944 went into force, three quarters of the districts were using the so-called Moray House tests of intelligence and attainment to place the brightest pupils in grammar schools.

During the last decade or so, starting in London in 1963, eleven-plus examinations have been largely abandoned. Now fewer than a dozen local school districts select pupils for places in grammar schools, because "comprehensive" secondary schools enroll virtually all pupils. Most of the reasons for giving up these tests have been political rather than educational: social-class differences among pupils and school districts, political squabbles over social policy, financial and population trends, arguments over the worth of the tests themselves, disagreement over the proper age for selection. Briefly, the central problem was that what started out to ensure just *allocation* of pupils to appropriate schooling (with places sufficient to educate everybody as they deserved) turned more and more into competitive *selection* of some pupils for highly valued but insufficient places. Vernon called this eleven-plus selection "indeed a peculiarly English institution" (1957, p. 14).

Trends in France, Germany, and Sweden

The pattern of differentiated schools has been widespread in Europe. A few pupils have gone right through to the university, attending selective elementary and secondary schools along the way. The masses have gone to their own elementary schools, leaving eventually to become apprentices, to attend technical schools, or to take jobs. As in England, the crucial question throughout Europe has been whether a bright child would get onto the university track. If this track has its own expensive feeder schools, there has been little hope for poor children. But along with the move toward providing common elementary schooling for everyone have come several solutions to the problem of giving all bright children the opportunity for appropriate schooling. Mainly the strategy has been to delay the critical decision until pupils are older.

France and West Germany have developed elaborate guidance schemes. At school and with their families, pupils between the ages of eleven and fifteen explore their capabilities and related vocational possibilities. Those for whom schools and families agree a university education will eventually be appropriate take examinations for entry into selective secondary schools: in France, the *lycée,* in Germany, the *Gymnasium.* These examinations do not give weight to tested intelligence but to cumulative academic skills and knowledge. This is in marked contrast to British and American practice, which have included tests of both academic achievement and general intelligence.

Germany has remained relatively conservative in trying new approaches. W. D. Halls (1966) has ascribed this conservatism to postwar reaction against Nazism, a desire to resurrect the traditional Humboldtian *Gymnasium,* and opposition during the occupation to a pattern of comprehensive schooling that was associated with the United States. France, with tight national control over education, prepared a number of ambitious plans to broaden opportunity while protecting the legendary quality of the prestigious *lycée.* In both countries, and in most others in continental Europe, the selection of pupils for secondary schools has continued to be based largely upon school performance and even more directly upon examinations of academic achievement.

There is an important distinction between Britain, on the one hand, and many continental countries on the other. The secondary school in Britain has been a relatively specialized school, whose pupils prepare for examinations in only a few subjects. On the Continent, the examinations cover a much broader range of subjects. As a consequence, British graduates enter the university on the basis of limited options, mainly to major in fields which they have studied to some depth in secondary school and in which they have superior marks in final examinations taken at the close of their secondary-school career. On the Continent, the final examinations cover many more topics. According to some figures from the 1960s, a very large majority of university entrants in Britain chose to major in fields closely related to their secondary school "A-level" examination specialties. In West Germany, on the other hand, almost half the science majors in the universities had taken the classical or modern language curricula rather than the science curricula at the *Gymnasium.* These German students were not at a great disadvantage, because they had continued to study science, along with everything else, up to the close of secondary school. British students did not have such freedom to choose because, in effect, they had already made their choices in secondary school. This contrast in emphasis is still evident.

Sweden has developed still another approach to preparing students for higher education—maximizing opportunities for all pupils, including the gifted. Their well-publicized school reforms began after World War II. The major change was to abolish separate schools in favor of a single, unified, nine-year elementary school. Secondary and higher education would be chosen according to the interest and ability of the individual student. Thus, any selection of the gifted was delayed until rather late in a pupil's career. There was the same emphasis on guidance during early adolescence as in France and on the same national scale. But Sweden went further by insisting that the decision be made essentially by the pupil and his or her family. The school would provide its records and advice, but it was forbidden to allocate the pupil.

Debates have raged over this policy, partly because it is also a Swedish tradition to thoroughly air major changes in social policies throughout the country. A major reason for the nine-year school and for the delay of crucial decisions came out of research sponsored by the government while reform was being studied and while it was being introduced. The official Swedish position emerged early. Neymark (1945) reported that a secure basis for vocational guidance does not appear until a girl is fourteen or fifteen years old, a boy fifteen or sixteen. Husén (1960) and others pursued this problem, concluding that earlier selection of the bright for special and separate schooling was inefficient and often unfair because a pupil's pattern of talents did not mature sufficiently until the years of secondary school. Preliminary guidance toward the end of the nine-year elementary school would prepare the way, but a decision before mid-adolescence would be neither accurate nor equitable. This policy contrasts with that which informed the British Education Act of 1944—namely that early differentiation (at age eleven) was feasible and desirable so as to "stream" pupils properly.

Approaches in the United States

In the United States, various techniques have been used to identify bright children for appropriate schooling. One postwar survey (Havighurst, Stivers, & De Haan, 1955) gives us a good picture of the means of selection typically employed at that time. In it, almost all the schools questioned used standardized intelligence tests (usually group, not individual tests). They also depended upon attainment tests, school marks, and recommendations from school personnel. Harry Passow (1962) referred to a more intensive survey of nearly one thousand schools. Almost all (95 percent) used most or all of the following to choose their brightest children: standardized tests of intelligence and attainment, anecdotal reports from teachers, recommendations from counselors, tests of special aptitudes, and information and requests from parents. In nearly all schools, an intelligence test was administered, but it was neither the sole basis nor the single best index for selection.

A 1962 yearbook on the gifted (Bereday & Lauwerys, 1962) urged that educators use a very broad definition of intelligence, thus allowing for very diverse selection criteria. Gifted pupils can be those who show consistently superior performance in any worthwhile activity. Talented children can also be brought to notice fairly systematically by other techniques, such as science fairs, National Merit Scholarship examinations, and competitions to enter specialized schools in subjects like music, science, and art. In Chapter 6 we shall discuss how gifted children are educated. Here let us look briefly at certain school practices that reflect the variety of selection procedures used.

Flexibility

In the United States for many decades, differentiation—if it occurs at all—has usually taken place within a school, rather than by segregation into separate schools. Thus, as in Sweden, critical decisions can be delayed, and if they turn out to be wrong, it is easier to correct them later. The bright, however, may be recognized as early as four or five years of age, allowing them to start school early.

It is not unusual in elementary schools to put bright children into special groups for certain subjects. It is also fairly common to make a formal identification before entering junior high school, based on accumulated intelligence test scores and other data. But this selection does not usually induce the trauma that the British eleven-plus examination often does. Because curricula in the elementary school and in most secondary schools are broad, ultimate decisions for the bright about such matters as university study and occupational choice can be deferred until middle or late adolescence.

Flexibility is further ensured because there is less attention to matriculation examinations than there is elsewhere in the world. As part of their entrance requirements, many American colleges and universities, especially the more selective ones, require students to take aptitude and achievement tests toward the end of high school. But higher education is so diversified that there are colleges for almost any level of score on these matriculation examinations. In addition, the open admissions policies discussed in the preceding chapter make it possible for students to enter some colleges on the strength of a high-school diploma alone. For bright persons who have done poorly in school, this form of flexibility is a welcome opportunity. "Late bloomers" may therefore take a long time to find their places, without serious repercussion. Flexibility of both kinds is thus evident in the United States: bright children can be identified quite early, or they can be found much later and still be guided into suitable programs.

New techniques

Two recent developments in the U.S. are promising for the gifted. One is the bold use of advanced-level tests to identify young gifted children. The SMPY at The Johns Hopkins University (which we have already discusssed) has successfully tested eighth-grade pupils with tests designed for twelfth-graders, in order to identify high mathematical skill. This is an excellent example of coping with the "ceiling" problem in tests of any kind. This problem occurs whenever the highest scores are bunched together so closely that the important differences within the group at the top are lost. Stanley et al. (1976) have documented how well these more difficult tests permit finer assessment of talented children and more accurate prediction of their later development. It is the same solution that Terman chose when he devised his demanding Concept Mastery Test.

This technique should be encouraged. The norms that come with published tests (based on older pupils) must be carefully adapted to the actual group of younger pupils taking the tests. But this kind of adaptation has long been employed whenever local communities needed it. For example, educators connected with the Cleveland Major Work Program (designed for that city's gifted children) found that the national norms for general intelligence tests were inadequate. For years now, educators in Cleveland have referred to their own accumulated statistics, assigning to each pupil a "probable learning rate" score. This score replaces the IQ that national norms would provide. If one cannot devise an entirely new test for local conditions (as Terman did), adapting existing tests that are difficult enough can be useful. With concentrations of very high scores, finer and more appropriate distinctions can thus be made.

A related effort to be sensitive to special demands has occupied persons who wish to assess creativity. The many definitions of creativity, as we have seen already, have complicated test making. Most tests are verbal, depending upon fluency with original ideas to signal fertile imaginations. Critics have thought this kind of verbal approach too close to the academic realm, especially that of reading and writing. So other strategies have been tried. E. Paul Torrance's tests (1966) employ objects, pictures, conversation, and observation. For economy, one situation can be scored according to several of the dimensions of creativity under study. For older students, Raven's Matrices (1965) are sometimes used. This test uses patterns of designs that are free of cultural significance to call upon the individual's ability to sense very subtle and complicated relations. However, exactly what the Matrices tap is a matter of some discussion. It may be more a test of pure g (Spearman's general intelligence), or of spatial and visual perception, or even of a leaning toward science and mathematics (Marolla, 1973). Unfortunately, the attempts to measure creativity in children are complicated by the difficulty investigators have had in deciding how creativity and intelligence are related. Many schools have been trying to offer programs that stimulate children to high levels of imaginative activity. But analyses of these programs have provided no dependable evidence that they have fulfilled their promise.

Equity for all children
In the United States, the intense campaign in behalf of equity for all children has brought certain changes in selection procedures. In some places, mass screening with group intelligence tests has been abolished. New York City, San Francisco, and Washington, D.C., are the most prominent examples. The impetus has come mainly from retesting to show that group intelligence tests have too often assigned minority children to classes for the mentally retarded when more accurate individual tests later demonstrated normal intelligence. As an indirect result of this discovery, selection of gifted pupils has been improved to make it more obviously and conscientiously fair to minority children, whose high potential might be missed by tests developed for majority children. This closer scrutiny will produce, in the long run, more accurate assessments. Already there are national and local regulations in force, requiring that children who are being considered for possible participation in a special program for the gifted be tested (and otherwise judged) in a way that fits their background.

To the same end, Wallach and Kogan's 1965 study of intelligence and creativity was unusually sensitive. They believed that other investigations had tested children without allowing enough "warm-up" time. Children could not get over feeling unsure or threatened by the tests, and the results might thus be distorted. Especially when Wallach and Kogan wanted to elicit not only valid measures of intelligence but also free-flowing, imaginative responses by the children, they determined to be quite sure each child would feel at home. To do this, they had their testers spend two weeks in school with the children, getting acquainted and in every possible way avoiding any suggestion of examinations, pressure, authority, or threat. In fact, their aim was to make the whole situation more like a natural and playful game. Seldom has the basic demand for rapport been so rigorously honored. The clear implication is this: most gifted children are able to respond readily and enthusiastically to questions and tests of many kinds, but care is required to prevent missing the children who for various reasons do not freely respond.

SUMMARY AND A PERSPECTIVE

The most obvious fact to emerge from a survey of national and international selection practices is that they employ a great variety of approaches. Just as there is no easy or universally accepted definition of intelligence, there is no wide agreement on which kinds of gifts to seek or how to locate the children who have them. In China, the civil service examinations were biased toward literary skill; in the Ottoman Empire, great attention was given to physical beauty; in the United States—because of reliance on the IQ—rate of mental development has been primary. The key is the dominant values a society cherishes. We have even noted how a strong commitment to equality leads some people to demand that no special attention go to anyone. Let us summarize the kinds of variety that appear in the patterns for selecting the gifted.

Levels of Control

Some countries set a policy and enforce it nationwide. In China, the use of identical measures to find the brightest throughout the land was the result of a conscious effort to unify the nation. Since Napoleon's time, France has had a school system centrally controlled in Paris. This school system, which includes the universities, has test hurdles to decide which children will continue how far. On the other hand, the United States, from its beginning as a nation, has delegated responsibility for most aspects of education to state and local bodies. As a result, greater variety probably exists in American selection processes—from nothing at all to elaborate and costly schemes—than anywhere else in the world. With so many programs, different methods of selection have flourished. What similarity there is across America comes not from federal fiat, but from widely distributed tests and the similar training needed to give and interpret them.

Bases of Selection

Another aspect of variety is the basis for selecting gifted persons. In most countries "brightness" means "academic superiority." In some (chiefly the English-speaking countries and most consistently the United States), a more or less separate and parallel basis for selection has been some direct measure of high intelligence. Of course, intelligence and academic attainment are hard to separate, in tests as well as in school learning. Where school marks and achievement tests bear the entire burden, bright pupils whose native gifts have not developed into conventional intellectual skills usually escape attention. Unfortunately, it does not follow that intelligence tests will catch all the potentially bright children whom the achievement measures miss.

Increased Scope

In very recent years selection has become more flexible. This is partially due to the expansion of the definition of *gifted* to take in gifts not traditionally measured, such as creativity and special talents. It is also the result of increased pressure to seek the bright wherever they are, including neighborhoods and ethnic groups where high intelligence has not taken the forms that were previously required in order to qualify for typical selection.

Changes may be ordered by a national legislature in order to break up the monopoly an elite has had over advanced education. This was the case when England introduced the eleven-plus tests in 1945. The government's goal was to use an impersonal, fair instrument to find the brightest youngsters, regardless of family status or location. In contrast, many instruments for selection are used in the more decentralized United States, from screening for early enrollment in kindergarten to assessing talent in secondary school or university.

Many countries are also trying to extend the ages during which people can continue to develop their talents. In France, for more than a century the universities were open only to students who had successfully passed the *baccalauréat* examination at the end of secondary school. Now, recent provisions have been instituted in favor of persons who never prepared for or took this examination. In Scandinavia, "folk high schools" offer short and long curricula for adults, sometimes for vocational retraining but more generally to stimulate enjoyment in continuing education. "Sandwich courses" in Britain and elsewhere consist of alternating periods of study and work, especially in technical fields. "Extension" education (in the United States, sometimes called "lifelong learning") reaches out from the campus to the entire community, offering courses in a wide range of fields. All these adult programs build on the implicit assumption that maturity brings with it a high degree of self-selection, so that formal examinations for entry are not necessary.

Attention to working-class students has similarly increased the breadth of selection. The People's Republic of China provided the most extreme example of such reorientation in recent history. During the Cultural Revolution of the 1960s, formal examinations and traditional preparation for university study were replaced by requirements for political orthodoxy and experience working in factory or field. For about a decade, this change brought into higher education students from the working classes, which had always been badly underrepresented. In 1977, however, this policy was abruptly reversed, and more traditional university entrance examinations were revived. The reason given was a decision by the government of Hwa Kuo-feng, Mao Tse-tung's successor, to improve high-level training as part of a plan to make China into a major industrial country by the year 2000. It had been found that students chosen mainly for their work experience and ideological loyalty during the Cultural Revolution were not adequately prepared for university work. Their studies had been a mixture of theoretical and practical work that gave decisive priority to the practical. As a result of lower ability and weaker academic demands, the quality of education fell. Corrective measures have now been adopted, including the examinations for entrance and stiffer course curricula, to reassert the importance of rigorous academic study. However, the government is determined not to lose the broad representation of working-class students won during the Cultural Revolution. In the 1977 university matriculation examination, only "a very small minority" of applicants came from the families of bureaucrats ("Educational Policy," 1978). It remains to be seen how successfully this three-way challenge will be met: to keep university doors open to students from all backgrounds, ensure adequate academic aptitude, and maintain tough course standards.

An interesting aspect of the 1977 examinations in China was that they were available not only to recent graduates of secondary schools, but also to two other groups. One was a large number of persons who had finished secondary school as far back as 1968 but who had not been able to attend universities. The other was very capable younger pupils still attending secondary school. Almost half the 1977–78 university places went to these two groups of students, so that the age range of the freshman class that year was from fifteen to over thirty years. Unfortunately the four hundred Chinese universities and colleges had places for only about 5 percent of the 5.7 million who applied to take the examinations. From 1978 on, plans are to provide more places and to open the examinations only to recent graduates (up to age twenty) and younger pupils still in school (down to about age fourteen).

It is still debatable what effect changes in broad social policy will have on selection procedures or how effectively gifted students will be recruited from outside the mainstream. What is clear is that no one technique will suffice. The conventional intelligence test remains, but it is now accompanied by many other tools: teacher recommendation, games to show creativity, nonverbal estimates, tests of special skills, even self-nomination. In Chapter 7, we shall investigate some of the major issues arising from a broader and more varied population of gifted children and from some stubborn social problems connected with selection and education of the gifted.

6

Educating the Gifted

If a man has a talent and cannot use it, he has
failed. If he has a talent and uses only half of
it, he has partly failed. If he has a talent and
learns somehow to use the whole of it, he has
gloriously succeeded, and won a satisfaction
and a triumph few men ever know.

Thomas Wolfe, *The Web and the Rock*, 1939

Bright children usually go to school for a long time. What happens to them
there? Does it make any difference whether or not they get special attention? How is such attention provided? What academic or personal problems do the bright have as they go through school? Are there discernible
patterns of schooling that may develop in the future for them?

These are serious questions; anyone who has known clever children in
school can appreciate their importance. Earlier chapters have touched
upon various school patterns and problems arising from educational policies toward the gifted, and the collection of vignettes in the opening chapter is dramatic evidence that these children learn in different ways and
under different conditions. In this chapter we shall deal with schooling in
detail, considering first some programs developed in several communities
across the nation that have proved particularly successful. Then we shall
examine the more traditional teaching arrangements for the gifted, and
move on to a closer look at the difficulties gifted children most often face
in school. Finally, we shall discuss a few innovations that should increase
the flexibility and scope of learning activities for the bright.

In this discussion, there are no prescriptions compounded to serve all
bright children everywhere. In developing methods to teach the bright, we
lack the confidence so evident in recommendations for other kinds of
"exceptional children," such as those with specific and treatable crippling.
We do not see attempts to subclassify types of giftedness as we've seen
with types of retardation, and we rarely find gifted teachers with the degree of sensitivity and skill we find among specialists who can teach a deaf
child to speak or a blind child to read braille or to walk safely. In fact,
among all kinds of exceptionality, brightness has failed most often to call
up sustained support or sure methodology.

A telling reason is that the bright show us no insistent handicap to evoke our sympathy or to tug at our conscience. On the contrary, the bright are often so capable of making their own way that people find it hard to believe there could be any problem. Frank Copley, a classicist who surveyed American work with the bright in the late 1950s, recognized that the majority of brilliant pupils have been educated in ordinary schools, for most young scholars and scientists of today have gone through the public schools (Copley, 1961). But he emphasized that we don't know how many potential scholars and scientists we have lost because we didn't educate them well enough. If, within the framework of mass education, we are to assure the full development of our brightest children, then we have a major challenge—to educate them effectively. Ironically, as Ruth Martinson (1973) pointed out, we may not realize any urgency so long as gifted pupils do so well in school without any special attention. They thrive on any opportunity to read widely and independently, and to pursue their own interests.

There is much stronger objection to special education for the gifted than merely noting that these pupils get along well in any case. One often hears the stubborn argument that "it's undemocratic to set children like that apart—you know, to give them special favors." Charles Telford and James Sawrey (1977) suggested that we have spent more energy guarding against undue privilege than we have serving individual differences.

PATTERNS OF EDUCATION

As a consequence of the attitudes discussed above, the number of gifted children in special programs, in the United States or elsewhere, has been remarkably small. But organized curricula and unusual teaching techniques have emerged, especially when pressure or fear has catalyzed their development. Because there seems to be another wave of interest in them now, successful programs warrant renewed attention.

Early Programs

A useful guide to American programs for the gifted over the past two decades has been a monograph titled "A Survey of the Education of Gifted Children," published in 1955 by Robert Havighurst, Eugene Stivers, and Robert De Haan. They gave brief descriptions of school provisions in over forty cities, emphasizing for each its salient characteristics. They also discussed in several short chapters more general considerations prompted by their survey, including the great variety of approaches they found, the wide use by schools of community resources, and the crucial importance of finding and motivating as many gifted pupils as possible.

Over the years, the most systematic programs for the bright have been concentrated in big cities, where enough children go to school to permit planning for large groups and where significant funds can be made available. The oldest continuing American program is in Cleveland, Ohio, where since 1921 pupils with high test scores and other recommendations have devoted part of their school day to special curricula and methods— their so-called Major Work projects. These children join other pupils for general classes in subjects such as physical education. New York City has had a variety of separate classes and schools since the 1920s, notably the several experimental programs at Public School 500 (where Leta Hollingworth helped develop the curricula) and selective schools for pupils with scientific and artistic talents. Since the 1930s, laboratory schools on university campuses, such as the one at Ohio State University, have provided opportunities both for bright children and for researchers interested in them.

Smaller communities, especially those with well-educated and prosperous families, have sometimes set up their own programs: New Trier Township, Illinois; Racine, Wisconsin; Quincy, Illinois; Scarsdale, New York. A few departments of education in state governments have stimulated statewide activity, most comprehensively in California, Connecticut, Georgia, Illinois, and North Carolina. In these states, regulations are usually permissive, and extra funds are usually provided. Some states mandate special provisions wherever there are a certain number of eligible children. Alaska is an example. The state governments occasionally pay most or all of the expense incurred.

Recent Educational Programs

The examples we have been citing span several decades. In general, the pattern for educating gifted children in the United States has been cyclic, alternating between apathy and interest. One peak of support in the late 1950s followed the launching of the first Russian satellite. Legislatures and local school boards moved hastily to improve education, especially for prospective engineers and scientists. Supporting federal legislation carried the title, "National Defense Education Act."

Financial support
In the past few years another wave of support has been gathering. In 1972, Sidney Marland, the U.S. Commissioner of Education, set up an Office of the Gifted and Talented, responsible for authorizing expenditures for model school programs, teacher training, research, and dissemination of information regarding the gifted. At first, support for expenditures came from funds of other programs, such as the Educational Professional Development Act and the Bureau of Occupational and Adult Education (Sisk, 1978). During the period from 1972 to 1974, the total dollars spent rose from about $300,000 to $1 million per year. In August 1974, the passage of Public Law 93–380 (The Elementary and Secondary Amendments) included what is perhaps the most important result so far of the awakening concern for the gifted: the Special Projects Act. This Act provides funds specifically for the Office of the Gifted and Talented, and since this 1974 legislation,

the level of spending has risen significantly (to about $2.6 million per year). Like the 1950s legislation, this law reflects the growing shift of responsibility for education to the national government. Historically, this responsibility was vested in the states and local districts by the federal constitution, so that there has been no long tradition of national direction over the public schools. But during the past few decades, people have looked more and more to the federal government for leadership. Educational problems have come to demand financial support on a scale more suited to the entire nation than to a particular state.

One reason for the sudden rise in funding stems from the language used in the legislation, that is, "gifted and talented children." Reflected in these words is an official sanction for a broader definition of giftedness; as such, more children can benefit from the funding. Specifically, children are eligible if they show achievement or potential ability in any of the following areas, singly or in combination: general intellectual ability, specific academic aptitude, creative or productive thinking, leadership ability, talent for the visual and performing arts, psychomotor ability. In practice, these children, picked by professionally qualified people, are to be in the top 3 to 5 percent of the school population. Evidence used in selection must come from at least two sorts of assessment. No longer may a pupil be chosen or excluded on the basis of only one intelligence test score.

The initial allocation was about $2.6 million for fiscal year 1976 to be distributed through various state and municipal bodies. These funds have so far been used for a wide range of programs and research, for classroom instruction, teacher training, and for model projects. The 1976 allocation for model projects illustrated this breadth with the inclusion of preschool children in Seattle, high-school science students in New York City, pupils in a sparsely populated area of northern California, disadvantaged children in New England, and children with handicaps in rural Idaho. In 1977, the same amount was allocated ($2.6 million). The scope of the program was increased to include thirty-one states and seventeen local school districts, leadership programs in colleges and agencies, and six model projects and services in public and private organizations (Sisk, 1978).

Support variables

States have not, however, been immune to budgetary restraints. The 1974 federal law offers encouragement to which many states and districts are responding. But three related forces act as brakes. One, the result of a general economic slump, is an attitude of skepticism toward school spending, especially for new or expanded activities. In better times, the federal law itself might have been more generous, and local initiative to supplement federal grants stronger. Recently, a 1978 California election focused national attention on tax support for schools and other public services by passing "Proposition 13." The voters of California put a ceiling on property taxes, with results that will take some time to see clearly. Clear enough, however, was the electorate's frustration with rising taxes. California's gifted children were quickly affected. In the summer following the elections, special programs all over the state were scrapped, including a major project planned for Los Angeles. The 1978–79 appropriation for state assistance to the gifted, $15 million, was trimmed by 10 percent. California's experience will probably become more and more representative, as citizens everywhere face the hard choices that a troubled economy exacts. As it has in the past, the education of the gifted may be an early casualty, especially in regions without any tradition of support for the gifted.

A second inhibition toward expansion of programs is a widespread suspicion that the schools are not doing a good enough job to warrant it. This suspicion is sharpest in opposition to experimental tendencies dating from the 1960s, against which a demand has arisen for efficiency, for accountability, for proof that the public schools are making effective use of the taxes they collect. Programs for the gifted that appear to be experimental are therefore vulnerable. They fare better if they stress conservative educational values and the contribution that the bright will eventually make to the community.

A third problem that programs for the gifted face is competing demands for other kinds of worthy programs. The most notable competition in recent years has been from those who want dramatic improvement in education for handicapped children. The public schools in Portland, Oregon, for example, have faced this choice (Schneider, 1977). Their program for the gifted, which had earned wide recognition during the 1950s and 1960s, was abandoned when priority for scarce funds went to handicapped children. Signs of interest in the gifted are visible again in Portland, but any new programs in this area will, in the interest of equity, share available funds with those for other kinds of children.

Even when public interest in education for the gifted mounts and pressure for expanded programs is applied to governments and local boards, the responses are often slow and piecemeal for a variety of reasons. Rural districts are the most difficult places in which to develop organized programs. Finances there may be strained, parents themselves may not cooperate, the number of children is so small as to preclude concentrated attention and professional services. At the least, such districts usually expect a larger government unit to assume all the extra cost, and few state legislatures find that total state support would be fiscally or politically wise. In the United States, the federal government has begun to take on some of the burden, distributing funds to individual states in order to stimulate innovation. Illinois sponsors regional centers which serve particular children and which also act as models to other regions. In 1964 Massachusetts enacted legislation that included expenditures for research on the education of gifted children. All these schemes depend ultimately on favorable public opinion: willingness to see the problem, to approve potential solutions, and to pay for them.

METHODS OF TEACHING THE GIFTED

Gallagher (1975) believes that the key to teaching the bright is in the classroom, because that is where any new methods must prove their worth.

Nevertheless, he recognizes that good administrative arrangements can stimulate good teaching. Three such arrangements predominate in school systems: sending the brightest pupils through school faster; teaching them separately with other bright children; and leaving them in classes with agemates but offering them supplementary work. True, these schemes overlap. In elementary school, a pupil who skips a year may also be put into a special group; in high school, some advanced classes may also be especially enriched. Or the arrangement may be part-time, allowing the pupil to spend time in both worlds—the advanced and the conventional classrooms. Summer study has become an effective way to bring pupils together temporarily when nothing unusual is done on a regular basis. Beyond these overlapping school plans, there are many ways for families and social agencies to stimulate talent: private music lessons, Saturday art classes, athletic leagues, library programs, and so on, to the end of resources and ingenuity. Let us look now at the classical arrangements in schools: acceleration, grouping, and enrichment.

Acceleration

Two basic arguments support the practice of allowing bright children to skip a year or otherwise to telescope their school experience. First, it is the easiest administrative expedient: putting children in already existing classrooms where they seem to fit better causes the least disruption of regular school activities. Harassed administrators like the simplicity of this approach, and budgetmakers like its economy. Of all the ways to "do something for the bright," it has been the most common because it has caused the least intrusion. The other argument for acceleration is more fundamental: it may help keep pupils intellectually engaged in school instead of bored, and it allows them to graduate and enter their careers sooner.

Critics attack both such arguments. Skipping is an oversimplified method, they say, because it ignores (and perhaps creates) social and emotional problems. Children should enjoy childhood and not be forced to grow up too quickly. In other words, society is looking after its own interests more than it is considering a bright pupil's needs.

Approaches to acceleration
Before examining the arguments for and against acceleration, we should define it more fully. Historically, it has been skipping a year or two, usually in primary or elementary school. A related procedure is early enrollment in school, probably after a test of intelligence and reading, and other checks on maturity and home background. Either way, a bright pupil is able to start secondary school sooner than is typical.

Recently, in America, many elementary schools have erased distinctions among the first three or four years. Under this ungraded primary system, a child may go through what would ordinarily take three or four years in as short a time as seems appropriate, perhaps in only one or two years. In secondary school, where pupils attend different classes, they do not ordinarily skip over a whole term or year at once. Instead, they may take a heavier schedule or enroll in summer courses, thus covering the curriculum faster. A popular American plan has been to permit secondary-school pupils to study college-level material in high school: the so-called Advanced Placement courses. In schools that are near college or university campuses, pupils may also take regular college courses. This latter arrangement usually applies to pupils in the last year or two of secondary school, and it may be restricted to advanced work in fields that the high school offers, such as foreign language or mathematics. With either Advanced Placement or concurrent college courses, pupils do not necessarily graduate from high school early. Instead, colleges may admit them with advanced standing. Some highly selective American colleges thus enroll high-school graduates who already start out with as much as two years of credit toward a bachelor's degree.

There have also been other approaches to acceleration. For many years the undergraduate College of the University of Chicago, under the aegis of Robert Hutchins, admitted younger students after the second year of high school. During Hutchins' regime all Chicago students earned the bachelor's degree in the European pattern—by passing examinations rather than by accumulating course credits. Early admission to college could thus be coupled with accelerated examinations, and very clever students could complete secondary and higher education in a much shorter time than usual.

In our opening chapter, the story of Lisa Skarp introduced us to an experiment at The Johns Hopkins University that deserves special attention in any discussion about acceleration. In 1969 Professor Julian Stanley learned from a colleague about a thirteen-year-old boy who had just taken a summer course in computer operation (Stanley, 1973). The instructor found the boy to be very precocious and asked Stanley what could be done to provide him with a continuing educational challenge. Stanley tested the boy for mathematical and other aptitudes, and decided that his scores were so high that the best solution seemed to be for him to enter the university right away. The boy did so, even though he had only finished the eighth grade. While still thirteen, he took a regular university load that included honors work in calculus and a sophomore course in physics. He earned high marks and stayed on to take a bachelor's degree in four years and a master's degree in computer science after another three months. He then started work on his doctorate at an age when under ordinary circumstances he would have been starting his freshman year in college. Stanley's experience with this boy, and with a few others with whom he worked shortly thereafter, awakened his interest in gifted children and especially in acceleration.

Stanley and his associates have since designed several acceleration programs for bright junior high school pupils who display precocious achievement in mathematics and science. Their guiding principle is detailed assessment. They examine each pupil's unique pattern of aptitudes, skills, and interests in order to devise an appropriate form of acceleration.

Only after extensive testing and interviewing (including careful attention to family background and attitudes) do they make their recommendations. Sometimes, as with the first boy, they propose immediate enrollment as a college student in a university or perhaps in a community college close to home. Sometimes they recommend that the student stay in the local school but take college-level mathematics courses as well.

For the majority of precocious mathematics pupils discovered in annual statewide competitions, Stanley's group has relied upon accelerated secondary-school instruction. One of the most successful tactics has been to start with intensive summer courses taught by a superb teacher. In the first summer program Stanley's group conducted, pupils who had completed sixth grade covered first-year algebra in 18 hours of Saturday classes (as against 135 or more hours in a regular class). The pupils were so successful and enthusiastic that the next summer the experiment was expanded. Pupils who had finished eighth grade, who showed high aptitude, and who had passed an achievement test covering first-year algebra studied second-year algebra in the summer. During the following school year they were excused from regular mathematics classes to study third-year algebra, plane geometry, trigonometry, and analytic geometry. As a result, most of these pupils were ready in tenth grade for Advanced-Placement calculus, usually taught to twelfth-graders.

Stanley's group has found the kinds of assessment tests that seem to work best at determining potential candidates for acceleration, the personality characteristics associated with successful acceleration, and the most effective ways to work with cooperating school people in various specific settings. He is convinced—and he has ample evidence—that accelerating skillful young mathematicians is not only feasible but essential. He is aware that problems may arise as a result of acceleration; for example, there is risk of social or emotional strain, and there is difficulty in motivating high-scoring girls. But he has tried systematically to deal with these problems, always starting with an assessment of each pupil as a whole person before deciding what to do next. Impersonal, mass acceleration would maximize risks and court public rejection. But Stanley is showing that careful, individually devised acceleration is something that can be done successfully. The most useful single result of Stanley's research may be his observation that accelerating pupils not only builds their confidence and aids in their social adjustment but also increases their enthusiasm for mathematics.

Concerns regarding acceleration

Unfortunately, although we have wide acquaintance with acceleration, we do not use it often enough. Where schools avoid acceleration, it is not usually because they do not understand it or because they are already practicing something else, like enrichment. Rather, it is because they fear acceleration will harm pupils. We have had a curious dialogue on this issue. On the one hand, there are those persons who cite the possibility of severe psychological harm to the student. On the other are those who press the case that individual pupils should not be held back to the pace of the mediocre—that society needs the services of its talented citizens as soon as possible. The dialogue persists despite the evidence, which is preponderantly in favor of acceleration. There are undoubtedly individual cases of a student's maladjustment while at school, of remembered unhappiness later, and of chronic adult bitterness—all linked to rapid schooling. Most of us have heard of these unfortunate consequences. But they are exceptional, not at all typical.

Noel Keys (1938), a conservative investigator, conducted a thorough study at a time when acceleration was relatively popular in California. He reviewed the arguments against rapid promotion: social development is allied more to age than to mentality; young children will not learn to be leaders if they are pushed ahead; skipping grades leaves serious gaps in information and skill; and brightness alone cannot compensate for the experience that only comes from longer living.

To test these objections Keys combed the University of California's records for the 1920s and 1930s. He found several hundred students who had enrolled one or more years younger than average. As compared to normal students, these underage students had distinctly superior academic records at the university and more extensive and successful athletic and social activities. When asked how they recalled their school days, most of them thought their experience had been satisfactory. A minority (about one in six) expressed some disappointment or wished they had waited to enroll in the university. Some men and several of those who had entered at age fourteen or fifteen remembered that social relations had been awkward, but others were glad they had entered the university early.

Keys concluded that the evidence clearly favored acceleration. He pointed out that adjustment difficulties are often more acute before college, citing one scientist (from an earlier study) who had entered ninth grade when he was ten years old. This man recalled that high school had been a tortured, bitter experience. But in college he felt no sense of maladjustment because he was younger than his fellow students. Keys stressed that most (over 85 percent) of his students had skipped grades in the elementary school, where he thought social readjustment was probably easier than it would have been later.

Keys' general conclusion, amounting to advice, is worth quoting:

> That gifted students uncommonly young for their group face certain special difficulties may be supposed. If so, the great majority appear entirely adequate to the demands. . . . Parents and educators should be encouraged to learn that, when faster advancement is effected with due regard to individual circumstances of intelligence, temperament, physical development, and prospects of higher education, and with suitable provision for the mastery of essential skills and contents, there is nothing to indicate it to be harmful. On the contrary, . . . acceleration, up to two years at least, makes for better adjustments, social as well as intellectual. It might well be practiced both more widely and more wisely than at present. (1938, p. 266)

No systematic research has unseated this firm conclusion. A steady if modest series of studies has reinforced the point that Keys made. To cite only three, there are Terman and Oden's report (1947) on their gifted children; Pressey's evidence (1949) about the Ohio pupils he followed; and Martinson's California study (1961). As Newland (1976) put it, the evidence is remarkably consistent that those pupils who are accelerated tend to do well later. Advancement timed to fit intellectual ability need not bring serious side effects of maladjustment or awkwardness.

Research on acceleration
The qualifications that Keys mentioned are now customary in many schools when a child is being considered for advancement. A typical regulation is that children with high test scores and superior academic achievement may be accelerated only if they also have average or larger than average body builds, adequate social skills, and emotional maturity suited to their age. At the start of school, a child may safely enter kindergarten or first grade a year or more early under similar precautions, as the schools in Brookline, Massachusetts, and many other communities have shown. Given these safeguards, the argument that social and emotional adjustment as well as academic achievement in the higher class will be better is almost beyond rebuttal. The challenge will be more nearly commensurate to the talents, and the basis of friendship more dependable. On the other hand, it is quite likely that holding bright children to the standard schedule may not only bore them, but may lead to behavior that would alienate them from potential friends and keep them from building self-confidence.

The other argument for acceleration—that it permits talented students to complete their education and enter the world of work earlier—is one that Sidney Pressey (1949) supported with convincing evidence. Pressey followed students who in 1939–1940 entered Ohio State University early. He found that 50 percent of those who entered at age sixteen graduated, compared to only 38 percent of eighteen-year-olds of similar ability studying similar subjects. After graduation, the accelerated students were more successful in their careers as shown by responsibility, advancement, salary, and satisfaction. A later organized program sponsored by the Ford Foundation in the 1950s reported that little or no harm resulted from skipping and that accelerated pupils usually had an advantageous start on careers (Paschal, 1960). Further, Lehman (1953) showed that people may mature earlier in certain fields than in others, notably in mathematics, music, and science. It is of special importance, therefore, to allow young people aiming toward these fields to finish their preparation in time to take full advantage of their most creative years.

As we have seen, mental prowess tends to persist well into old age, so the productive life of a person who gets an early start can be fruitful indeed. Arbitrarily holding a child back for fear of maladjustment is, according to existing research evidence, unfair, unnecessary, and unwise. The evidence, gathered mainly in the period from the 1930s to the 1960s, is consistent. Since then, investigators have apparently not found it necessary to raise questions or to replicate the earlier studies.

However, simple acceleration does not guarantee superior education. If Megan skips the third grade and lands in a mediocre fourth grade, she may still suffer from unimaginative teaching, stale syllabi, and a flabby regimen. All we can say is that such mediocrity would have been even worse for her in the third grade. Based on extensive clinical work with children, John Mordock (1975) found this problem to be acute for the most creative. After they have skipped to a higher grade, they may get no more stimulation to develop divergent thinking or problem solving than they had in earlier grades. In fact, they may find less. Mordock referred to the "fourth-grade slump": the stifling influence of straight rows, feet on the floor, and neat papers that are intended to impress pupils that the upper grades are serious, and that the fun and games of the primary school are over. Divergent thinking does not thrive under drab teaching, nor does a talented child—nor, for that matter, does convergent thinking or an average child.

To be truly successful, acceleration must be coupled with vital, sensitive teaching. As a device for focusing on a bright child's individuality, it has the convenience of administrative simplicity, if nothing else. Skipping ahead does no inevitable harm, and it may be surprisingly beneficial. But dependable and effective results demand that a teacher work closely with the pupil after acceleration. This devotion is, of course, what all pupils deserve. A gifted one needs it, especially in the early weeks after acceleration, to help adjust to a new group of classmates and perhaps to a new pattern of assignments or demands.

The evidence suggests that acceleration should be available to very bright children on a much larger scale than it is at present. It need not be imposed on all of these children, especially on those who are immature emotionally or who need a deliberate pace. Choosing carefully is only sensible caution. But systematic research shows unmistakably that most bright children can be safely and routinely accelerated provided we take ordinary precautions and especially if we see that they get sustained help when they have moved up. To forbid acceleration, as so many school officials do because they assume it will bring harm, is to base policy on exceptions. Accelerating more pupils would probably improve their attitudes toward school and help them finish their extensive education a year or more earlier.

However, acceleration is only one way to fit the school to the child, and in many respects it is only an administrative move. What goes on in the classroom—the critical question—must still be considered.

Grouping

The prevailing practice in schools has been for all children to advance together—the familiar lockstep that has come to be the marching order of mass education. Pushing clever children ahead according to their natural pace is a logical way to break the lockstep. But here there is a hidden assumption: learning faster, being confronted by more advanced work, will keep interest high and make learning more effective. Those who advocate assembling children together into special groups or classes do not trust this assumption. They want to provide work at a suitable level, but they also want to ensure a classroom climate in which the curiosity, enthusiasm, and concentration so characteristic of the bright will flourish.

Bright children may need to be advanced in school in order for the work to be a challenge to them. But they need even more to be with those who share their excitement, who can follow their ideas, who understand and accept their way of learning, who may even outstrip them. Putting bright children into higher classes may not alone provide the stimulation, any more than shortening the length of their education may. Somehow bright children should mingle freely with each other, lest they fail to realize their full gifts. James Dunlap (1967) put the case well. He reminded us that fewer than 10 percent of children possess the degree of curiosity, wide interests, and power to grasp ideas peculiar to the gifted child. Compatibility, he said, thrives on similar interests in any activity, be it physical, social, or intellectual. Lack of stimulating companionship, not high intelligence, can make social adjustment difficult. More important to optimal attainment and adjustment is the company of intellectual rather than chronological peers.

Few pedagogic assertions have been more controversial. We shall examine the arguments proposed and the evidence generated, but first let us note the various ways in which schools have tried to bring clever children together.

Approaches to grouping
Generally, as we have seen, British and American schools in the past several decades have depended on intelligence tests and direct assessment of academic achievement to identify pupils for special instruction. Elsewhere the intelligence test has not been widely used, and in many countries it has been pointedly ignored. But in both traditions a variety of programs have been used. The cleverest pupils have sometimes been put together for part of their schooling or for all of it; for quite intensive and specialized study or for less intensive, broader work. Grouping may be into rather small clusters or classes, or into entire schools or communities. Special consideration sometimes goes to developing particular gifts, especially in aesthetic and scientific study. This may be part of an otherwise unsegregated experience, or it may involve the student's isolation and deep immersion into a specific discipline. A few patterns of homogeneous grouping are new, but most of them have been traditional somewhere in the world.

We may forget that educating the most promising children has been the chief preoccupation of schools from the beginning. Prospective rulers or priests or professionals were the only persons who received much formal schooling at all. By the standards of modern intelligence tests, they were not necessarily the brightest children in a society. But they were the children destined for responsibility on hereditary, political, or financial grounds, and they had to be prepared for their responsibilities. Everybody else learned what was needed while growing up at home. For them, adult responsibilities did not require much skill in reading, writing, or reckoning.

In the eighteenth century, reformers argued more and more for educating everybody. But there still remained a cleavage between what was taught to the majority of children and what continued to be reserved for the very few. However chosen, these favored children went to school longer than their fellows, and they were more likely to have a fully academic education culminating in university study and professional training. In this sense, segregating a small number of pupils for special, intensive, and abstract study is an old tradition.

Academic, as opposed to occupational, curricula are still dominant in European schools, especially in the secondary schools that prepare pupils for the university. For generations these have been separate institutions: the *lycée* in France and the *liceo* in Italy, the *Gymnasium* in Germany and Scandinavia, and the grammar school and public school in England. They all share high prestige and enforce tough standards of admission and progress. They have virtually monopolized university preparation and eventual entry into positions of influence and prosperity.

Up to the nineteenth century, a child who was expected to qualify someday for a university place would not only attend one of these secondary schools but might also go to special preparatory elementary schools as well. Some schools, like the Boston Latin School in the eighteenth century, took pupils at age seven or eight and prepared them during seven or more years for the higher education of the day. In the United States the nineteenth century was a period of educational expansion and transition. Most children went to elementary school, and increasing numbers went on to high school, although they were still only a minority of their age group. In the last quarter of the century the new land-grant universities completed a pattern of broad opportunity for a full education.

In our century, as secondary schools have opened up to a wider range of pupils, not all of whom plan to go to university, it has become necessary to offer different curricula geared to a variety of occupational goals. But whether in a separate school catering only to the most favored, or in a preuniversity stream flowing alongside others, it seems that brighter pupils in Europe have found heavier demands than those in the United States. Let us look at some examples.

Since World War II, Sweden has made a major overhaul of its schools, installing a nine-year elementary school for all pupils between the ages of seven and sixteen. Then, when pupils go on to secondary school, they choose among courses for university preparation or occupational training. In the preuniversity curriculum (according to the early 1970s stage of the reform), a typical first-year student, about sixteen years old, studies the following subjects: Swedish, English, one or two other foreign languages, history, civics, mathematics, science, art, music, and physical education. Mathematics and science occupy five hours a week; languages and civics, three; history, two; and the rest, one. Three years later, the student's course load is similar, except that religion, philosophy, and psychology replace mathematics, science, art, and music. In addition, students devote more time to civics, language, and physical education. Preuniversity students planning to major in science or mathematics take more work in these fields throughout the three years. These curricula are designed to build upon the unified elementary school, where each week all ten-year-olds, for example, study Swedish, mathematics, English, music, drawing, handicraft, physical education, religion, civics, history, geography, and nature study. These last five are spoken of together as orientation subjects, something like social studies in an American school.

France and England make an interesting contrast between general and more specialized secondary studies. In the last year of the *lycée,* French pupils traditionally study philosophy, modern language, mathematics, physical and biological science, physical education, and electives. (French itself is not a formal subject.) Proficiency in these subjects is tested in the *baccalauréat* examination, a hurdle that is the aim of secondary schooling and the prerequisite to university matriculation. English pupils, on the other hand, who have studied many subjects in earlier years, concentrate in the last, or sixth form of grammar school, on the subjects that they have chosen for "A-level" examinations. These are three or four subjects, either from the arts (English, history, languages) or the sciences (mathematics, chemistry, physics, biology), but seldom from both.

Long arguments have explored the merits of secondary-school specialization. The English defend it as necessary for high standards in the university. Continental Europeans cite the proportion of university students who choose—and follow successfully—a major subject that is quite different from the one they had chosen in secondary school. It is not unusual, in fact, for them to cross all the way over from the sciences to the humanities. One study conducted during the 1960s showed that about a fifth of the pharmacy students at French universities had followed the philosophy option when they were in the *lycée,* rather than a science option (Halls, 1965).

In the United States, university-bound high-school pupils take neither so specialized a program as British pupils, nor so broadly based a one as Continental pupils. Nor are they—except in the most demanding of special school programs—required to work so intensively. The academic track in a comprehensive high school, along which most pupils travel toward college, normally includes four or five "solid" or academic subjects (e.g., English, science, mathematics, social studies, and foreign language) plus physical education and "soft" electives like music or art. A more intensive program rarely adds more than one "solid" and perhaps an extra elective.

One may recall the cliché that American pupils bound for college are generally about two years behind their peers abroad. The more apt comparison would then be with what an American college student studies in the second year. Here the variety of expectations and standards is bewildering, but at the more demanding schools the typical student takes three to five different courses, attending class twelve to sixteen hours a week. A nineteen-year-old counterpart in European secondary schools has an average weekly load of more subjects, studied in thirty or more class hours. Such comparisons across boundaries are tricky, and they rarely settle the crucial questions. When indulging in comparisons, however, most informed observers find that the intellectual demands on bright American pupils, even in selective special classes, could be substantially increased without resulting harm or distortion. Even the barest outline of the academic programs available elsewhere shows how much could be done.

The most sustained challenge to American pupils is probably to be found in some of the special schools set up specifically for very bright children. Two of the best known of these are the Bronx High School of Science and neighboring Hunter College High School with its associated elementary school. Hunter has traditionally selected the brightest of a large number of candidates to enter between the seventh and tenth grades. The average IQ at both schools borders 150, with virtually nobody scoring below 130. Similarly, the Laboratory Schools of the University of Chicago enroll very bright pupils throughout the full range of elementary and high-school grades.

Lowell High School in San Francisco draws bright pupils from all over the city, and while it is not as well known as other special schools, it has enjoyed an unusually strong record dating back to 1856. As a public high school, it is an example of a special-purpose school without university associations, philanthropic support, or a location isolated from modern urban tensions. This school has managed to keep its identity despite sharp demographic changes in San Francisco, big-city problems of poverty and frustration, fierce competition over school taxes, and opposition from educators and civic activists who do not believe in segregated schools of any kind. In 1974 it won a critical court battle defeating a suit that would have changed it into a comprehensive neighborhood high school like most others. As the trial progressed, an astonishing number of alumni came out to support the school. An important aspect of the school's defense was the overwhelming evidence demonstrating its impressive and consistent accomplishments over the years.

While maintaining a strict policy of admitting students from all ethnic and economic backgrounds, Lowell High School continually has heavy enrollments in Advanced Placement courses (in some fields, near the highest in the nation). It has also sent a larger number of graduates than any other high school to the University of California (for which only the top 12 percent of California pupils are eligible) and has graduated a large number of scholarship winners each year in both local and national competitions. The staff has an impressive range of training and talent, and the school has developed an extracurricular program involving nearly all students in activities that have included prize-winning musical ensembles and championship athletic teams. After decades of absence, classical Greek was revived in 1975, at the same time that courses in horticulture and aeronautics were introduced.

Some other, much better known special schools for high-school students should be mentioned. In Philadelphia, Central High School and

Girls' High School have long records of rigorous academic study and successful graduates. They are open to pupils from the entire city. Admission depends on high marks and test scores, with special criteria for pupils who have backgrounds of inhibited academic achievement but who show strong promise. In New York City, there are several special-purpose high schools open to very bright pupils from every part of the city. There are also local high schools with enviable records of achievement serving pupils in their home districts, such as DeWitt Clinton in the Bronx and Erasmus Hall in Brooklyn. Admission, as in Philadelphia, requires superior school records and scores, with separate standards for promising pupils from disadvantaged environments.

Noteworthy schools for elementary and junior-high pupils exist in several parts of the country. For many years, the Colfax Elementary School in Pittsburgh experimented with large and small groups of gifted pupils. This school terminated its special program in 1971, but in 1977 the city of Pittsburgh opened a "scholars' program" in all grades from kindergarten through twelfth. This new plan selects pupils with IQ scores of 130 or more and/or other characteristics related to special abilities. Each child attends a special resource center with other gifted children from all over the city for one day a week and then spends the rest of the week in flexibly enriched study at the home school. University City, Missouri, has also shown a long-standing interest in the gifted. It now offers special classes for about one hundred pupils in two junior high schools.

The durable Cleveland Major Work program combines special academic work with special-interest clubs and projects outside of the classroom. At first, the program was restricted to pupils with scores equivalent to IQ 125 or higher on a test using local norms that provided "probable learning rates" (see Chapter 5). There are now variations as well for children who do not score as high, but who display other talents. Children enroll from all parts of the city, including the severely depressed ghettos. Academic work is serious and intensive, and is accompanied by regular art, music, and physical education classes, and by a variety of special-interest clubs. Two special emphases are pupil research on individually chosen topics (their "major work") and the cultivation of skillful leadership. Teachers are a powerful force, stimulating high standards in both academic and social realms, but they are trained to shift much of their responsibility to their pupils as the year progresses. Experienced Major Work pupils know how to do their own work, how to help others, and how to conduct class sessions. This program, like the one in San Francisco, has managed to maintain strong public support through a depression and several recessions, wars, and fluctuating big-city problems. Alumni loyalty is an important reason for its survival, as an elaborate 1939 survey showed (Sumption, 1941) and as the Major Work staff has validated since then (Barbe, 1955; Hall, 1956). However, in the 1978 crisis over pupil integration and budget deficits, the Cleveland schools cut out funds for Major Work supervision. The classes themselves were to continue, but only time will show how well they survive without the close and helpful attention from supervisors that has been an important feature of the program. If this cut is only the first step toward dismantling Major Work itself, a landmark in the education of gifted children will soon be lost.

Much more widespread in the United States than separate schools for the gifted are the several kinds of "ability grouping" for elementary- and secondary-school classes. As many as half the elementary schools and over three quarters of the high schools in the U.S. employ grouping of some kind, though it may be confined to certain subjects, such as reading in the lower grades or mathematics in the high school. As with English "streams," some school systems place brighter pupils in classes that are all at the top level, particularly in smaller towns where schedules are tight and options few. Other schools assign a pupil in each subject to what appears to be the most appropriate class. Very bright pupils might then be in the top-level section of every class they take, but they might possibly be in some top-level sections and in some lower-level sections if their skills are unevenly developed. Schools have experimented with flexible "cluster groups," which bring bright pupils of various ages together periodically to study a topic. These groups do not require a formal, year-round classroom situation, but they do require a willing teacher who is well informed about the topic under investigation and the ways to study it. This arrangement is useful in small schools, particularly.

In addition to groups, schools may also give considerable freedom to individual pupils who wish to pursue independent projects. Independent study can be the most effective tool of all for children who prize time to themselves and who respond to encouragement and to hints about strategy or resources. Examples of independent study can be found at any level, even in the kindergarten. They are most abundant in secondary school and college.

Individual attention has recently flourished in so-called ungraded classes, notably in the elementary school but also in some secondary schools. Pupils may be assigned to a teacher rather than to a class or grade, remaining with the teacher for up to two or three years. This assignment, of course, can be the basis of their entire school program, or it can be—as it usually is—something that affects only part of their schedule. A variant of this tactic is weekend or summer programs in which many unusual topics might be studied—from haiku to the Crusades. Pupils often share their work, taking turns teaching and criticizing.

Thus one may find special programs at any scale: an entire school, separate classes, part-time clusters, individual and independent study. The methods that teachers employ vary according to the tradition of a region (as in the classical *lycée*), the techniques stressed by a program (as in the Major Works Program), or the teacher's own personal experience and success (as in most programs, no doubt). Bringing bright children together is just the beginning, after which great variety is the rule.

Concerns regarding grouping

Against this background of very different ways of grouping children, let us look at the broad disagreement over whether we should form groups at all.

Arguments range over several topics: how accurately a school program can select the brightest pupils, how we can defend giving attention to skillful pupils when the unskillful need help so desperately, what place there is in a democratic society for segregated curricula, and what impact special study has on a pupil's personality and social effectiveness.

The first problem concerns how to pick bright pupils for special groups. We have already seen that there are different definitions of intelligence and different intelligence tests. In the classroom the major difficulty is the spread of talent that still remains after selection, as many psychologists have demonstrated. In 1948, after studying many American classrooms where pupils had been picked for similar abilities, Walter Cook made a forceful statement about this difficulty. Suppose, he said, we choose sixth-grade pupils who should be able to do well in reading and arithmetic. According to data he collected in many schools, he found that when pupils were put into groups on the basis of achievement tests aimed heavily at reading and arithmetic, there was at best a 20 percent reduction in variability. Instead of the full range of eight grades in reading ability that one would find in an unselected sixth-grade classroom, the selection tests still brought together a class with a range of six and one-half years. This is a minor reduction, albeit helpful, if the extremely low-scoring pupils kept out are the ones who would have needed the most attention. But it is disappointing when we note that the screening tests were supposed to put together pupils of quite similar arithmetic and reading ability.

Alfred Yates (1971) found a similar situation in England: a primary school class streamed for homogeneous attainment in English often showed much variation in mathematics. He considered streaming to be "a coarse, unsatisfactory, and potentially unjust form of grouping" (p. 82). He would settle, but reluctantly, for quite specific selection; for example, a reading test to distinguish advanced readers from slow ones. And, as Cook pointed out, among the high scorers in English, there would nonetheless be those who have trouble with spelling, others with grammar, and still others with paragraph construction. If as much as 80 percent of the original variation in ability were to remain, the idea of a "homogeneous group" would still be deceptive.

If we move from a reading test for a class in English to an intelligence test to select pupils for a whole school, difficulties increase. We return to the problem of general intelligence and its relation to academic skill. This relation, while positive and dependable, is not close enough to permit confident prediction for all individual pupils. Hence the difficulty that has always dogged selection, the overlap between pupils who barely qualify for a selected group and those who barely miss. Some of those who are chosen will do poorly, and some of those left out would have done rather well. However, the Cook-Yates line fades as we approach the upper limits of intelligence. Jane, who scores 180 on an IQ test given individually and sympathetically, may well have a "true" IQ closer to 160; Bill, whose score is 90, may actually be closer to 115. A program geared to pupils of 150 and above (roughly Terman's cutoff), or more likely to 125 and above (a typical cutoff in city programs), would not be unfair to either Jane or Bill, because their scores would be well above or below the cutoff. What causes concern, of course, is the scores clustering near the 150 or 125 cutoffs. Most of the disagreement between psychologists who recommend and those who oppose grouping refers to the milder levels of brightness. This is no small matter, because there are many more children (over twenty times as many) who test at IQ 120 than at IQ 150 and, therefore, a larger number who hover near the lower cutoff. The later experience of pupils near the cutoff may be markedly different, according to whether they were selected or rejected.

Recent attention to self-fulfilling prophecies has emphasized the potential influence of knowing a child's status beforehand. Robert Rosenthal and Lenore Jacobson (1968) called this the "Pygmalion effect." Jacobson studied this effect with elementary-school pupils and their teachers in a San Francisco suburb. She assigned numbers at random to some of the pupils. Then she told their teachers at the start of school that these numbers were from the "Harvard Test of Inflicted Acquisition" (the teachers were not told that there was no such test) and that according to the test certain pupils would probably show a growth spurt during the coming year. Later, on real tests of achievement and intelligence, these growth-spurt pupils actually showed greater progress than the rest of their classmates: achievement was higher, IQ scores had risen. Teacher reports gave special commendation as well to the better adjustment of the growth-spurt pupils. In another phase of the study, Rosenthal and Jacobson analyzed the scores of some other children who had not been put into the growth-spurt category, but who had made substantial intellectual improvement during the term. Their teachers reported that these pupils were less friendly, less well adjusted, and less interesting than the others. They succeeded, apparently, without encouragement from teachers, perhaps even—in a reverse Pygmalion effect—despite their teachers' perception of poor potential. This study has been widely cited and also strongly criticized on technical and statistical grounds. But the general principle accords with wide experience. The children picked for a group will tend to respond to teachers' expectations, so that the borderline children are more likely to organize their efforts and meet standards than they are to collapse under strain. Unfortunately, the obverse is that the pupils who are not selected miss out on this stimulating encouragement. They are not so likely to be challenged and thus to grow.

Teachers are not so sensitive as psychologists to the data on how imprecise scores can be. They have strong convictions based on their experience with the children whom the tests—fallible as they are—send to them. They are confident that they can more easily respond to each pupil if the others in the class are not very different. Many teachers believe that some students learn academic subjects more readily than other pupils and that these pupils can be put into appropriate groups. Then teaching is more effective, there are fewer discipline problems, and class cooperation is easier to stimulate (Copley, 1961). Burt (1969) found the same strong opinion among veteran teachers in London. They said that in mixed groups they could not deal fairly or effectively with the potential ability latent in either dull or bright children.

Perhaps what we have here is, at least in part, a difference in perspective. Psychometrists by training look specifically at particular and carefully bounded domains. They question how sharply they can detect the things they try to measure. Teachers, generally less dependable in their estimates of intelligence, are nonetheless surrounded by and concerned with a total experience in a classroom. They draw upon the data they are given but also depend upon their own insights, impressions, and intuitions.

Research on grouping

Given these diverging views about selection, how do pupils actually fare once they've been selected? Only a very few large-scale studies have systematically analyzed and compared students who have been segregated in school and those who have not.

Three surveys have attracted international attention: one each in Britain, Sweden, and the United States. The British study, conducted by the National Foundation for Educational Research, was performed in two stages. The report written at the close of the first stage concluded that junior high school pupils in segregated classes did better work in arithmetic, English, and reading than those in heterogeneous classes (Barker Lunn, 1967). The second phase of the testing did not point to such superiority, but critics have argued that there were important errors in the methodology of this latter segment of the research (Barker Lunn, 1970). The Swedish study compared two sections of Stockholm—one where segregated secondary schools persisted, the other where there was a shift to the new comprehensive schools (Svensson, 1962). Often quoted, this report concluded that segregation favored the less able but did not significantly aid the bright. But Dahllöf (1969) recalculated the data to find what he considered a consistent trend for segregated bright pupils to excel peers of equal ability in comprehensive classes. The American study was conducted in Utah and involved four thousand children in junior high schools. This study found that segregation was a benefit to bright children, but was less beneficial for the less able (Borg, 1966).

In an unusual experiment that has not been widely known, Wilhelm Sjöstrand (1967) studied the general problem of segregation in Sweden by conducting a well-designed survey of education in the city of Växjö. After the first six years of school, during which all pupils studied the same subjects, they were offered, in the seventh and eighth grades, a choice. They could take either a second foreign language (German) or a less academic subject. In addition, they could choose either harder or easier sections of certain required courses (mathematics, science, English). The schools had found that the brighter pupils chose the second language and the harder section. One year Sjöstrand arranged to have all seventh- and eighth-grade pupils assigned at random to segregated or mixed classes. Half the brighter pupils were thus taught all their subjects in homogeneous groups; the other half remained with less-talented pupils in most subjects (history, art, and so on) but were placed by themselves in the foreign language courses and the harder sections of mathematics and science. (This experiment is one of the few in which random assignment to type of class according to academic aptitude permitted control of other variables, such as home background, earlier achievement, and parental traits.)

Let's examine carefully what Sjöstrand found. He studied the effect of mixed versus segregated instruction on both academic achievement and on the promotion of the student's awareness of civic equality and human individuality. Equality and individuality are prominent democratic goals that leading Swedish school reformers believed would be attained better in mixed classes than in segregated ones. What Sjöstrand found, however, was that bright pupils not only made better academic progress in segregated classes but also developed a more stable appreciation for equality and individual differences in others. Sjöstrand proposed that there is a connection between these academic and personality variables. In totally mixed classes, bright pupils grow increasingly aware of their superiority and less tolerant of others, and they find they can get by with less work. However, less-bright pupils who have some classes filled with other bright pupils learn increasing humility and respect for their brighter fellows and are stimulated to work harder. Sjöstrand's results reinforced his skepticism about current Swedish school reform, which has aimed to eliminate segregated instruction as much as possible in order to strengthen democracy. His research deserves to be replicated and extended, in and out of Sweden, in order to probe further the relations among academic, personal, and social development.

We have some systematic evidence about how grouping works in comparison to nonsegregated schooling of the bright. This evidence does not support claims of serious harm, and some of it shows important benefits. But, partly because it is difficult to conduct research that would be thoroughly convincing, we do not have decisive data. A comprehensive review of research in the United States has found several recurring faults in studies of grouping (Anderson, 1961). Academic achievement was the only criterion used to judge success of a program, tests used in assessment had poor reliability, and the effect of other children in the school upon the gifted was not properly checked. The most serious flaw was that "homogeneous" grouping was only "a little less heterogeneous"—the weakness that we found Cook emphasizing earlier in this chapter. This review concluded that there is no sound evidence to show that grouping has adverse effects on social or personal attitudes.

Gallagher (1975), after analyzing a number of studies, concluded that grouping, like acceleration, is not as potentially harmful as critics have thought. Martinson (1973) was more aggressive, citing her own survey as well as those by Terman and Oden (1947), Barbe (1955), and others. Why, she asked, have special groupings been so controversial, in the face of the evidence? As Hildreth (1966) said—after looking at the empirical data—there is no evidence that grouping has brought children lasting harm. As for how much benefit it brings, that seems to vary according to the effort, flexibility, and support in individual programs.

Where grouping has seemed to be successful, it has been no simple matter of bringing children together. It has meant watching for personal development, maintaining flexible options, finding committed teachers, and carefully cultivating public support. At an international conference on gifted children, Lord James of Rusholme argued for a "critical mass" of *both* bright pupils and well-trained specialist teachers, especially in secondary schools (James, 1975).

We probably have a basic lesson to learn from Cleveland's Major Work program. It has lasted for over half a century because it has been carefully managed by officials who know children, teachers, and the politics of public institutions. It has changed some features of the program to meet new demands, without losing its basic determination to work specifically with bright children. Above all, it has insisted that "gifted" mean more than a narrowly defined ability with abstractions. Adding to this definition criteria that include personal attitudes and social skills, it has greatly expanded the possibility for developing a wide range of talents among its pupils.

The Major Work idea is broadly conceived. A list that was drawn up to tell the curious what the program is trying to foster includes: increased knowledge and skill, alertness, initiative and creativity, critical thinking, independent work habits, ability to share ideas and efforts, and leadership. These are lofty goals, and officials try in various ways to reach them. Classes are organized to make sharing a major activity, especially in preparing and presenting research reports. There is, from the earliest grade, a class structure that rotates responsibility for chairing discussions, accomplishing specific tasks, and talking about the qualities that help or hinder leadership. Teachers do not dominate their classrooms but insist that pupils regularly take the initiative for their own individual work and for that of the entire group. The scope of this initiative broadens as a pupil progresses through the several grades. But observers usually remark at how large a responsibility is given in the earliest grades and at how well pupils rise to it.

Enrichment

The third classic way to help the bright is through enrichment. It takes place in school and out, whenever something extra is provided: lessons, travel, hobbies, new responsibilities, sympathetic listening. It can be an effective response to bright children's curiosity and their intense search for reasons or causes. Indeed, gifted children normally enrich their own lives whether they get help from others or not, when they are bored with repetition or afflicted by loneliness.

Most teachers recommend enrichment. In theory, it should be the right of all students—with each getting as much individual attention as possible, with lessons geared to ability and remedies devised for difficulties. For the gifted, this individual attention logically implies teachers who give assignments that fit a quick mind, develop opportunities to extend knowledge by wide reading, and welcome variant explanations. To the purist, enrichment for the gifted is found whenever education is differentiated for them—whether in a regular classroom, in a special group, or in an accelerated program. Whatever, enrichment should be beneficial (Cutts & Mosely, 1957). It may be repetitive (drill has its place), and it may permit apparent idleness (reflection has its place, too). But it must produce beneficial learning.

Approaches to enrichment

What do schools do for the bright to meet this definition? Long ago the little red schoolhouse inevitably enriched the experience of younger pupils whenever they sat in the same room while older pupils were reciting. Henry Adams (1918) told of how in the 1870s he did away with history textbooks at Harvard and put his students to work for themselves. Nowadays any list of enrichment activities would include extra subjects, such as foreign language or typing; exposure to research techniques and the art of careful study; forays into the world outside the classroom; visits to experts in various fields—either in the school or in the expert's own work place; intensive exploration of hobbies and inventions; experiences in the arts; and systematic collections of all kinds. Enrichment does not require separate education or a fast pace (though all the activities above can take place in segregated classes or in accelerated programs). What it does require is some modification in the schedule and activities of the regular classroom. It nearly always means that the bright pupil will be freed from some routines necessary for (or at least imposed upon) pupils who work more slowly, or who are not so interested in wider horizons. It is truly enriching to the extent that a pupil is challenged to undertake problem solving and original work beyond the interests and abilities of the rest of the class.

So far, so good. The catch is that in a regular classroom this enrichment does not automatically take place. The teacher can scarcely spare the time to prepare genuine enrichment exercises for a few bright pupils and do justice to the others as well. Hence most successful enrichment programs provide two kinds of help to the teacher: some free ("released") time in which to plan and some special assistance (curriculum consultants, resource persons). Time for planning is vaguely defined. It may be an hour or so every week away from class to consult references or to arrange for visiting experts. It may mean time in class when somebody else—an aide, perhaps—takes over, so that the regular teacher may just watch certain children and think about them. It may be subsidized study in the evening or the summer, so teachers may continue their own education in areas where their pupils require special help.

All of these provisions, however, eventually reach the limit of any one teacher's ingenuity and endurance: hence the need for a consultant. Sometimes this person is an employee of the central administration who compiles inventories of resources in the district, makes up bibliographies, and assembles other facts that would take too much of the regular teacher's time. Consultants may also go directly to the classroom to demonstrate scientific experiments or conduct discussions. Or they may be on call for private talks with pupils.

One of the best organized resource services was pioneered in San Diego, California. There, since the 1950s, the entire system has tried to give greater depth to the education of pupils in about the top 2 percent of intellectual aptitude. San Diego has avoided setting up special schools or separate classes. Instead, small and flexible "cluster groups" of bright children within a school have studied together, and the general curriculum has been strengthened through added assignments and experiences. Thus the gifted have wide and continuing contact with all the children their age in school, from kindergarten on. Here, the definition of gifted has broadened to include criteria appropriate to the large number of children who come from backgrounds outside the middle class, English-speaking mainstream.

The most important reason for the continuity of this San Diego program is the solid support it gets from the community, including its support of elaborate services. Over the years, bibliographies and lists of specialists on an enormous range of topics have been compiled. When a pupil or a group wishes to study a subject, teachers can routinely ask for authoritative assistance well beyond their own personal experience or study. Teachers occasionally have time off from regular duties to prepare or contribute to new syllabi and bibliographies. Pupils may go from the schools into the community to visit museums and parks. Conversely, experts regularly visit classes to discuss their work and interests. School officials and teachers often make unusually sensitive assessments of this program, and pupils and parents are called upon for detailed evaluations. Since the enactment of state-subsidized programs for gifted pupils, San Diego has harmonized its regulations with those of the state and is able to continue its efforts with even firmer support.

Research on enrichment
All these forms of enrichment are difficult to judge because evidence is scanty. Defenses and speculations abound, but they are mainly hortatory and descriptive, not critical or evaluative. Certainly, published analyses are few. Gallagher and Crowder (1957) studied the adjustment of very intelligent pupils in unselected classes, and they assembled useful case studies. Various city schools have described their programs, and the compilation by Havighurst and his colleagues (1955) gives capsule descriptions of a great many.

However, there is some firm consensus on enrichment. Where it seems to succeed, it enlivens the classroom for bright children by keeping them constructively busy, by stretching their understanding, and by allowing them to share what they discover with their classmates. They continue to mix with children their own age and to have an easy rapport with them on the playground. They have ample chance to exercise leadership and thus bolster their self-confidence. Teachers who are able to stimulate these pupils in their regular classes often find the challenge exciting, especially if they can keep the entire class together, cooperating on lessons and projects to which all contribute their particular gifts.

This is not, however, what usually happens. Much of what has been written about enrichment is discouraging. Gallagher (1975) flatly stated that it has failed, because it so often consists of more assignments at the same or even a lower conceptual level than ordinary classwork. This is the result of a very difficult predicament for teachers. They face a wide range of backgrounds and abilities among a large number of children all in the same room. Teachers have their own limits no matter what their strengths, and gifted pupils will often push hard at these limits. The special techniques inculcated by good enrichment (guiding, discussing, enlisting collaboration—even the cardinal, "Let's look it up") do not come easily or naturally to harassed teachers. The democratic tone that commends enrichment to many teachers may deteriorate into the sterility of low motivation and repetition.

Determining that the bright must be kept busy may become a hazard. This is quite clear in the case of one elementary-school girl who was asked to help the art teacher, to do library research for the English teacher, to be the liaison between her class and the audiovisual department, to teach a second-grade class when the teacher was absent, to give extra science reports, and to come to school early to study French (Isaacs, 1971). This potpourri might have been stimulating to the girl, but it was hardly a well-planned regime, and it probably seemed like exploitation to her.

Copley (1961) caught another temptation in secondary schools—that of "pseudo-intellectual play"—which emphasizes enthusiasm, not learning. Studying the incidental music to *Midsummer Night's Dream* as a way to introduce the play, or making posters and soap carvings are all fun, but they bear "about the same relation to genuine enrichment that conversation does to critical thinking" (p. 23). And Copley pointed out a more subtle problem: the premature study of a topic that depends for proper understanding on a thorough mastery of fundamentals. He used as an example the conducting of public-opinion surveys and the risk that the misinformation such surveys will surely include will not be properly interpreted. He admonished that enrichment is acceptable only if it brings intellectual discipline and competence. It cannot be just "study in breadth."

Stanley (1973), too, has found enrichment dangerously tempting, and believes that little of it actually goes on in most regular classes. Other veteran observers are equally pessimistic. "Teachers just don't have the time." "Easier to state [the program] than to execute it." "Useful if nothing else is available." "Easiest to give lip service to."

There is no doubt about it. There can be quite a distance between good intentions and enrichment. But it remains a tantalizing technique because it *can* work—and not only as a last or sole resort. After quoting doubt or despair, we owe time to affirmation, often from the same persons, who themselves are sensitive to imperfections because they know how far enrichment can go. Here is Copley again, summarizing the advantages of enrichment:

The advantages of enrichment, as opposed to acceleration, are numerous. It does not displace the student from his normal age group. . . . He is enabled to study more intensively, to follow out in greater breadth and depth, those subjects for which he has shown aptitude. In the end, . . . the content of his education will be literally "enriched"; he will have acquired knowledge and skills more nearly commensurate with his [gifts]. In actual fact, enrichment . . . simply makes educational capital of the natural tendency of the highly intelligent youngster to explore his environment, to read, to observe, to investigate, and to experiment. (1961, p. 21)

This is a formidable recommendation. Accounts of the drawbacks that can impede enrichment are sound warnings, but they should not drive out enrichment, when with care it can be very stimulating.

OTHER CONCERNS

There are educational concerns beyond the availability and effectiveness of special programs that must be considered when dealing with bright students. Inside the school, there is the problem of recognizing and encouraging the so-called underachievers and late bloomers, and of dealing with other personality patterns peculiar to the gifted. Equally important is the need to determine those qualities that make some teachers adroit with clever pupils and then to foster those qualities. Outside the school are issues that lie squarely in the larger society and its values.

Underachievers

If we test a lot of children and then follow them in school, we usually find a number whose scores are higher than their achievement. If we believe the tests, then we fret because these pupils are not "realizing their potential." Even if we discount the tests, those scores remain stubbornly in the back of the mind to raise questions. Among teachers, the so-called underachiever begets frustration and sometimes hostility or guilt. Gallagher believes we must distinguish two sorts of underachievers: those who come from average or privileged families, and those who come from low-income or minority families. The first (who are more often the ones teachers have in mind) should do well because they were tested with a suitable instrument and have available more of the opportunities a school expects. The second (who achieve high test scores despite a language or culture outside the test's normal purview) may be even brighter than scores suggest and thus be even more disappointing when their schoolwork lags. Gallagher (1964) noted that such children may be shrewder and more realistic than we suspect because they may recognize that "opportunities through academic channels seem particularly limited for youngsters in minority groups." Such an attitude is reinforced when counselors only recommend to them training or jobs currently available to minorities.

Why do apparently bright children fail to produce? There are some provocative hunches. Several studies have examined the inner working of families. Some find that low producers (especially boys) often have overbearing fathers. Most of them have family problems that interfere with school. Gough (1955) suggested that these pupils are showing in school only one part of a broader rejection of all social values. Terman (1954) found (in the comparison between his A and C groups) that underachievement went back to early childhood. Pierce and Bowman (1960) followed underachieving children into adulthood, to find personal maladjustment common. Shaw (1961), in a series of particularly thorough studies, associated underachievement with feelings of inadequacy, aggressiveness, and hostility. For whatever reason, a large number of underachievers are apt enough for superior schoolwork but thoroughly uninterested. It is the problem of low motivation that often accompanies underachievement. Teachers, of course, may try to make schoolwork appealing and to relate it to pupil concerns; but they cannot supply the motivation itself.

Some persons who have looked closely at the initial clue to underachievement—the intelligence test—are not so surprised at school performance. Given the difficulty that teachers have in stimulating the bright in the midst of everything else they should do, they say we should expect to find some discrepancy. In the mid-1950s, the Los Angeles city schools arbitrarily lowered expectations for pupils, by about one third of a year for each 10 IQ points above IQ 100. For example, an eight-year-old boy with an IQ of 150 and a mental age of twelve does not function in all respects the way average twelve-year-olds do in the seventh grade (Telford & Sawrey, 1977). This strategy has something defeatist about it, but the same school system has consistently offered splendid opportunities to bright children. It is an interesting attempt to quantify the school's contribution to underachievement and perhaps to alleviate some frustration.

The so-called "late bloomer" is a special case of underachievement. Typically a boy, he may not display any special brightness as a young child, in tests or in class work. But then something seems to happen, and he starts to move more rapidly and surely, to do work whose quality surprises the teachers who have looked him up in the school records or watched him in years past. The older he is when he shifts his gears, the harder it may be for him to do all that he wants, because he may have missed taking prerequisites or acquiring basic skills. He may also have come to believe he is mediocre and thus have trouble rearranging his attitudes to incorporate superior academic work and new aspirations.

This "late-bloomer" problem may be particularly prevalent in the United States, because the intelligence test has become such a fixture in schools. Two aspects of this test affect the late bloomer. One is the belief that the IQ endures, impervious to all but the rudest shocks. The other is its arithmetic: a bright child is one whose mental age is larger than chronological age. That is, the IQ is a measure of rate, and the high scorer is fast. A child who is thoughtful and deliberate suffers when the test questions have time limits or require facile adaptation. Piaget long ago abandoned this form of inquiry, which concentrates on quick and accurate answers, because he found it much more revealing to probe behind the answers— especially answers that were technically wrong. The late bloomer is often the child who prefers to think about things, to consider another view, to question the questions. A teacher who looks very closely is not so likely to be fooled, because clues will be there. But for a teacher mesmerized by the score in the register, these clues may go unnoticed or be rejected because they do not fit into the official profile. This attitude, which violates the basic notion of test validity, makes the late bloomer's situation all the more distressing. Which is right, the score or the behavior?

In the early years, when behavior is only infrequently or tentatively clever, offering the proper encouragement can be a delicate maneuver. In a culture that deifies speed, the deliberate child may look dull. But if the same society keeps opportunities open well into late adolescence, as in the United States, the late bloomer can still have a real chance. Nonetheless, many of them would have bloomed earlier under more watchful and understanding cultivation.

There is a rhythm to children and cultures. Some cultures do not encourage precocity. A recent study of children in Guatemala found that they live a stable, relatively monotonous life. At age eight or nine, they were already three years behind children in the United States in tested intelligence (Kagan & Klein, 1973). They did not remember how to solve a problem after instructions had been given to them, nor could they put together different bits of information learned at different times. Fortunately, the researchers said, they suppressed a tendency to make gloomy forecasts about "the future potential of the young Guatemalan." By the time these children were eleven, they had been inducted into the much more vigorous and exciting life reserved for older children, and their test scores rose accordingly. One is reminded of another culture—of the old tale of the Chinese farm boy who tugged too hard at the corn shoots, when he was only trying to help them along.

Maladjustment

We have enough evidence now, especially from Terman's long study, to destroy the stereotype of the bright child as inherently neurotic, unstable, and prone to early insanity. Some talented youngsters have serious personality disturbances, of course. But the data are unambiguous: the great majority of the gifted have superior emotional health. Nonetheless, schools do encounter adjustment difficulties in bright pupils, some of them exacerbated in the classroom.

This is not the place to examine in any detail the personality problems that clever children may develop as a result of serious strains at home. It is appropriate, however, to note how school procedures can either initiate or reinforce maladjustment. Kellmer Pringle's admirable work, written up in *Able Misfits* (1970), offers many case studies, two of them excerpted in the first chapter of this book. Most of her children had troubles that centered in the home (too high or too low aspirations, for example, or emotional friction between the parents). She found that school behavior often resembled what we have discussed as underachievement. The school regimes that she recommended were ones that bore in mind the home's contribution but that also grappled with the academic problems that were the direct responsibility of the school. "The most frequent single suggestion was . . . for remedial work and play therapy" (p. 86). Other suggestions were for a change of school or school stream, to allow a fresh start.

In America, Dunlap (1967) pointed out in what ways high intelligence can be a hazard at school. It should be an asset, but it sometimes evokes reactions that send the pupil off into unhappy and unproductive behavior. Some of the behaviors that he singled out include adopting an aggressively nonconforming attitude, revolting against the demands for rote work, and being outspoken—often with great fluency. He also pointed out some less aggressive behavior patterns, such as putting on the mask of mediocrity ("I can do better, but if the teacher found out she would expect more of me") or choosing to be timid rather than to try new skills ("Oh, no! I'd make a fool of myself"). These hazards, especially in young children, require the foresight and wisdom of teachers. One cannot list all the strategies that may help, but they nearly all begin with understanding what brightness is and looking directly at a bright child's behavior. They also include talking frankly with the children about problems that might otherwise build up unseen. Many a program for the bright involves spending some time in candid discussions of hubris, boredom, responsibility, and humility. One principal gave a very effective lecture every summer that she called "The Big I," followed by sharp discussion and private talks with pupils.

If the key is the classroom, the teacher must turn it. And all too often the teacher is not as smart as the pupils and cannot depend on seniority and experience alone to bridge the chasm. Bright children regularly say that they appreciate most the teachers who know their subjects and how to help children learn them, who are willing to deal humanely and fairly with pupils, and who are enthusiastic about learning (Hildreth, 1966). Paul Brandwein's 1955 survey of the teachers of brilliant science pupils found a similar group of characteristics: they are well versed in science, alert and vigorous, splendid demonstrators, and they enjoy children.

Of course, all children deserve skillful, sensitive, and enthusiastic teachers. The gifted especially need persons who are themselves bright and observant. The new teacher, hired to be part of a special program for the bright, should be willing to be taught. The more structured the program and the larger the student body, the more important it is for teachers to offer suggestions or criticism in ways that will get serious attention from school administrators. Inevitably, bright pupils and eager teachers will resist bureaucracy. As the Cleveland Major Work program demonstrates, it is desirable to strike a balance between the regulations from headquarters and the teacher's ingenuity in the classroom. But there are only a few organized programs to train or retrain teachers for gifted children. The programs available actually depend more upon very careful selection of persons than upon specific ingredients in the training. A typical training course includes the following topics: survey of bright children's traits, some bases for identifying them, curricula available at the several school levels, and discussion of matters like motivation and home cooperation. These topics are important, but if the prospective teacher is not a lively and intelligent person, they will be sterile.

Individualization

In the best of worlds each pupil would receive a great deal of attention. For bright pupils—as for other kinds of pupils with unusual strengths or handicaps—personal attention is more than an idealistic possibility; it is an urgent necessity. Acceleration, grouping, and enrichment all start from the premise that what most children get routinely isn't enough. The radical position is that individualization must be as nearly comprehensive as possible, because gifted children are not really alike even if their scores and grades appear to be quite similar. Stanley's project on acceleration has led some participants to believe that a uniquely compounded prescription for study, derived from lengthy assessment of traits and background, is essential for each pupil (Weiss, Haier, & Keating, 1974). They do not think enough individualization takes place by enriching regular classes, or even in classes restricted to gifted pupils. Anastasi (1974) applauded the Hopkins acceleration program because it is so carefully tailored to the needs of individual students.

Partial individualization is also desirable, and usually more feasible. British teachers defend classes and other school arrangements that break up schedules to allow for more flexible offerings (Ogilvie, 1973). These teachers recognize that a program designed entirely around a tutorial model is neither workable nor desirable, but they say that a "cafeteria-like" curriculum, offering a variety of interesting and more specialized subjects, will foster individual attention to bright pupils.

Upon careful inspection, most successful programs for the gifted, whatever the administrative plan, bring pupils into close touch with teachers prepared to deal with the special questions that curious and insistent pupils pose. Most gifted children have learned early how to investigate on their own. They can go a long way with a little individual help from a teacher or a fellow pupil. Even so, the child in greatest need of all is the exceedingly gifted one. As Lynn Fox (1974), one of the Hopkins investigators, pointed out, we have very little experience with children in the top one half of 1 percent, whereas we know the top 10 or 15 percent fairly well. Because they are rare, they may attract notice when they appear in school. But there is still insufficient recognition of just how radical an appropriate curriculum may need to be if it is to be truly effective. It takes very individual and careful attention to reach a confident decision about whether or not to send an eighth-grader to college rather than to ninth grade. But a decision to do so may be the most sensible one if the child in question is not only very bright over all, but remarkably advanced in mathematics as well. Fox pointed up that in high school and college, instruction comes in specific courses, so that great flexibility is possible in arranging a good individual fit between pupil and studies.

Social Values

The *Zeitgeist* surrounding gifted children is powerful. Pressey (1955), a veteran agitator for gifted children, compared the musical prodigies in central Europe during the eighteenth century to the champion athletes in the United States during the twentieth. Both types of talented individuals received support that was similar in several respects: early opportunities and encouragement from families and friends; superior instruction; ample chance to practice; close association with others like them; and recognition of mature performers. But the types of talent valued, and consequently supported, by the two societies was different: musical ability in eighteenth-century central Europe and athletic ability in the American Midwest today.

Gallagher (1975) cited a rough parallel that he called the "Palcuzzi Ploy." Palcuzzi was the principal of an elementary school where parents were grumbling about giving special attention to gifted children. At a school meeting with parents, Palcuzzi presented the following proposal for gifted pupils: group them by ability, give them special instruction during the school day, share activities with talented pupils at other schools and at school district expense, advance each pupil according to talent rather than age, and have specially trained and highly salaried teachers. There was a storm of protest, but after several minutes, Palcuzzi pointed out that he had only been describing what the school had been doing for years—for gifted basketball players. Similarly, Copley (1961), in defending Advanced Placement courses, said that it is no more undemocratic to reward superior academic ability than to reward superior athletic skill. Democracy means equality of opportunity. Talented students who don't have appropriate schooling are missing out on their democratic inheritance.

Social pressures and traditions that stand in the way of school programs for the bright are, to a large extent, beyond the school's manipulation. But the many kinds of special help that are already being given show that some groups of people will support school proposals and demonstrate to other groups what can be done. Public interest in the bright is sometimes mobilized by "emergencies," like the launching of Sputnik I in the 1950s. It is often deflected, as when segregating the bright became more a political than an educational issue in England in the 1960s. Interest in the gifted can occasionally support an organized effort over centuries, as in imperial China, or it can be frustrated by competing claims for scarce funds. A *Zeitgeist* that places high value on intelligence is one upon which schools can count for support, even heavy pressure for expansion, where programs for the gifted are concerned. A *Zeitgeist* that values other things more, or that has a truncated view of intelligence, can still be influenced. Fear and pride were the most dramatic influences, when in the 1950s the Russian Sputnik brought quick action to improve mathematics and science instruction for bright American pupils. It is hard to tell the reasons for the rise in state and federal spending for the gifted in the late 1970s, especially when we keep in mind that it has been a time of economic troubles. As Dorothy Sisk (1978) noted soon after she took charge of the U.S. Office of the Gifted and Talented, funds for the gifted rose between 1972 and 1977 from about $300,000 a year to over $2.5 million, and the number of pupils served by state and federal funds from about 100,000 to nearly half a million. In 1977, California alone enrolled more gifted pupils in programs than the entire country had in 1972, only five years earlier. In the same year (1977), ten states each allocated over $1 million of their own funds for gifted pupils. All of this rise in expenditures is impressive against the background of lean years. As Sidney Marland (1972) reported when he was federal commissioner of education, provisions for the gifted and talented are toward the bottom of the priority lists of local, state, and national governing bodies. Even so, despite marginal allocations in most places, there are signs of progress, perhaps of a mild shift in the American *Zeitgeist*.

Trends

Because countries and regions differ so, it is impossible to draw a simple picture of all the programs for the gifted currently in operation, or what is most likely to develop for them in the future. At present, however, Florence Goodenough's (1956) preference has wide support. She favors a combination of acceleration, segregation, and (with each) enrichment. She reached this conclusion without all the empirical support she would have liked. But she recognized what is increasingly accepted, that no one method of teaching clever children will do. Just as the gifted are a various group, so are their teachers and the schools where they study. This variety dictates several approaches rather than one. What Goodenough stressed was not merely *tolerance* of variety. She recommended a combination. And this is what is being put forward more and more widely now—flexibility among several options offered to pupils. Martinson (1973) spelled out this flexibility: increased emphasis on conceptually advanced learning, less reliance on exercises and workbooks and other artificially contrived devices, student participation in designing curricula, and incorporation of creativity into the curriculum as a cognitive learning style and a personality expression. In addition, Gallagher (1975) recommended "adjunctive services" such as counseling for underachievers. He also urged wider use of outside resources—experts, field trips, and any other alternative programs that allow the bright to explore the links between their books and the outside world.

In England, a stubborn problem remains in the unequal status of various schools. The 1945 regulations froze for a long time a three-tiered system of secondary schools in which only one school seemed to fit the bright. The implicit assumption that all types would eventually attain "parity of esteem" has failed to be realized. If a more integrated pattern (as Sweden has fashioned, in open imitation of the American system) gets more support, bright children will have broader opportunities—but only if provisions are made for them in a comprehensive scheme. The future of streaming in Britain and elsewhere is not clear, but it seems unlikely that the schools will return to relatively rigid choices at an early age and the resulting difficulty in making later adjustments.

A strong trend in the United States is for local districts to formulate their own definitions of giftedness and to devise programs for such pupils. Definitions and programs vary from the narrowly academic to those

loosely inclusive of other traits such as leadership. The new federal regulations that govern distribution of funds stimulate this diversity. In several
states, a related trend is to avoid large-scale separation, as in special
schools, in favor of smaller groups or alternate study in regular and special
settings. In Ohio, for example, only the established special classes in big
cities, like the Major Work program in Cleveland, have resisted this trend.
Elsewhere in Ohio the typical program is in a fairly small community,
which sponsors resource rooms to which pupils go for particular projects
or assignments. These rooms are staffed with teachers who have special
training and are designed to serve children with similar interests and skills,
as when six or seven sixth-grade pupils collaborate on mathematics or
science at certain times during the week. They come together for mutual
stimulation, without the relatively major investments in equipment and
staff that a large-scale special class might require.

Still another trend is to increase the scope of activity for bright children with an unusually high degree of creativity. The traditional outlets
have been music lessons or creative writing seminars or Saturday art
classes. Now, especially since E. Paul Torrance (1966) began stimulating
teachers to encourage creativity in all their class activities, the gifted have
more opportunities to exercise their talents. Some schools systematically
seek the gifted, whether they have high IQs or not. They use tests that
Torrance has designed or other tests that do not depend upon verbal or
traditional test questions. Other schools infuse essentially academic routines with opportunities for unusual applications or presentations, designed to enlarge their pupils' vision and to emphasize fresh perspectives.
The most arresting examples are not those from aesthetic or scientific
fields, where creativity and discovery have habitually been stressed, but in
such fields as history and mathematics. There, rote memorizing, which
often dampens the creative force, is carefully counterbalanced by encouragement to explore and to explain, activities that bright pupils undertake
with zest.

If the past is a guide, school programs for the gifted will continue to
vary, to change slowly, and to be uneven. But we must sustain a commitment to educating our brightest children well. For, like Wolfle (1969), we
should recall the historian Herbert Muller's inference from earlier civiliza-
tions: "the greatest achievements will always be due . . . to the gifted few"
(Muller, 1952, p. 231).

7
Current Problems and Issues Concerning the Gifted

What is honored in a country will be
cultivated there.

Plato

Interest in the gifted has fluctuated over the years. It has reflected social patterns, educational traditions, and in recent times research in psychology, sociology, and allied fields. At the present time, this interest has produced a number of unresolved issues, ranging from the venerable question of what giftedness is to increased pressure for the fair treatment of bright minority children. Let us examine a few major issues where agreement is difficult and implications are important: (1) the remarkable resurgence of debate over heredity; (2) the widely studied pattern of unequal distribution of brightness among social groups; and (3) some recent controversies over testing children's intelligence in order to select the very brightest among them. These three topics are broad, so broad that they overlap. As we discuss them, we shall see that some aspects could have been put under more than one heading, or could arbitrarily have been assigned to other headings. But these three broad categories are at least useful starting points from which to consider the underlying and very complex problems concerning the gifted.

HEREDITY AND ENVIRONMENT

What makes bright children bright? This question is really a special case of the broader question, What is the origin of intelligence? Curiously, the broader question has occupied psychologists extensively over the decades, but the specific question of what causes brilliance has received little attention. Both questions are important, on theoretical and practical grounds, for they get at a fundamental human quality that requires understanding. Even our cursory look in Chapter 1 at the young Mill raises our curiosity about how he could have been so precocious. The same curiosity grips anyone who rears or teaches bright children.

The Source of Intelligence: A Continuing Debate

Let us go over briefly the classic positions taken by those who have investigated intelligence. Historically, the conventional explanation for the level of an individual's intelligence has been *heredity:* the mind is part of the child from the beginning. Experience would, of course, shape this mind, but the basic stuff was given. Experience could only work within limits already laid down. At various times in history, however, greater responsibility has been assigned to experience, or *environment.* During periods of social reform, above all, revolutionary programs have depended on making massive changes in "human nature" through education or training. Helvétius (1795), in eighteenth-century France, put it succinctly: "Education is everything."*

Today the environmental position, shorn of statistical trimmings, reflects the belief Helvétius had, that we are really nothing but the product of our education. As for those who are unlike their peers, Helvétius pointed out that "education, which must be different for different persons, is perhaps the cause of unequal mental abilities that until now we have attributed to unequally developed brains." He explained further that "people are not put in exactly the same circumstances, so they do not receive precisely the same education." Helvétius believed that we all begin with the same capacity for thinking. So the obvious differences among us as we grow up must come from our different circumstances. For him, this word meant not only formal schooling but also private experiences, family expectations, and the pervasive culture—in short, everything that surrounds and happens to us. This is the pure environmentalist position: equal potential, unequal experience, unequal mentality. "Education is everything."

John Watson, the American behaviorist, echoed this argument. Although in his early work he had recognized the role of heredity, saying that habit is largely reducible to hereditary connections, when he concentrated on children, he restricted the influence of heredity. In the 1920s, he formulated the following proposition that has been identified with him ever since.

> Our conclusion, then, is that we have no real evidence of the inheritance of traits. . . .
> . . . Give me a dozen healthy infants, well-formed, and my own specified world to bring them up in and I'll guarantee to take any one at random and train him to become any type of specialist I might select—doctor, lawyer, artist, merchant-chief and, yes, even beggar-man and thief, regardless of his talents, tendencies,

---

*Helvétius quotes are author's translations.

abilities, vocations, and race of his ancestors. Please note that when this experiment is made I am to be allowed to specify the way the children are to be brought up and the type of world they have to live in. . . .

Let us, then, forever lay [to rest] the ghosts of inheritance of aptitudes, of "mental" characteristics, of special abilities . . . . (Watson, 1924, pp. 82–83)

It is interesting to note that Watson insisted on having complete control of both the child and the child's world, well beyond what is actually available to the most dedicated environmentalist, then or now.

Years later, Watson was embarrassed by the oversimplification inherent in this and later dicta he gave to parents. In a 1930 edition of the work quoted above, he stated, "I am going beyond my facts, and I admit it, but so have the advocates of the contrary and they have been doing it for many thousands of years" (p. 104). Recently, in a memorial tribute to Watson, Mary Cover Jones (1974), who had been one of Watson's graduate students, said she believed that had he continued to work with children, he would have mellowed and recognized the subtlety and complexity of their responses to the total environment.

In the 1930s the debate about the source of intelligence shifted to the proportionate contributions of nature and nurture. A "hereditarian" found in genetic background the major influence; an "environmentalist" emphasized the flexibility of children's minds and the consequent heavy influence of experience after birth. For decades, these two points of view provoked intense debates, with both sides citing empirical data from genealogical studies, especially comparisons of identical twins. The hereditarians often proposed that heredity contributes 70 to 85 percent to an individual's intelligence. Such claims were vigorously attacked by environmentalists.

In the course of argument, the either-or focus of debate dissolved into serious and increasingly sophisticated examination of how heredity and environment were related and how they worked together to produce mature intelligence. In 1961 J. McV. Hunt said that trying to decide exactly how much heredity or environment contributes to intelligence is an unfortunate enterprise. He suggested that we ask instead much more specific questions that would be directly useful to social agencies like the school and that would lead to solid theories of human development and human nature. Such questions include the effects of prenatal diet, nursery school, hormonal controls, and sensorimotor patterns. Hunt proposed, too, that we try to discover what Dobzhansky (1950) had earlier set as a prime goal: how genetic factors may indirectly determine the range of variation within which environmental stimulation can work.

But in 1969 Arthur Jensen's article appeared in the *Harvard Educational Review;* with it the debate over the influence of heredity versus environment suddenly bounded back into public and professional notice. In the article, Jensen summarized research over many years, discussed his conclusion that heredity was probably the major influence on intelligence (the ubiquitous 70 to 85 percent), and presented his own data to support two levels of intelligence: I and II. Intelligence I, he contended, involves associative ability, as in memorizing. Intelligence II is conceptual ability, as in abstracting or in solving complicated problems. Level II is what most discussions of intelligence refer to, especially those dealing with academic learning.

It is ironic that Jensen's distinction between Levels I and II has been one of the chief reasons for labeling him a racist. What he actually wrote in his 1969 article (pp. 109 *ff.*) was that his research seemed to contradict what some others (notably G. S. Lesser) had found: that patterns of intelligence test scores differed among Caucasian, Chinese, Jewish, Black, and Puerto Rican children. Instead, Jensen found in his own work at Berkeley that it was socioeconomic status, not ethnic origin, that produced different score patterns. The major difference was in Level II, where middle-class children, regardless of race, earned better scores than lower-class children. Jensen pointed out that school success is heavily dependent on the conceptual thinking that Level II requires, so that middle-class children progress more quickly and surely doing what seems to be inherently easier for them. He urged schools to recognize the difference between these two levels by giving more opportunity and encouragement to children who learn better at Level I. Then, as he wrote in closing his article, "The reality of individual differences thus need not mean educational rewards for some children and frustration and defeat for others" (p. 117).

The fact that most minority children in America come from lower-class homes seriously confounds the issue, so that Jensen—like many others—did not find it possible to measure definitively the hereditary contribution to intelligence among different races. He thought, however, that the question was important enough to warrant investigation. His position, fundamentally, was that we don't *know* (that is, we can't prove) the specific ways in which genetics and intelligence are linked. Therefore, we can't prove that either heredity or environment is what explains differences in intelligence. But for proposing careful study of the question, he was damned as a racist and an anti-democrat in the storm of protest that greeted his 1969 article. One effect of his personal travail was to keep others from studying hereditary or racial aspects of intelligence, for fear of the same savage treatment.

It is too early to assess the lasting effect of the Jensen controversy. But it is already clear that he touched a sore, if dormant, problem. Unhappily, for him personally and for the community of scholars generally, the debate over "jensenism" has strayed far from careful dialogue and empirical data into political and emotional pronouncements. Jensen's own apologia, presented in a preface to a collection of his articles published in 1972, gives a dogged recital of the events leading up to and following the publication of the 1969 article. He shows how much of the discussion, especially in the more popular press, either distorted his actual work or argued against him without ever having read him closely.

Among people who have read Jensen closely and who know his record for careful research—people working in population genetics and psychometrics—there are those who do not seriously fault either his data or his conclusions. Much of the argument has been political, rebuking him for returning at this time to the heredity issue with its racial overtones; for using IQ tests that are biased in favor of middle-class whites; for proposing differential schooling in an egalitarian era. However, the basic questions, to Jensen, remain scientific: How can we account for intelligence? How can we apply population genetics to a fundamental and crucial human characteristic? How can we improve mass schooling?

In a perceptive article surveying the IQ-testing movement, Lillian Zach (1972) concluded that the Jensen paper has the major merit of reminding us that we are dealing with a biological organism and that the educational environment is only one of the many influences affecting the growth and development of a given individual. The furor surrounding the man has called wide attention to basic questions. But the kind of attention has not made it easy to pursue the answers.

Despite the Jensen episode, research may eventually gather the evidence to assess hereditary contributions to mental development and to analyze the critical roles of diet and health in the earliest years—quite apart from the tricky matter of comparisons between racial or economic groups. Meanwhile, the position most widely accepted is that there is an interaction between genetic potential and experience. Let us cite briefly some examples that suggest the present pattern of thought about the interaction.

Shortly before the 1969 Jensen article appeared, Ernest Caspari (1968) drew an analogy of the interaction in the acquisition of language to the interaction in disease: the genotype controls, in part, the reaction of the organism when it becomes infected with a pathogenic organism. Or, considering language, Caspari wrote, "the genotype determines the sensory, central, and motor structures and mechanism necessary for the development of language, and in addition possibly the time of development of the character. The nature of the language is completely determined by learning" (p. 54). Caspari suggested that it is not very important to seek to know how much variance is due to environment or heredity. To him, the important factor to know is the nature of the interaction between heredity and environment needed to produce optimal intelligence.

At the same time Caspari made these observations, H. J. Butcher (1968) conducted a survey of the data on intelligence in which he cited A. H. Halsey, a well-known British investigator of social-class influences on learning. Halsey's view was that even given the power of environment, the fraction of variance in test results attributable to inheritance may be between a half and three quarters. Philip Vernon (1960), another respected British authority on intelligence, also attributed initial, or potential intelligence to the genes. But he stressed that a child's early environment could either stunt this innate ability or encourage it to develop and deepen in adolescence and early adulthood.

Richard Herrnstein (1971), pilloried for a time with Jensen because he pursued the heritability thesis, conceded that existing knowledge justifies us only in treating people individually, without regard to race or origin.

And Benjamin Bloom (1969), looking at the implications for schools, left speculation about the gene pool to geneticists. He concluded that if heredity imposes limits, teachers have to work with what is left, whether 20 percent or 50 percent.

So we do not know exactly how heredity and environment interact. We have no consensus to support the extreme positions, those of the 100 percent nature or nurture advocates. And we have considerable confidence that each component to the interaction is powerful; that we should pay attention to individuals as individuals, being alert to the possible effects of both nature and nurture; that we should avoid the trap of confusing broad intelligence with specific test scores; that political positions can affect how we deal with intellectual development, but they should not supplant careful inquiry. The Jensen debate has sharpened awareness of these fundamentals.

Giftedness

Turning attention directly to the bright, we find little contemporary information and no sustained research concerning how heredity and environment affect their development. What material we have is derivative, reflecting more general views about intelligence. This scarcity is ironic, considering that Galton's seminal work sprang in 1869 from curiosity about hereditary genius. But even he was applying ideas from elsewhere, interpreting the genealogy of eminent families according to his cousin Darwin's evolutionary biology.

Today, however, there are still considerations about the bright child that call up the old questions of nature and nurture. Some of these considerations are the origin of brightness, the nature of cognitive development, and the rationale for our social policy toward bright children.

Origins

The brighter a child, the harder it is to avoid suspecting innate hereditary gifts. At a superficial level, how much credit for extreme precocity can we give to eager parents and their diligent "hothousing"? For example, J. S. Mill learned classical Greek at age three. Some of the children Terman studied were reading before they were age three or enjoying chess before age six. Pascal at age eleven secretly constructed his own geometry "as far as Euclid's thirty-second proposition" because his father had deprived him of his beloved mathematics books in fear that the boy's Latin and Greek would suffer. Other pupils have entered college before they were age twelve, or received a Ph.D. before they were age fifteen. All these children were involved in activities that are quite abstract. They began with direct experience, but they always transcended it through analogy, deduction, and all the other coordinating activities of the mind. Of course, these unusual children needed opportunity and encouragement. But they so far outstripped their peers that the methods and the regimens of their families and teachers are inadequate explanations for their precocity.

The thoroughgoing environmentalist, fresh perhaps from studying severe deprivation in retarded children, can only explain genius by calling upon extreme stimulation. It is relatively easy to argue that mental potential could be submerged into imbecility by a constricted environment. But is extreme intellectual accomplishment sustained from an early age merely the reverse, a response to unusual stimulation? Interaction of natural endowment with environment, each component affecting the other, seems a more satisfactory explanation. A quick and responsive nervous system reacting and growing with richly varied experiences provides the optimal conditions for unusual intellectual achievement. Neither heredity alone nor environment alone is sufficient.

Cognitive development

Just as there are differences among the highest IQ scorers, there are also differences in their performances as they grow. Nowadays, most research on this growth reflects the stages in cognitive development that Jean Piaget has proposed. Piaget was, by early training, a biologist, so he sees a child's intelligence as something with a secure bodily basis. But in his biological studies, he was strongly attracted to the relation between physical growth and surrounding conditions that affect growth. His contention has been that growth occurs as a reciprocal relation between bodily potential and stimulation to activity. The environment alone will not induce a new activity, nor will increasing age be sufficient without opportunity and encouragement from the environment. The progress that more children obviously make in their cognitive skills is thus neither constitutionally nor environmentally ordained—it is not the result alone of physical tendencies or of training regimes. Piaget is not, therefore, a hereditarian or an environmentalist in the old meanings of these terms. He is, perhaps, an interactionist, stressing as he does the active role a child must take, sensing and reacting to experience. Though Piaget has shown little interest in bright children—or even in broad individual differences among children—he does go so far as to recognize that social surroundings play a part in hastening or retarding intellectual growth. But his real interest is in the strategies of cognitive activity that most children employ, rather than in differences between them.

Piaget's carefully constructed theory includes four stages in children's cognitive growth. The first, during early infancy, is the time for exploring with the senses: touching, tasting, seeing, hearing. Infants acquaint themselves in a rudimentary way with central elements of thought like space, objects, and time. In the second stage, up to about seven years of age, children begin to learn how to represent their experiences in some indirect way, through speech, gestures, mental pictures. In the third (ages seven to twelve or so), they start to fashion logical relations among things and experiences, ways to hold together the many aspects of their lives. They find out about dimensions, changes in surface appearance, representation through maps, appreciation of others' viewpoints. All three of these stages are in one way or another tied to direct experience. It is in the fourth stage, which Piaget has found to emerge in early adolescence, that the powers of abstract thought become evident. Children go well beyond immediate experience, considering all the possibilities suggested by a particular event. They discuss how things might be (but aren't), reason with symbols that do not resemble what they stand for, figure out relations among various abstract principles or symbols. This fourth stage, "formal operational thought," is where a very bright child's gifts flower.

Piaget has rather consistently held that this stage does not come until about age twelve, perhaps because he has never been much concerned with individual differences in intelligence. Certainly one must raise a question about persons like Oppenheimer, about children who learn elements of the calculus in first grade. Perhaps the normal schedule of stages is telescoped; perhaps the gifted are an important exception to Piaget's theory. There are also objections to other elements in the theory, especially about the stage of formal operations. Apparently, formal operations are not, as Piaget has assumed, universal around the globe (Kohlberg & DeVries, 1971). Some cultures, mostly nonliterate, do not employ them (Berry & Dasen, 1974). In industrial societies, as many as 40 percent of adolescents do not achieve them (Niemark, 1975).

On several counts we must realize that Piaget's theory, widely heralded and often accepted without question, has yet to be validated. But in less strict terms it squares with some broad tendencies in development. Younger children are ordinarily practical, here-and-now people. By contrast adolescents argue endlessly about religion and politics, dream about better worlds, care passionately about ideas. Inhelder and Piaget (1958) noted that formal thinking about the physical world, which is a child's chief source of evidence about formal operations, affects thinking about other parts of experience, such as personal relations and social problems. Gardner (1978) suggested that this broader, less strict interpretation of formal thinking is characteristic of most adolescents, fewer of whom may ever reach Piaget's stringently defined formal thought.

Whether one accepts Piaget's theory or sees important flaws in it, the major premise on which it rests commands wide respect: without activity, intelligence does not grow. Bright children, like all children, function within the limits of the strategies they have learned. They will learn more sophisticated ones as they find the existing ones inadequate and as they feel challenged by puzzling possibilities. They usually do so much sooner than average children, and their explorations are often very rich and complicated indeed. But they need opportunity and stimulation to engage in an active mental life in order to realize their gifts. The American publisher of two of Piaget's rare popular essays (written for UNESCO) chose the happy title, *To Understand Is to Invent* (1973), to convey the spirit of the man's work. The several stages, arising ultimately from a neurological base that cannot be tampered with, depend in part on social facilitation, on good teaching, on encouragement of invention and ingenuity. The underlying, physical source of intelligence, being inseparable from activity, thus requires stimulation, probably most of all among the bright.

Assumptions behind social policy

Social theorists who believe there are natural differences in mentality from the earliest years usually propose seeking out these children and developing their talents, so that they may better serve society. This is particularly true where a complex social order—whether a dictatorship or a democracy—requires highly trained citizens. The stronger the assumption of native gifts, the earlier the search begins. As we have seen in Chapter 5, the net will be cast wide. Officials (through the use of tests, for instance) look for clues to potential talent, so children who fall short of expectations—"late bloomers" and "underachievers"—may be caught in time. Social barriers—poverty, poor education, sluggish mobility—will be attacked so that as many bright minds as possible will come to full fruition.

Stephen Wiseman (1966), in industrial Manchester, found that homes and neighborhoods without intellectual stimulation or expectations were harder on the bright than on any other kinds of children. His findings reinforced those of Cyril Burt (1962a) and E. D. Fraser (1959), who also concluded that an adverse environment has its greatest effect on children with superior ability. Wiseman, Burt, and Fraser assumed that children have underlying differences in intelligence, and that those with more acute minds need maximum stimulation.

Much earlier, in the 1800s, Helvétius had another assumption: there are no basic differences except those that come from experience in one's environment. This assumption is implicit in attempts to improve or make up for a poor environment. Recently, campaigns in minority schools have assumed that brightness and school aptitude stem inevitably from a child's immediate background, just as "disadvantaged" homes diminish aptitude and send children ill-prepared to kindergarten. The argument runs: fix up the home and the neighborhood, and all the children will have the proper spirit and learn the proper things.

Wilhelm Sjöstrand, after a brilliant study (1973a) of freedom and justice in Western thought, stated that "if democracy must be governed by 'the wisest and the best' and if there are natural differences, it must be a sine-qua-non for democracy to take care of the gifts of nature." On the other hand, he said that if we follow Helvétius, "there will be no possibility to find reasons for who will be educated to what" (1973b). Edmund King (1973) saw the same assumption in Soviet education: "Soviet educators hold that everyone, given the right opportunity, is equally educable" (p. 329). However, the brightest Soviet pupils also get "the right opportunity" in intensive schooling: special academies for future ballerinas or competitive entry into Akademgorodok (the University City near Siberian Novosibirsk). Presently, the elected few are the Soviet pupils who have worked hardest and who show the most cooperative spirit.

But regardless of whether theorists emphasize heredity or environment, typically they join in one major prescription: give as much stimulation as possible. Hereditarians want to capitalize on gifts; environmentalists want to create them.

Carl Bereiter (1970) made an important distinction between educational policy for the individual and social policy for the community. He pointed out that teachers do not know their pupil's hereditary makeup nor can they manipulate it. Furthermore, teachers must deal with children individually, so that data about a hereditary group (even if available to the teacher) would not necessarily apply to a particular child from that group. For teachers, heredity is seldom a consideration that enters into their daily encounters with pupils. Their concern, and their only tool, is the environment, which—however weak—is all they can control. But Bereiter did point out that heredity may well count when general policy has to be decided. Policies cover entire groups, and if we know of heredity-environment links that affect certain groups, we can set policy to see that schools provide appropriately for these groups. Bereiter noted that by viewing heredity and environment as interacting upon each other, we can avoid two specious oversimplifications: that a school can do nothing about group IQ differences if they are genetic, or that group differences can be eliminated by social amelioration if they are entirely due to the environment.

As individuals, bright children need the attention any child needs, experiences that will test their abilities and develop their unique pattern of possibilities. As a group, they deserve a policy that recognizes their unusual development. If Bereiter is correct, the interactive model of intelligence is particularly appropriate for the bright. Their talent must be consistently enhanced from the beginning, lest they suffer early arrest. They can be expected to respond increasingly to stimulation as they grow, to sharpen their skills, and to gain confidence.

SOCIAL AND CULTURAL ENVIRONMENT OF THE BRIGHT

Bright children grow up in surroundings that affect their development. What backgrounds tend to accompany brightness? What backgrounds stifle it? The answers are clouded by disagreement over intelligence tests, which critics claim are not fair to children outside the middle-class mainstream in most countries. Hence a cycle: tests probe certain skills; the high-scoring children come from backgrounds that enhance these skills; other children, hobbled by their backgrounds, are not properly prepared for the tests, however bright they actually are. We shall examine this problem later, when we concentrate on testing. For the moment, let us look at some patterns discovered by using the tests available, recognizing their fallibility.

Distribution

High-scoring children consistently come from certain groups. Witty, like Terman, found that his gifted children had a preponderance of English, Scotch, German, and Jewish ancestors. This preponderance was out of scale to the proportion of these peoples in the total United States population during the 1920s and 1930s. Inversely, children with high scores have been relatively scarce among American blacks, Chicanos, native Americans, and among families of Portuguese and Italian ancestry. The reasons for this scarcity include the lack of social opportunities and prejudices, as illustrated strikingly by J. H. Rohrer. In 1942 he reported that American Indian children generally got low scores, but Osage Indian children performed much as did average Caucasian children. Gallagher ascribed this exception to "the accident of oil discovered on their reservation," and a consequently better educational environment (1966, p. 71).

Almost every intelligence test survey has identified more high-scoring children among whites than among blacks. This discrepancy is usually interpreted as the result of prejudice and poverty and of questions in the tests that cover material more familiar to white children. Audrey Shuey's 1966 survey of blacks in the United States during most of this century presented data from schools, colleges, the armed forces, and other populations. In studies of large groups, black gifted children were reported about one sixth as often as white gifted children. In studies directed specifically at the gifted, blacks appeared about one third as often as whites. However, since clear comparisons of races in the United States must await the day when minorities suffer no significant disadvantages as they grow up, critics emphasize that Shuey's survey refers mainly to present tests, under present conditions. It does not support definite inferences about the underlying genetic origin of intelligence. As in other genetic research, the data may be revealing about a given group (whites, blacks), but they are not conclusive when comparing one group to another.

Many studies have classified families according to the income and occupation of the parents, the status of their neighborhood, and other signs of social standing. In most of these studies, bright children have been concentrated in families where the parents hold professional, managerial, or highly skilled positions. Gallagher's table, noted on page 37, shows up to six times as many children of superior IQs in communities with higher average income than in ordinary communities. Martinson (1961) found that among California children averaging 140 IQ, 40 percent came from professional-managerial backgrounds, 48 percent from the broad middle-income group, and only 2 percent from the lower-income stratum. Havighurst (1961) reported a similar pattern among secondary-school pupils in a large midwestern city. Heuyer and Piéron (1950) derived a close association between family station and scores on a French intelligence test. In London, Burt (1962a) reported various surveys from the early 1900s where the pupils bright enough to qualify for scholarships came disproportionately from upper-income families. Parkyn (1962) found the same tendency in New Zealand, where class lines are less definite than in England.

In broadly inclusive summaries, Floud and Halsey (1961) for England and Wolfle (1960) for the United States have documented the presumption of an overwhelming tie between the father's occupation and the probability that his child will enter and be graduated from college. Anderson (1961) broadened this discussion to take in two dozen countries at varying stages of industrial prosperity, including the United States, Mexico, Greece, Hungary, Spain, and Yugoslavia. University students in all these countries form an elite coming unevenly from favored backgrounds, whether in a country where more than 20 percent attend (the United States) or fewer than 1 percent (Hungary). Regardless of whether he compared according to the proportion of adolescents attending college or the industrial-agricultural mix of the work force, Anderson found a steady tendency across countries for the children of professional and managerial homes to be the ones who move most consistently up the school ladder to the top.

The major contemporary exception has been mainland China. There, after the Cultural Revolution of the mid-1960s, the total number of students going to universities was reduced, with eligibility confined mainly to persons from peasant or worker families. Graduates of middle schools (who formerly would have taken examinations to qualify for university places) have had to go for a year or longer to work in a factory or on a farm. University entrance then depended on recommendations from fellow workers, not from secondary-school teachers or test administrators. The specific criteria for admittance to the university stressed political reliability and willingness to work hard. Not much attention was given to conventionally defined aptitude for technological training, which has dominated the university curricula. But, as we noted in Chapter 5, this radical change in university selection was itself reversed in 1977, in order to reinstate entrance examinations and higher standards of scholarship. The government is determined to ensure, however, that this new policy will not bring back the old preponderance of students from middle-class families.

Interpretations vary concerning the relationship between social status and intelligence. A recent report on the gifted and talented, prepared for the United States Congress, questioned the assumption that the gifted come from privileged environments (Marland, 1972). Terman is quoted, when he stressed that his group included representatives of all ethnic groups and all economic levels, with 19 percent of the parents representing labor. In Martinson's California study, 30 percent of the parents were in a range of occupations that included agricultural, service, and unskilled occupations. But if once more we compare the proportion of families in the population to the proportion of bright children they send to school, what stands out is disharmony. True, bright children come from farm homes and unskilled laborers' families. But these children do not come as often as we would expect. Terman's own study illustrated the situation: semiskilled employees were about a third of the adult males in California, but they were only about 8 percent of the fathers in his group; laborers were almost 20 percent of the male population, yet among Terman's fathers they were fewer than 1 percent. At the other extreme, professionals were about 6 percent of the males in the state, but they were about 33 percent of the fathers in the study. This imbalance, although the percentages vary, occurs in most surveys. It is too consistent to be ignored.

Philip Vernon (1977) has brought these two lines of argument together. He has pointed out that in recent years the majority of the gifted have come from working-class families, not from middle-class families. The latter produce a larger *percentage*, but the working class so far outnumbers the middle class that its relatively small proportionate contribution yields a larger *number* of children. Sandra Scarr-Salapatek (1971) went on from Vernon's observation to pose the question, "How many more disadvantaged children would have been bright if they had had middle-class gestation and rearing conditions?" She added that "high IQs will always be found among lower-class adults, . . . thereby leading to upward mobility for many offspring. Similarly, middle-class parents will always produce some offspring with debilitating personal characteristics which lead to downward mobility" (p. 1226), because factors other than IQ are at work.

More important than average differences between groups is the relatively wide spread of differences within any one group. This means that any group randomly chosen will have some very high scorers. Hence, all the races and all the levels of socioeconomic status have some very intelligent children. Fascinating attempts to seek out bright children in non-Western societies further corroborate the assumption of a wide spread. Biesheuvel (1962) reported construction of a test designed for African children, using film and requiring neither literacy nor verbal understanding. More ambitious batteries tap abstract reasoning, mechanical comprehension, and vocational interests, with material explicitly familiar to the children being tested. Vernon (1965) has sampled behavior among a variety of children—Eskimo, Jamaican, African, and others—establishing that wide ranges of ability exist among them all. Top scores, he noted, may be depressed during adolescence. He adapted Gordon Allport's description of personality as "becoming," saying that intelligence may depend on the future as well as on the past. Vernon noted especially the drop in tested intelligence among North American Indians during adolescence, when they realize the depressed status of their minority culture—the absence of opportunity for progress and advancement. He emphasized the different patterns that children show from one culture to another. A high score is not the same everywhere, and understanding a child's intelligence requires close attention to what the test has demanded and how experience has fashioned the child's response.

Motivation

One of the factors affecting high scores on tests is motivation. Very elusive to gauge, it may be inferred from persistence in school. Such an inference confounds intelligence with education on the ground that—especially in a selective, competitive curriculum—the more advanced and theoretical the schooling, the greater the intelligence needed to master it. But such confounding has been with us from the start, when Binet devised a test to pick out the children who would need special help in the early grades. The test "worked" to the extent that it correlated with school progress. We have already noted some studies, such as Terman's, which identify brightness with specific test scores, and others, like Halsey's, which assume brightness in the students who attain higher education after rigorous academic selection. This capacity to endure, to clear successive hurdles and eventually to complete an organized education, is only part of giftedness, because discouragement and apathy also characterize some very clever children. How is it that some talented children manage to persevere farther than others?

One answer is the very broad differences in opportunity. Raymond Cattell (1906) found long ago that more American scientists came from urban than from rural areas and that a surprisingly large number came from cities in just a few industrialized states like Massachusetts, New York, and Illinois. He believed the reason was better, more extensive schools, and he showed that as other states (notably in the Midwest) improved their schools, more scientists emerged. Ever since Kenneth Lindsay's pioneering analysis in the 1920s, studies of selective grammar schools in England have shown that the percentages of their students from different regions vary immensely: some regions send fewer than 10 percent, others over 25 percent. One researcher suggested that these admission figures result from local policies linked to regional differences of much deeper significance, reflecting industry, the distribution of social-class groups, family aspirations, and patterns of internal migration (Baron, 1965). Another researcher found that in London the richer boroughs had as many as four times the scholarship winners as the poorer boroughs (Armytage, 1964). He concluded that socioeconomic patterns were the chief reason.

Some of the most intimate and direct sources of variation must be the aspirations of a child's family. Joseph Kahl (1953) studied intensively the ambitions of a small number of secondary-school boys of high intelligence who came from lower- and middle-class homes. He called them "common-man boys." Some of them were content with the general way of life which identified the common-man class; others were not. The discontented ones reflected their parents, who encouraged good schoolwork in order to climb in society. Only sons who internalized such values were sufficiently motivated to overcome the obstacles which faced the common-man boys in school; only they saw a reason for good school performance and college aspirations.

Douglas Pidgeon (1970) carried the theme further in class-conscious England:

> It is the motivational factors in the home background, such as the interest and attitudes of the parents, that [are] important in influencing children's school performance, and not the more fixed material and economic conditions. It is the interest which parents will consistently show in their children's school progress, if not the actual help they may provide in explaining homework difficulties, which will lead to better school work, not the fact that the parents have good jobs and are themselves well educated. (p. 54).

Pidgeon reached this conclusion after having studied boarding school pupils who lacked continuing and "intimate contact with . . . the encouragement given by parents."

One concrete result of family encouragement is deciding to stay on in school. Vernon (1957) found that many parents of English eleven-year-olds, at the time for assignment to secondary school, preferred the selective and university-oriented grammar school. But the pattern was not uniform, since this preference occurred in 82 percent of professional parents and in only 43 percent of semiskilled parents. However, such class links got much weaker when pupils passed beyond the age of compulsory schooling. By the sixth form (about age seventeen), Furneaux (1961) reported that the selective effects of social-class determinants had ceased to operate. At this point, the most important determinant seemed to be whether pupils had developed a personal desire for a university education. The influential Robbins Committee report in the 1960s made the same point: that pupils from less prosperous homes who remain in school until eighteen or older are, on the average, as successful as children of the same ability in other social groups. This pattern is obscured by the severe competition to enter Oxford and Cambridge, whose students come overwhelmingly from the upper levels of society. But even this aberration comes indirectly from family aspirations, since admission to Oxford and Cambridge is based on examinations for which the successful candidates have been prepared in strong schools, often at heavy financial sacrifice.

There is the same pressure to enter the elite universities and colleges everywhere: the Harvards, the Sorbonnes, the Tokyos. But equality is not the rule at *every* university. Britain is again an example:

> The general increase of grammar school places has benefited children of all social classes, but working class children proportionately rather more than others. The general increase of university places has perhaps, if anything, benefited . . . the upper and middle strata more than . . . the lower stratum. Certainly, the overall expansion of educational facilities has been of greater significance than any redistribution of opportunities. (Little & Westergaard, 1964, p. 312)

As opportunities increase, artificial economic barriers fall, and the telling force is family striving. If the home is uneducated and the neighborhood unaspiring, larger grants and fairer tests will not be enough. From all classes, students who enter the university usually survive. It is getting them to persevere that far, to learn how to achieve academically, that is the difficulty. The French phrase, *"la famille éducogène"* refers to the family that exerts pressure to reinforce school expectations. Nason (1958) studied the heartbreaking data about counseling among bright pupils from poor homes in southern California. School officials saw to it that these pupils took university preparatory courses in high school, and they badgered business firms for scholarships. But many pupils did not finally enter the universities that had accepted them, mainly because of opposing family pressure. The wages that these graduates would earn immediately were needed too desperately to allow further schooling. Many surveys show that as many as half the secondary-school pupils who have the aptitude to succeed in college do not go. The chief reason is lack of encouragement, especially if at home the family is not *"éducogène."*

Floud (1961) examined how to encourage a supportive family attitude and to weaken the hold of social class on school opportunities. Affluence alone is not the key, she noted. Better schools, fewer children per family, and more secure employment will help pupils stay in school longer and match their studies to their talents. Thus, general economic advance will result in the education of more children. In Sweden, Husén (1960) found that increasing the number of flexible and comprehensive schools and expanding their curricula have held bright pupils longer and given them a better education. In rural districts, for instance, when the new comprehensive elementary school was introduced, attendance at the selective secondary schools doubled over that in areas where the older, shorter elementary school persisted.

King (1974) recently studied pupils who stayed on after the minimum leaving age in five Western European countries. He found the usual tendency for children from higher-income families to remain students. He also looked at the specific educational experience of their parents. While on the average, the parents had not gone very far (fewer than half had stayed on into upper secondary school), the longer they had stayed, the more likely they were to encourage their children to finish.

Wolfle (1961), referring to potential scientists, compared countries with different degrees of prosperity. In nations that were less well developed economically, industrially, and educationally, he believed attention should be given to increasing the number and quality of schools. He advocated attacking rigid class structures where such barriers prevented poor children from securing higher education.

If bright children can be motivated to complete their education, they usually do well and find rewarding occupations. It is intriguing to compare this pattern to that in an early much-debated study (Skodak & Skeels, 1949). The researchers studied a small group of mildly retarded infants, mostly illegitimate, who were separated from their parents when very young. The homes in which these children were raised varied in intellectual stimulation, emotional warmth, and adult guidance. The children who were stimulated showed remarkable gains in IQ, while those who were not slipped badly. The study was widely censured as badly designed and therefore inconclusive. But thirty years later, a follow-up study tracked down all these persons in their adult lives. Those who had been in lively circumstances showed normal intelligence and led normal lives; those who had not, remained subnormal, and most of them were living in institutions (Skeels, 1966). All told, the study dealt with a very small group, an arguable statistical design, and many influences could not be controlled. But the themes of intervention, encouragement, aspiration, and persistence stand out—as they do with gifted children.

Wastage and Amelioration

Children with similar levels of brightness do not all have the same test scores, school achievement, or adult careers. Is this ragged pattern inevitable?

The evidence of talent loss and wastage is impressive, and is closely related to motivation—either the lack of it or a kind of reverse motivation. Husén (1960) has written about the problem, with reference to his native Sweden and to other countries. He attributes much wastage to early selection and segregation: fine for those who are picked, perhaps, but disastrous for those who mature late or whose backgrounds do not prepare them to pass the selection tests. He has been a prime mover in Sweden's school reform, where all children now go to the same kind of elementary school for nine years, until age sixteen. There is minimal segregation, and pupils themselves are expected to make voluntary choices with their family's participation required. As a result, more pupils stay in school longer, among them bright ones who would probably not have gone so far under the prewar system. Husén's conviction is that severe competition in a highly selective program should give way to broader opportunity and more options.

The school, of course, is part of the larger society, whether the whole nation or the local neighborhood. Denis McMahon illustrated this with an anecdote from his own early life:

> In the industrial north of England where I was brought up I knew many able working-class people whose reaction to the suggestion that they should use their talent occupationally was "It's not for the likes of us." . . . Motivation to remain with the social group of one's kith and kin was stronger in the working class than in any other social class. ("Keeping down with the Smiths.") . . . A testable hypothesis could be erected: that the tighter the kinship relationships and the greater the neighborliness then the stronger the tendency to stay put and be relatively unambitious. . . . (1962)

McMahon went on to insist that the major "target group" to forestall talent wastage was working-class families. Such a task is beyond the school's power to undertake alone. Indeed, in the United States, researchers have found rather little leverage in the classroom, as against the power and inertia of society (Coleman et al., 1966; Jencks et al., 1972). But without the school's active participation, amelioration seems unlikely.

In the United States, the recent history of intervention among the poor—not at all restricted to the bright—is ambiguous, but some results are suggestive. Head Start for preschoolers, Follow Through and other programs for older pupils, and various kinds of special assistance in college have tried to stimulate academic progress. One successful program of intervention for older minority students started in the early 1960s, under the acronym "ABC" ("A Better Chance"). Privately funded, ABC had placed over 5000 students in secondary schools by 1977. These schools, more than a hundred all told, were very selective, including well-known private schools like Choate and Exeter. With the considerable boost that challenging study provided—and a great deal of special help in tutoring and allied activities—these students (mainly black or Spanish-speaking) were able to enter some of the most selective colleges in America. Their test scores were lower than those of typical students at these schools and colleges, but their achievement record was similar to broad averages. The most gratifying figures are those showing that of the ABC students, 70 percent have graduated from college compared to 75 percent overall. William Boyd (1977), president of ABC, cites his organization's experience as evidence that minority students can succeed if given encouragement and shrewd help. At all levels, from Head Start for children to Follow Through and ABC for adolescents and college students, the key is continuity. Otherwise intervention has only a temporary effect. If interrupted, it may leave behind the bitterness of hope denied.

TESTING AND SELECTION PROBLEMS

In the United States, difficulties have beset psychological testing to the point where some American cities have banned intelligence surveys, government agencies have restricted personality questionnaires in research, and court cases have challenged psychometric assessment in employment. Work with bright children is inevitably affected. Let us look at several controversial issues where testing and selection are currently involved: the definition of intelligence, the tests themselves, and their efficiency in picking out talented children.

Definition of Intelligence

What we mean by intelligence is, once again, a pointed question. Perhaps, as Butcher (1968) suggested, we still suffer from the grammar of it all:

> "Intelligence" is a noun, and nouns often refer to things or objects. Even when we know perfectly well that intelligence is not a "thing" but a sophisticated abstraction from behavior, we may sometimes half-consciously endow it with a kind of shadowy existence distinct and separate from the intelligent organisms which alone give it meaning, or, more insidiously, think it is a "thing" that these organisms "have," rather than a description of the way they behave. . . . It is better, therefore, to think of the adjective "intelligent" as more basic (and less dangerous) than the noun, and perhaps of the adverb "intelligently" as still more basic. (p. 22)

Similarly with highly intelligent children, we no longer think of them as having a lot of just one kind of intelligence, or, as Butcher might prefer us to say, behaving very intelligently in just one way. We include various kinds of behavior.

In its charge to the United States Commissioner of Education in 1970, the Senate meant this broader scope when it ordered a report on the status of education of "gifted and talented" children. The Commissioner's eventual report (Marland, 1972), written with the collaboration of leading specialists, spelled out the broad definition used: consistently superior scores on standardized tests; recommendations from teachers and others familiar with the pupil's abilities and potential; demonstration of advanced skill, imagination, interest and involvement; and the judgment of specialized teachers (as in art and music) and other persons qualified to assess special talents. Note "imagination," "interest and involvement," and "talent." The report recommends a high degree of flexibility. Such flexibility is often urged in behalf of pupils who stand out for qualities of imagination, social leadership, and technical inventiveness.

Taken together, "gifted and talented" now mean marked academic achievement, imagination, aesthetic accomplishment, technical and scientific facility, and social skill. As we have already seen, others (notably Hildreth and Witty) have emphasized creativity, especially if it should appear in children who do not get top scores on typical intelligence tests. This expanded definition harks back to Wechsler's influential address in 1950, in which he spoke out strongly for "conative and non-intellective" aspects of intelligence. This implies not unitary *g*, general intelligence, but something foreshadowed by Henri Bergson's *élan vital*—the components that remain *after* we have factored out abstract thinking and the use of geometric and logical symbols: drive, temperament, and curiosity.

But expansion has its price. The measurement specialist is always happiest with a precise, specific (and usually rather narrow) definition, because it is easier to make a test for it. To the general public, however, a narrow definition may be only an escape from the complexity of reality. Robert Ebel (1963) noted the circle of history when he reminded us that William Stern,

> the German psychologist who suggested the concept [of IQ in 1912] . . . saw how it was being overgeneralized and charged one of his students coming to America to "kill the IQ." Perhaps, we would be well advised, even at this late date, to renew our efforts to carry out his wishes. (p. 135)

The IQ is not dead, but some tests now cover broader intellectual activity. Both narrowly and broadly defined measures are being used with more discretion, with greater awareness of exactly how they should and should not be interpreted. In the same way, bright children are being selected with more caution across a broader range of intellectual activity.

Intelligence Tests

Some current problems call the tests themselves into question. Because schools most often use group tests (as high as 95 percent of the time), bright children usually come to notice after surveys of classrooms or of entire schools. Individual tests are more accurate, because they are given to one child at a time, taking the undivided attention of a carefully trained tester for as long as an hour or more. Such attention is expensive, and it may only be given to check on a dubious group score, or as one of the requirements for finally approving a child's entry into a special program. Most schools cannot afford individual tests on a scale large enough to locate all the bright children, so they depend upon other clues: teacher recommendations, high marks, parents' applications, accounts of creativeness, and so on. The nominated children may thus have a wide range of talents. The more precise and expensive individual test can be used with maximum efficiency, mainly for children who may have slipped by the group tests.

Children from minority families present a number of challenges to intelligence testers. Most countries have such children, whose racial, ethnic, or economic backgrounds may not acquaint them with the general culture of the society. Whether their families voluntarily isolate themselves or whether prejudice keeps them outside the mainstream, these children may not have what intelligence tests assume: a normal opportunity to learn.

In the United States, we are seeing more and more clearly that "normal opportunity to learn" has meant "opportunity to learn what middle-class children learn." So what about all the non-middle-class children? Do they need special tests based on their experiences and standardized on their real peers? Can we adapt our regular intelligence tests, perhaps by translating them into the languages the children know, or by leaving out questions about things they can't have met, or by developing new norms based specifically on their performance? These and other solutions have all been proposed and tried, but without general agreement about the results.

There is, however, some consensus about the problems posed when we ask minority children to take regular intelligence tests. Above all is the fact that most minorities are poor. They have their own cultural characteristics that distinguish them, but they all suffer economic hardship. So they and their children may lower their expectations to realistic levels and remain wary of contacts with the prosperous and powerful. The children learn about their own milieu; they may not learn much about the one the tests take for granted. Consequently, there are important differences between minority and majority children when they take intelligence tests. Jerome Sattler (1974) summarized these differences, chiefly from studies or observations about black, Spanish-speaking, and American Indian groups. An outstanding characteristic of many minority children is their lack of motivation to do well in school, or on the test in question. They may be more concerned to get the test over with than to do it right. Or they may try desperately to please without understanding quite how.

The language employed in tests is another problem. In the early days, testers made up questions for children in their native tongue. Now, decades later, the same linguistic problem has a vexing twist: What about black pupils who nominally speak English but whose English is not standard, whose experience with standard English has not made them fluent in it?

In the late 1960s, Adrian Dove, a black sociologist, devised the "Chitling Test," thirty questions drawn from ghetto life. Black children who know what a "handkerchief head" is, what a pimp means when he talks about "Mother's Day," or what the best way to cook chitlings is, do well. White students at elite colleges—or middle-class black students—fail

(Dove, 1974). Dove's test was not intended as a serious intelligence test. Rather, it was intended to dramatize how traditional tests use language and cite situations that are alien to many children. Linguists have been attracted to this psychometric problem because they regard standard English as just one of the languages with which children can think. They have parried the claim that minorities have inferior intellectual tools if they cannot speak the standard language easily. Yet William Labov (1972) analyzed the grammar of black English in the United States and found it to be highly structured, sensitive, and flexible:

> When linguists hear black children saying "He crazy" or "Her my friend," they do not hear a "primitive language." There is no reason to believe that any nonstandard vernacular is in itself an obstacle to learning. . . . Teachers are now being told to ignore the language of black children as unworthy of attention and useless for learning. . . . As linguists we are unanimous in condemning this view as bad observation, bad theory, and bad practice. (p.67)

Translating a test, or its directions, from standard English into a more appropriate language or dialect may not solve the problem at all, however. For example, children may not understand the Spanish used, depending on whether they come from Mexican or Puerto Rican backgrounds, because the two vocabularies are not identical. Often children who must become bilingual to some degree do not do well in either language. In fact, there are studies in which both black and Spanish-speaking pupils have done about as well (or even better) on traditional tests given in standard English as they have on tests prepared especially for Spanish-speaking or black children (Galvan, 1967; Quay, 1971).

A third problem related to intelligence tests for minority children involves the question of what happens when the tester comes from a different background than the child. Sattler (1974) found that what evidence we have suggests that the tester's race does not usually affect the performance of black or white children. However, Sattler emphasized that there are not many studies, and there is disagreement about results.

For many years, psychologists have been trying to deal with the general problem of majority-minority differences in tests by developing "culture-free" or "culture-fair" tests. Kenneth Eells and several colleagues in the 1940s and 1950s produced various "games" that played down language and used situations familiar to children from many backgrounds (Eells et al., 1951). In succeeding years, other people have used these and other approaches, trying to rule out the bias they believed was inherent in giving a traditional test to nontraditional children. Three decades of investigation have not shown that a "culture-fair" intelligence test works as it should. Alexander Wesman (1968) explained why. He noted that intelligence involves all that a child has learned, and therefore a test cannot be made that will rule out the widely different experiences children have. Both traditional and experimental tests reflect children's backgrounds.

What should be done? One proposal is to declare a moratorium on group intelligence tests (Williams, 1970) because they have become so closely identified with prejudice against minority children. Other proposals fall short of abolition, stressing that tests can be used carefully to provide objective, economical estimates of children's abilities. Sattler summarized the areas requiring special consideration in order to test minority children effectively: language, motivation, attitudes toward competition and achievement, and cultural traditions. Following Sattler's advice demands informed experience with a variety of tests, to know which ones are best for a given child. Where possible, separate norms that reflect the group a child belongs to should be used to complement the national norms most tests supply. Sattler also urged two broad reforms. One is to change curricula and methods of teaching in schools so that minority children are more likely to become involved in actively learning school assignments. Once the school accepts these children and how they learn, the children will be more likely to trust school people who give them intelligence tests. The other broad reform is to produce better tests of cognitive processes and of the various styles of learning that children employ at school.

It is important to realize that much of the criticism aimed at tests given to minority children has concentrated upon low performance. The examples cited in most research, discussion, and litigation refer to scores in the retarded range much more often than they do to scores at the top. But the problem is potentially the same at both extremes: scores that are lower than they might be if testing were more accurate. Even if a child gets a high score—high enough to qualify for some program that will be stimulating and profitable—what if the score might have been even higher, and the program that much more demanding?

It would seem that abolishing intelligence tests for minority children would be itself unfair, provided we can use tests more wisely. Whether or not the questions and the language in traditional IQ tests are significantly unfair to minority or to other "disadvantaged" children, it is ironic that they should be attacked as systematic despoilers of the poor. As Butcher (1968) recalled,

> Many of the pioneers of psychological testing . . . saw [intelligence tests] as a potent means of furthering social equality and of ensuring that able children, whose ability would otherwise have been submerged by poverty and environmental handicaps, should have the opportunity of an education commensurate with their talent. (p. 20)

It is now clear, however, that linguistic barriers may keep some bright children from being recognized. To that extent we probably have an inaccurate survey of the pool of talent. The children from outside the mainstream are underestimated whenever some of them score low because of language or culture. Children from middle-class families may be overestimated because their backgrounds have prepared them to deal with the problems in tests and with the competitive ethic in the schools. The problem is, surely, most acute at the border of brightness, where minority children are probably lost more often and more systematically than middle-class children.

Finally, there is the question of what age children should be when we check for brightness. If a child is talented we should act quickly, some say, at the time when the mind is malleable. Benjamin Bloom has been quoted widely for estimating that half the adult intelligence is formed by about the age of four. Sidney Pressey (1967) has urged us not to delay stimulating the brightest to their highest efforts. But, on the other hand, the younger a child, the less reliable is an estimate of intelligence. From the standpoint of accurate testing, whatever the initial age, we should take more than one reading, to settle on the correct level.

Test specialists are particularly sensitive to the effect of regression when very young children are selected. Regression occurs to a high score when it slips as the child is tested later. A seven-year-old may earn an IQ of 135, but two years later a similar test may show 130 or 125. Suppose the first score is barely above some minimum for special assignment, say 120. Then the second, lower score will not only prompt a question about the real level of intelligence, but it will jeopardize the special assignment. (The same phenomenon of regression occurs with borderline children who are assigned to mentally retarded curricula, but who later raise their IQs.) At either level of intelligence, underlying ability has not changed, but only the scores. Tests are not precise, and one predictable clue to their imprecision is this tendency for a score to move toward the average over a series of testings. Therefore, a bright child should not be locked into a program after a barely passable score, nor should others just below the cut off be permanently bypassed. Passage into and out of special programs should be routine to correct for test imperfections.

A prominent flaw in many curricula for the gifted is inflexibility, when programs cannot be changed or when esteem might be threatened. The so-called eleven-plus tests in England, on which so much of a pupil's later life can depend, were originally part of a far-reaching school reform plan that would also allow pupils to shift schools after age eleven. Pupils not originally assigned to selective schools were thus to have a second chance (usually at age thirteen) if their performance belied the test results. But such changes, which with fallible tests should not have been rare, have turned out to be rare indeed. The reasons may be curricular, as, for example, when catch-up study is required in fields like mathematics and foreign language. They may be personal, especially the sense of failure when reassigned to a lower-prestige school. They may be social, as when class-consciousness insists on tying school assignment to status and power. But pointing out that tests always have a built-in error is not enough to solve this problem, and the British example has parallels in most countries where selection of the most apt for secondary or higher education is stressed.

Validity and Parsimony

No discussion of intelligence tests would be complete without considering validity, which in one sense is the key to testing. A test is valid if it measures what it purports to measure. An intelligence test used to pick bright children should pick the children who are brightest. If it is more sensitive instead to good reading or persistent effort or ready memory, it may still be a useful test, but it does not thereby measure intelligence. In many ways this is the basic consideration in the discussion above about definitions, test conditions, and social attitudes: What are we doing when we think we are choosing the brightest children?

The puzzle is better understood if we distinguish between two standard ways of checking validity: substance and prediction. If the questions in a test cover what we had in mind (as when a chemistry test asks about chemistry, not about history or arithmetic), it is a valid test because its content is what the label specifies. By the same logic, an intelligence test has the proper substance if the questions require a child to exhibit intelligence. If some questions ask the child to be merely a mimic, or to show off what has been drilled in, the test is less valid because no definition of intelligence recognizes rote memory as the core.

The other way to determine if an intelligence test is valid is to see if it picks children whose later behavior is what the test would lead us to expect. It is here that apparent conflict arises, for though the questions in the test may not appear to get at what we want to measure, they somehow help to pick children who turn out later to do well in school. A ludicrous, hypothetical example of this situation might be to ask whether a child were left-handed, red-haired, and fat. None of these questions ought to point to brightness. But if the children who later excelled in school were in fact left-handed, red-haired, and fat, then the test could be a valid predictor. Not at all hypothetical is a case that is often cited nowadays. So-called intelligence tests, it is claimed, are constructed to favor—instead of the left-handed or the red-haired or the fat—those who speak the standard language well because they come from well-educated homes. But if they are the pupils who do best in school, a test that detected their language skill would be valid to the extent that it predicted school performance. The problem, of course, is with the pupils who do not do well on the test because they didn't develop enough language proficiency at home. Now it does not follow that all children whose language training at home is poor are potentially bright, any more than it follows that all children who speak well are inherently gifted. Some children who do poorly would probably respond to stimulation if only they could be identified in time. But this problem does not require us to abandon intelligence tests in the search for gifted children. These tests, after all, have a remarkable record of success in picking children who become very able pupils. We recall, in fact, that intelligence tests were originally proposed in order to find children who would need special consideration in the early grades—what we would now call the demand for predictive validity. It is ironic that they are under fire today because test results and school attainment go together in a way that seems to give the advantage to children from educated homes. As we shall see shortly in discussing test fairness, it is not logical to give up a valid test merely because there is something that it does not do, or because we try to use it in ways it wasn't designed for.

What about situations where tests are rarely given or used to find apt pupils? After all, it is only in the United States and Britain that there has been any consistent reliance on intelligence tests. In most other countries high marks and—more important—success in the examinations that measure attainment in school subjects are the basis for selecting. These marks and examinations also must be checked for validity. The correspondence should be close, for an arithmetic test should ask arithmetic questions (substance) and pupils who do well one year should continue to do well later (prediction). But home background and encouragement, understanding the language of instruction and testing, cooperativeness, and inner drive affect the results of attainment tests in the same ways that they affect intelligence tests. In fact, there is some evidence that tested intelligence is more highly related to home background than is school attainment. That is, measures of each are at the same time measures of home background and other aspects of development that ought, on the face of it, to be expunged from standardized tests or objective marks.

Test validity is related to test fairness, and as Lloyd Lovell (1977) has stressed, the question of fairness revolves around the use to which information from the test is put. If test scores (in school or employment or anywhere else) accurately predict different levels of later performance, and the questions in the test are fair and properly put, then test scores are going to be valid. If, however, these same test scores are then used to reinforce prejudice or to penalize persons or groups, the charge of unfairness is warranted. But the charge is against *unfair use* of test information, not against the test itself. Of course, not everyone is willing to accept this distinction. Those who believe that the only way to end discrimination is to root out everything allied to it will not allow tests to be given because they have been and might still be instruments of oppression. H. S. Dyer tried to counter this criticism in 1961. He said that it was specious to argue that tests should be abolished because they are misused, just as it would be specious to say automobiles should be forbidden because reckless drivers can kill people. Admitting imperfection is no charter for abandoning attempts to locate gifted pupils. Many minority children with great potential can only be discovered through testing. Underachievers, whom we often would not recognize without intelligence tests, are a particularly telling example. As Richard and Norman Sprinthall (1974) suggested, if we abolish tests, we may come to think there is no longer any problem since we don't find the children who need help. The prudent tactic is to pay closer attention to what tests and marks can and cannot do to help us identify and understand the gifted.

In addition to being valid, a good test is also parsimonious: it asks enough to find out something wanted, without wasting the time of the tester or the pupil. Arguments over the substance of test questions or the effect of social prejudice obscure a stubborn fact: that with all its shortcomings, a good intelligence test is a very economical source of information about a bright child. This is not to say that a child's entire mental life has been surveyed. Hildreth (1966) cautioned that brief tests do not portray the richness of imagination, the speed and quality of thinking. Better, she said, to make a thorough study of many aspects of a child's mental life. Nonetheless, she put considerable faith in the limited but concentrated information that a test can supply, so that a mentally advanced child can be recognized as early as kindergarten entrance—not "will always be recognized," but "can be," and this in the space of an hour or so. More time must be spent gathering further evidence, but the initial guess can be remarkably acute. The best test gives not simply a label—IQ 140—but a compact collection of critical clues to intelligent behavior. As Wesman (1968) cautioned when pointing to the various aspects inherent in a six-year-old's arrangement of three alphabet blocks to form the word "CAT"—for example, cognition, memory, perception—to assume that we can abstract from a host of such activities a pure and simple entity called *intelligence* is to ignore the psychological meaning of intelligent behavior.

CONCLUSION

We have now reached the end of a brief book about giftedness. I believe it is salutary to close with a hopeful statement, coming so close upon a formidable list of difficulties. These difficulties, as we have seen, are real and they are serious. They involve a whole society's attitudes, which go well beyond the purview of schools or families alone. They come up at the same time we are hearing more clearly and insistently about other kinds of children and their needs. They have received irregular and grudging attention.

But concerned people continue to persevere, because to each generation are born brilliant children to impress us with their talents. These children deserve proper help; society must have their trained minds. No social challenge offers so great a reward, whether it be the personal satisfaction of helping children fulfill their promise, or the social benefit from shrewd provision for the future. If enough of us realize how promising the gifted are, how they need sustained and special schooling, how varied successful stimulation can be, I am confident of progress. This book is the expression of my confidence, and my attempt to sharpen our awareness.

REFERENCES

Adams, H. *The education of Henry Adams.* New York: Modern Library, 1931. (Originally printed in 1918 by the Massachusetts Historical Society)

Anastasi, A. *Differential psychology: Individual and group differences in behavior* (3rd ed.). New York: Macmillan, 1958.

Anastasi, A. On the formation of psychological traits. *American Psychologist,* 1970, *25,* 899–910.

Anastasi, A. Commentary on the precocity project. In J. C. Stanley, D. P. Keating, & L. H. Fox (Eds.), *Mathematical talent: Discovery, description, and development.* Baltimore: Johns Hopkins University Press, 1974.

Anderson, C. A. Access to higher education and economic development. In A. H. Halsey, J. Floud, & C. A. Anderson (Eds.), *Education, economy, and society: A reader in the sociology of knowledge.* Glencoe, Ill.: Free Press, 1961.

Armytage, W. H. G. *Four hundred years of English education.* Cambridge: Cambridge University Press, 1964.

Barbe, W. Evaluation of special classes for gifted children. *Exceptional Children,* 1955, *22,* 60–62.

Barker Lunn, J. C. The effects of streaming and non-streaming in junior schools: Second interim report. *New Research in Education,* 1967, *1,* 46–75.

Barker Lunn, J. C. *Streaming in the primary school.* Slough, England: National Foundation for Educational Research in England and Wales, 1970.

Baron, G. *Society, schools and progress in England.* Oxford: Pergamon Press, 1965.

Bereday, G. Z. F., & Lauwerys, J. A. (Eds.). *Concepts of excellence in education: The yearbook of education, 1961.* New York: Harcourt Brace Jovanovich, 1961.

Bereday, G. Z. F., & Lauwerys, J. A. (Eds.). *The gifted child: The yearbook of education, 1962.* New York: Harcourt Brace Jovanovich, 1962.

Bereiter, C. Genetics and educability. In J. Hellmuth (Ed.), *Disadvantaged child* (Vol. 3). New York: Brunner/Mazel, 1970.

Berry, J. W., & Dasen, P. (Eds.). *Readings in cross-cultural psychology.* London: Methuen, 1974.

Biesheuvel, S. The detection and fostering of ability among under-developed peoples. In G. Z. F. Bereday & J. A. Lauwerys (Eds.), *The gifted child: The yearbook of education, 1962.* New York: Harcourt Brace Jovanovich, 1962.

Binet, A. *[Modern ideas about children] Les idées modernes sur les enfants.* Paris: Flammarion, 1911. (a)

Binet, A. [New research on measuring school children's intellectual level] Nouvelles recherches sur la mesure du niveau intellectuel chez les enfants d'école. *L'Année Psychologique,* 1911, *17,* 145–201. (b)

Binet, A., & Simon, T. [New methods for diagnosing the intellectual level of abnormal persons] Méthodes nouvelles pour le diagnostique du niveau intellectuel des anormaux. *L'Année Psychologique,* 1905, *11,* 196–98.

Binet, A., & Simon, T. [Intellectual development in children] Le développement de l'intelligence chez les enfants. *L'Année Psychologique,* 1908, *14,* 1–94.

Binet, A., & Simon, T. [The intelligence of imbeciles] L'Intelligence des imbéciles. *L'Année Psychologique,* 1909, *15,* 128–47.

Bisconti, A. S., & Astin, H. S. *Undergraduate and graduate study in scientific fields.* Washington, D.C.: American Council on Education Research Report, *8*(3), 1973.

Bloom, B. S. Letter to editor. *Harvard Educational Review,* 1969, *39*(2), 419–21.

Bock, R. D., & Kolakowski, D. Further evidence of sex-linked major-gene influence on human spatial visualizing ability. *American Journal of Human Genetics,* 1973, *25,* 1–14.

Borg, W. R. *Ability grouping in the public schools.* Madison, Wis.: Dembar Educational Research Service, 1966.

Boyd, W. SATs and minorities: The dangers of underprediction. *Change,* 1977, *9*(7), 48–49; 64.

Brandwein, P. F. *The gifted student as future scientist.* New York: Harcourt Brace Jovanovich, 1955.

Brody, E. B., & Brody, N. (Eds.). *Intelligence: Nature, determinants, and consequences.* New York: Academic Press, 1976.

Burt, C. The structure of the mind: A review of the results of factor analysis. *British Journal of Psychology,* 1949, *19,* 110–11; 176–99.

Burt, C. The gifted child. In G. Z. F. Bereday & J. A. Lauwerys (Eds.), *The gifted child: The yearbook of education, 1962.* New York: Harcourt Brace Jovanovich, 1962. (a)

Burt, C. The psychology of creative ability. *British Journal of Educational Psychology,* 1962, *32,* 292–98. (b)

Burt, C. Is intelligence normally distributed? *British Journal of Statistical Psychology,* 1963, *16,* 175–90.

Burt, C. The mental differences between children. In C. B. Cox & A. E. Dyson (Eds.), *Black paper two: The crisis in education.* London: The Critical Quarterly Society, 1969.

Butcher, H. J. *Human intelligence: Its nature and assessment.* London: Methuen, 1968.

Caspari, E. Genetic endowment and environment in the determination of human behavior: Biological viewpoint. *American Educational Research Journal,* 1968, *4,* 43–55.

Cattell, J. McK. A statistical study of American men of science. *Science,* 1906, *24,* 732–42.

Cattell, R. B. *Abilities: Their structure, growth, and action.* Boston: Houghton Mifflin, 1971.

Coleman, J. S., Campbell, E. Q., Hobson, C. J., McPartland, J., Mood, A. M., Weinfeld, F. D., & York, R. L. *Equality of educational opportunity.* Washington, D.C.: U.S. Government Printing Office, 1966.

Comenius [Jan Amos Komensky]. *[The great didactic]* (M. W. Keatinge, trans.). London: A. & C. Black, 1896.

Cook, W. W. Individual differences and curriculum practice. *Journal of Educational Psychology,* 1948, *39,* 141–48.

Copley, F. O. *The American high school and the talented student.* Ann Arbor: University of Michigan Press, 1961.

Covington, M. V. The cognitive curriculum: A process-oriented approach to education. In J. Hellmuth (Ed.), *Cognitive studies* (Vol. 1). New York: Brunner/Mazel, 1970.

Cox, C. M. *Genetic studies of genius: The early mental traits of three hundred geniuses.* Stanford, Calif.: Stanford University Press, 1926.

Cutts, N. E., & Mosely, N. *Teaching the bright and gifted.* Englewood Cliffs, N.J.: Prentice-Hall, 1957.

Dahllöf, U. S. *Ability grouping, content validity, and curriculum process analysis.* Göteborg, Sweden: Institute of Education, 1969.

DeBary, W. T., Chan, W. -S., & Watson, B. *Sources of Chinese tradition* (Vol. 1). New York: Columbia University Press, 1960.

Dewey, J. *How we think: A restatement of the relation of reflective thinking to the educative process.* New York: Heath, 1933.

Dobzhansky, T. Heredity, environment and evolution. *Science,* 1950, *111,* 161–66.

Dove, A. Soul folk "Chitling" test (The Dove Counterbalance Intelligence Test). In G. A. Davis & T. F. Warren (Eds.), *Psychology of education: New looks.* Lexington, Mass.: Heath, 1974.

DuBois, P. H. A test-dominated society: China, 1115 B.C.–1905 A.D. *Proceedings of the 1964 Invitational Conference on Testing Problems.* Princeton, N.J.: Educational Testing Service, 1965. Also cited in W. L. Barnette, Jr. (Ed.), *Readings in psychological tests and measurements* (Rev. ed.). Homewood, Ill.: Dorsey Press, 1968.

DuBois, P. H. *A history of psychological testing.* Boston: Allyn & Bacon, 1970.

Duff, J. F. Children of high intelligence: A following-up enquiry. *British Journal of Psychology,* 1929, *19,* 413–38.

Dunlap, J. M. The education of children with high mental ability. In W. M. Cruickshank & G. O. Johnson (Eds.), *The education of exceptional children and youth* (2nd ed.). Englewood Cliffs, N.J.: Prentice-Hall, 1967.

Dyer, H. S. Is testing a menace to education? *New York State Education,* 1961, *49,* 16–19.

Ebel, R. L. The social consequences of educational testing. *Proceedings of the 1963 Invitational Conference on Testing Problems.* Princeton, N.J.: Educational Testing Service, 1963.

Educational policy: Questions and answers. *Peking Review,* 1978, *21*(15), 13–15.

Eells, K., Davis, A., Havighurst, R. J., Herrick, V. E., & Tyler, R. W. *Intelligence and cultural differences: A study of cultural learning and problem solving.* Chicago: University of Chicago Press, 1951.

Ferrez, J. Regional inequalities in educational opportunity. In A. H. Halsey (Ed.), *Ability and educational opportunity.* Paris: O.E.C.D., 1961.

Fincher, J. The Terman study is fifty years old: Happy anniversary and pass the ammunition. *Human Behavior,* 1973, *2*(3), 8–15.

Floud, J. Social class factors in educational achievement. In A. H. Halsey (Ed.), *Ability and educational opportunity.* Paris: O.E.C.D., 1961.

Floud, J., & Halsey, A. H. Social class, intelligence tests, and selection for secondary schools. In A. H. Halsey, J. Floud, & C. A. Anderson (Eds.), *Education, economy, and society: A reader in the sociology of education.* Glencoe, Ill.: Free Press, 1961.

Fox, L. H. Facilitating educational development of mathematically precocious youth. In J. C. Stanley, D. P. Keating, & L. H. Fox (Eds.), *Mathematical talent: Discovery, description, and development.* Baltimore: Johns Hopkins University Press, 1974.

Fox, L. H. Sex differences in mathematical precocity: Bridging the gap. In D. P. Keating (Ed.), *Intellectual talent: Research and development.* Baltimore: Johns Hopkins University Press, 1976.

Fraser, E. *Home environment and the school.* London: University of London Press, 1959.

Furneaux, W. D. *The chosen few: An examination of some aspects of university selection in Britain.* London: Oxford University Press, 1961.

Gallagher, J. J. *The gifted child in the elementary school.* Washington, D.C.: American Educational Research Association, 1959.

Gallagher, J. J *Teaching the gifted child.* Boston: Allyn & Bacon, 1964.

Gallagher, J. J. *Research summary on gifted child education.* Springfield, Ill.: Office of Superintendent of Public Instruction, 1966.

Gallagher, J. J. *Teaching the gifted child* (2nd ed.). Boston: Allyn & Bacon, 1975.

Gallagher, J. J., & Crowder, T. The adjustment of gifted children in the regular classroom. *Exceptional Children,* 1957, *23,* 306–12; 317–19.

Galton, F. *Hereditary genius: An inquiry into its laws and consequences.* London: Macmillan, 1869.

Galvan, R. R. Bilingualism as it relates to intelligence test scores and school achievement among culturally deprived Spanish-American children (Doctoral dissertation, East Texas State University, 1967). (University Microfilms No. 68-1131)

Gardner, H. *Developmental psychology: An introduction.* Boston: Little, Brown, 1978.

Gardner, J. W. *Excellence: Can we be equal and excellent too?* New York: Harper & Row, 1961.

Getzels, J. W., & Jackson, P. W. *Creativity and intelligence: Explorations with gifted students.* New York: Wiley, 1962.

Ghiselin, B. (Ed.). *The creative process.* Berkeley: University of California Press, 1952.

Goodenough, F. L. *Exceptional children.* New York: Appleton-Century-Crofts, 1956.

Gough, H. G. Factors related to differential achievement among gifted persons. Mimeographed report. Berkeley: University of California Psychology Department, 1955.

Guilford, J. P. Three faces of intellect. *American Psychologist,* 1959, *14,* 469–79.

Hall, T. *Gifted children: The Cleveland story.* Cleveland, Ohio: World, 1956.

Halls, W. D. *Society, schools, and progress in France.* Oxford: Pergamon Press, 1965.

Halls, W. D. The education of the academically gifted in Europe: Some comparisons. *Comparative Education Review,* 1966, *10*(3), 426–32.

Halsey, A. H. A review of the conference. In A. H. Halsey (Ed.), *Ability and educational opportunity.* Paris: O.E.C.D., 1961.

Havighurst, R. J. Conditions productive of superior children. *Teachers College Record,* 1961, *62,* 524–31.

Havighurst, R. J., Stivers, E., & De Haan, R. F. A survey of the education of gifted children. *Supplementary Educational Monographs,* 1955, No. 83.

Hebb, D. O. *The organization of behavior.* New York: Wiley, 1949.

Helvétius, C. A. *[On understanding] De l'esprit.* Paris: Didot, 1795.

Herrnstein, R. J. I.Q. *Atlantic,* 1971, *338*(3), 43–58; 63–64.

Heuyer, G., & Piéron, H. *[The intellectual level of school-age children] Le niveau intellectuel des enfants d'âge scolaire* (Vol. 1). Paris: Presses Universitaires de France, 1950.

Hildreth, G. H. Three gifted children: A developmental study. *Journal of Genetic Psychology,* 1954, *85,* 239–62.

Hildreth, G. H. *Introduction to the gifted.* New York: McGraw-Hill, 1966.

Hollingworth, L. S. *Children above 180 I.Q.* Yonkers-on-Hudson, N.Y.: World Book, 1942.

Horn, J. L. Human abilities: A review of research and theory in the early 1970s. *Annual Review of Psychology,* 1976, *27,* 437–85.

Hudson, L. *Contrary imaginations.* New York: Schocken Books, 1966.

Hunt, J. McV. *Intelligence and experience.* New York: Ronald, 1961.

Husén, T. Loss of talent in selective school systems: The case of Sweden. *Comparative Education Review,* 1960, *4*(2), 70–74.

Inhelder, B., & Piaget, J. *The growth of logical thinking from childhood to adolescence: An essay on the construction of formal operational structures.* New York: Basic Books, 1958.

Isaacs, S. Being gifted is a bed of roses, with the thorns included. *Gifted Child Quarterly,* 1971, *15,* 54–56.

James, Lord, of Rusholme. *Gifted children: Is there a problem?* Address given at the meeting of the National Association for Gifted Children, London, 1975.

Jefferson, T. Bill for the more general diffusion of knowledge [1779]. In G. C. Lee (Ed.), *Thomas Jefferson on education.* New York: Columbia University, Teachers College Bureau of Publications, 1961.

Jencks, C., Smith, M., Acland, H., Bane, M. J., Cohen, D., Gintis, H., Heyns, B., & Michelson, S. *Inequality: A reassessment of the effect of family and schooling in America.* New York: Basic Books, 1972.

Jenkins, M. D. The upper limit of ability among American Negroes. *Science,* 1948, *66,* 399–401.

Jensen, A. R. How much can we boost I.Q. and scholastic achievement? *Harvard Educational Review,* 1969, *31*(1), 1–123.

Jensen, A. R. *Genetics and education.* London: Methuen, 1972.

Johnson, S. *Lives of the English poets.* Oxford: Clarendon Press, 1905. (Originally published, 1779)

Jones, M. C. Albert, Peter, and John B. Watson. *American Psychologist,* 1974, *29*(8), 581–83.

Kagan, J., & Klein, R. E. Cross-cultural perspectives on early development. *American Psychologist,* 1973, *28*(11), 947–61.

Kahl, J. A. Educational and occupational aspirations of "common man" boys. *Harvard Educational Review,* 1953, *23*(3), 186–203.

Keating, D. P. The study of mathematically precocious youth. In J. C. Stanley, D. P. Keating, & L. H. Fox (Eds.), *Mathematical talent: Discovery, description, and development.* Baltimore: Johns Hopkins University Press, 1974.

Keating, D. P. (Ed.). *Intellectual talent: Research and development.* Baltimore: Johns Hopkins University Press, 1976.

Kellmer Pringle, M. L. *Able misfits.* London: Longmans, 1970.

Keys, N. The underage student in high school and college. *University of California Publications in Education,* 1938, *7*(3), 147–271.

King, E. J. *Other schools and ours: Comparative studies for today* (4th ed.). London: Holt, Rinehart and Winston, 1973.

King, E. J. (Ed.). *Post-compulsory education: A new analysis in Western Europe.* London and Beverly Hills, Calif.: Sage Publications, 1974.

Kogan, N., & Pankove, E. Creative ability over a five-year span. *Child Development,* 1972, *43,* 427–42.

Kohlberg, L., & De Vries, R. Relations between Piaget and psychometric assessments of intelligence. In C. Lavatelli (Ed.), *The natural curriculum.* Urbana: University of Illinois Press, 1971.

Labov, W. Academic ignorance and black intelligence. *Atlantic,* 1972, *229*(6), 59–67.

Lange-Eichbaum, W. *The problem of genius.* New York: Macmillan, 1932.

Laycock, F., & Caylor, J. S. Physiques of gifted children and their less gifted siblings. *Child Development,* 1964, *35,* 63–74.

Lehman, H. C. *Age and achievement.* Princeton, N.J.: Princeton University Press, 1953.

Lindsay, K. *Social progress and educational waste, being a study of the "free-place" and scholarship system.* London: Routledge & Kegan Paul, 1926.

Little, A., & Westergaard, J. The trend of class differentials in educational opportunity in England and Wales. *British Journal of Sociology,* 1964, *15*(4), 301–16.

Lovell, L. Personal communication, 1977.

Lowenfeld, V. *Creative and mental growth* (2nd ed.). New York: Macmillan, 1957.

MacKinnon, D. W. The nature and nurture of creative talent. *American Psychologist,* 1962, *17*(7), 484–95.

Marland, S. P., Jr. *Education of the gifted and talented: Report to the Congress of the United States by the Commissioner of Education.* Washington, D.C.: U.S. Government Printing Office, 1972.

Marolla, F. A. Intelligence and demographic variables in a 19-year-old cohort in the Netherlands. Unpublished doctoral dissertation, New School for Social Research, New York, 1973.

Martinson, R. A. *Educational programs for gifted pupils.* Sacramento: California State Department of Education, 1961.

Martinson, R. A. Children with superior cognitive abilities. In L. M. Dunn (Ed.), *Exceptional children in the schools* (2nd ed.). New York: Holt, Rinehart and Winston, 1973.

McGinn, P. V. Verbally gifted youth: Selection and description. In D. P. Keating (Ed.), *Intellectual talent: Research and development.* Baltimore: Johns Hopkins University Press, 1976.

McMahon, D. The identification and use of talent. *Advancement of Science,* 1962, *19.*

Mill, J. S. *Autobiography.* New York: Holt, 1873.

Miller, B. *The Palace School of Muhammad the Conqueror.* Cambridge: Harvard University Press, 1941.

Mitchell, J. Evening with a gifted child. *New Yorker,* 1940, *16,* 28–32.

Mordock, J. B. *The other children: An introduction to exceptionality.* New York: Harper & Row, 1975.

Muller, H. J. *The uses of the past.* New York: Oxford University Press, 1954.

Nason, L. J. *Academic achievement of gifted high school students: Patterns of circumstances related to educational achievement of high school pupils of superior ability.* Los Angeles: University of Southern California Press, 1958.

Neimark, E. D. Intellectual development during adolescence. In F. D. Horowitz (Ed.), *Review of child development research* (Vol. 4). Chicago: University of Chicago Press, 1975.

Newland, T. E. *The gifted in socioeducational perspective.* Englewood Cliffs, N.J.: Prentice-Hall, 1976.

Neymark, E. *[Counseling youth for education and work] Ungdomens vägledning till utbildning och yrke.* Stockholm: Statens Offentliga Utredningar, 1945.

Oden, M. H. The fulfillment of promise: Forty-year follow-up of the Terman gifted group. *Genetic Psychology Monographs,* 1968, *77,* 3–93.

Ogilvie, L. E. *Gifted children in primary school.* London: Macmillan, 1973.

Parkyn, G. W. *Children of high intelligence: A New Zealand study.* Wellington, N.Z.: Council for Educational Research, 1948.

Paschal, E. *Encouraging the excellent: Special programs for gifted and talented students.* New York: The Fund for the Advancement of Education, 1960.

Passow, A. H. Introduction to Section II, Detection of ability and selection for educational purposes. In G. Z. F. Bereday & J. A. Lauwerys (Eds.), *The gifted child: The yearbook of education,* 1962. New York: Harcourt Brace Jovanovich, 1962.

Piaget, J. *Psychology of intelligence.* London: Routledge & Kegan Paul, 1950.

Piaget, J. *Origin of intelligence.* New York: International Universities Press, 1952.

Piaget, J. *To understand is to invent: The future of education.* New York: Grossman, 1973.

Pidgeon, D. A. *Expectation and pupil performance.* Stockholm: Almqvist & Wiksell, 1970.

Pierce, J. W., & Bowman, P. Motivation patterns of superior high-school students. *Cooper Research Monographs,* 1960, No. 2, 33–66.

Plato. *The Republic* (A. Bloom, trans.). New York: Basic Books, 1968.

Pressey, S. L. Educational acceleration: Appraisal and basic problems. *Ohio State University Bureau of Educational Research Monographs,* 1949, No. 13.

Pressey, S. L. Concerning the nature and nurture of genius. *Science,* 1955, *68,* 123–29.

Pressey, S. L. Fordling accelerates: Ten years after. *Journal of Counseling Psychology,* 1967, *14*(1), 73–80.

Quay, H. C. Language, dialect, reinforcement, and the intelligence-test performance of Negro children. *Child Development,* 1971, *68,* 73–82.

Raven Progressive Matrices. New York: Psychological Corporation, 1965.

Reischauer, E. O., & Fairbank, J. K. *East Asia: The great tradition.* Boston: Houghton Mifflin, 1958.

Riegel, K. F. *Dialectic operations: The final period of cognitive development.* Princeton, N.J.: Educational Testing Service, 1973.

Robbins Committee. *Higher education.* London: Her Majesty's Stationer's Office, 1963.

Roe, A. *The making of a scientist.* New York: Dodd, Mead, 1953.

Rohrer, J. H. The test intelligence of Osage Indians. *Journal of Social Psychology,* 1942, *16,* 99–105.

Rosenthal, R., & Jacobson, L. *Pygmalion in the classroom: Teacher expectation and pupils' intellectual development.* New York: Holt, Rinehart and Winston, 1968.

Sattler, J. M. *Assessment of children's intelligence.* Philadelphia: Saunders, 1974.

Scarr-Salapatek, S. Unknowns in the I.Q. equation. *Science,* 1971, *174,* 1223–28.

Schneider, E. Personal communication, July 18, 1977.

Sears, P. S., & Barbee, A. H. Career and life satisfactions among Terman's gifted women. In J. C. Stanley, W. C. George, & C. H. Solano (Eds.), *The gifted and the creative: A fifty-year perspective.* Baltimore: Johns Hopkins University Press, 1977.

Sears, R. R. Sources of life satisfactions of the Terman gifted men. *American Psychologist,* 1977, *32*(2), 119–28.

Shaw, M. C. The inter-relationship of selected personality factors in high ability. *Final report, Project 58-M-1.* Sacramento: California State Department of Public Health, 1961.

Shuey, A. M. *The testing of Negro intelligence* (2nd ed.). New York: Social Science Press, 1966.

Simpson, R. E., & Martinson, R. A. *Educational programs for gifted pupils: A report to the California legislature.* Sacramento: California State Department of Education, 1961.

Sisk, D. Education of the gifted and talented: A national perspective. *Journal for the Education of the Gifted,* 1978, *1*(1), 5–24.

Sjöstrand, W. School achievement and development of personality: Some results of a Swedish homogenizing experiment. *Paedagogica Europaea,* 1967, pp. 189–212.

Sjöstrand, W. *Freedom and equality as fundamental educational principles in Western democracy from John Locke to Edmund Burke.* Stockholm: Föreningen för Svensk Undervisningshistoria, 1973. (a)

Sjöstrand, W. Personal communication, Aug. 25, 1973. (b)

Skarp, L. [pseud.]. Personal communication with author, 1978.

Skeels, H. M. Adult status of children with contrasting early life experiences: A follow-up study. *Monographs of the Society for Research in Child Development*, 1966, *31*(105), 1–11; 13; 54–59.

Skodak, M., & Skeels, H. M. A final follow-up study of one hundred adopted children. *Journal of Genetic Psychology*, 1949, *75*, 85–125.

Spearman, C. S. *The nature of intelligence and the principles of cognition*. New York: Macmillan, 1927.

Sprinthall, R. C., & Sprinthall, N. A. *Educational psychology: A developmental approach*. Reading, Mass.: Addison-Wesley, 1974.

Stanley, J. C. Accelerating the educational progress of intellectually gifted youths. *Educational Psychologist*, 1973, *10*(3), 133–46.

Stanley, J. C., George, W. C., & Solano, C. H. (Eds.). *The gifted and the creative: A fifty-year perspective*. Baltimore: Johns Hopkins University Press, 1977.

Stanley, J. C., Keating, D. P., & Fox, L. H. (Eds.). *Mathematical talent: Discovery, description, and development*. Baltimore: Johns Hopkins University Press, 1974.

Stern, W. *The psychological methods of testing intelligence* (G. M. Whipple, trans.). Baltimore: Warwick & York, 1914. (Originally published, 1912)

Stern, W. *General psychology from the personalistic viewpoint*. New York: Macmillan, 1938.

Sumption, M. R. *Three hundred gifted children: A follow-up study of the results of special education of superior children*. Yonkers-on-Hudson, N.Y.: World Book, 1941.

Suzuki, S. Cited in *Newsweek*, March 23, 1964, p. 73.

Suzuki, S. *Nurtured by love: A new approach to education*. New York: Exposition Press, 1969.

Svensson, N. E. *Ability grouping and scholastic achievement*. Stockholm: Almqvist & Wiksell, 1962.

Telford, C. W., & Sawrey, J. M. *The exceptional individual* (3rd ed.). Englewood Cliffs, N.J.: Prentice-Hall, 1977.

Terman, L. M. The intelligence quotient of Francis Galton in childhood. *American Journal of Psychology*, 1917, *28*, 209–15.

Terman, L. M. *Mental and physical traits of a thousand gifted children*. Stanford, Calif.: Stanford University Press, 1925.

Terman, L. M. The discovery and encouragement of exceptional talent. *American Psychologist*, 1954, *9*, 221–30.

Terman, L. M., Burks, B. S., & Jensen, D. W. *The promise of youth: Follow-up studies of a thousand gifted children*. Stanford, Calif.: Stanford University Press, 1930.

Terman, L. M., & Oden, M. H. *The gifted child grows up*. Stanford, Calif.: Stanford University Press, 1947.

Terman, L. M., & Oden, M. H. *The gifted group at mid-life*. Stanford, Calif.: Stanford University Press, 1959.

Thorndike, E. L. *The measurement of intelligence*. New York: Columbia University, Teachers College Bureau of Publications, 1927.

Thorndike, E. L. *Human nature and the social order*. New York: Macmillan, 1940.

Thurstone, L. L. *Primary mental abilities*. Chicago: University of Chicago Press, 1938.

Time Magazine. The eternal apprentice [J. Robert Oppenheimer], 1948, *52*, 70–72; 75–78; 81.

Torrance, E. P. Torrance Tests of Creative Thinking. Princeton, N.J.: Personnel Press, 1966.

Ulich, R. *Three thousand years of educational wisdom: Selections from the great documents*. Cambridge: Harvard University Press, 1950.

U.S. Department of Health, Education, and Welfare. *H.E.W. News*, Nov. 18, 1976.

Vernon, P. E. *Secondary school selection: A British Psychological Society inquiry*. London: Methuen, 1957.

Vernon, P. E. *Intelligence and attainment tests*. London: University of London Press, 1960.

Vernon, P. E. *The structure of human abilities* (2nd ed.). London: Methuen, 1961.

Vernon, P. E. Ability factors and environmental influences. *American Psychologist*, 1965, *20*(9), 723–33.

Vernon, P. E., Adamson, G., & Vernon, D. F. *The psychology and education of gifted children*. London: Methuen, 1977. (Also Boulder, Colo.: Westview Press, 1977)

Wallach, M. A. *The intelligence/creativity distinction*. New York: General Learning Press, 1971.

Wallach, M. A., & Kogan, N. *Modes of thinking in young children: A study of the creativity-intelligence distinction*. New York: Holt, Rinehart and Winston, 1965.

Warner, W. L., Havighurst, R. J., & Loeb, M. B. *Who shall be educated? The challenge of unequal opportunities*. New York: Harper & Row, 1944.

Watson, J. B. *Behaviorism*. New York: Norton, 1924.

Watson, J. B. *Behaviorism*. New York: Norton, 1930. (Reprint of 1924 edition, with changes)

Wechsler, D. Cognitive, conative, and non-intellective intelligence. *American Psychologist,* 1950, *5*(3), 78–83.

Wechsler, D. *The measurement and appraisal of adult intelligence*. Baltimore: Williams & Wilkins, 1958.

Weiss, D. S., Haier, R. J., & Keating, D. P. Personality characteristics of mathematically precocious youth. In J. C. Stanley, D. P. Keating, & L. H. Fox (Eds.), *Mathematical talent: Discovery, description, and development*. Baltimore: Johns Hopkins University Press, 1974.

Wesman, A. G. Intelligent testing. *American Psychologist,* 1968, *23,* 267–74.

Williams, R. L. Testing and dehumanizing black children. *Clinical Child Psychology Newsletter,* 1970, *9*(1), 5–6.

Willis, M. *The guinea pigs after twenty years: A follow-up study of the class of 1938 of the University School at Ohio State*. Columbus: Ohio State University Press, 1961.

Wiseman, S. Environmental and innate factors and educational attainment. In J. E. Meade & A. S. Parkes, *Genetic and environmental factors in human ability*. Edinburgh: Oliver & Boyd, 1966.

Wiseman, S. *Intelligence and ability: Selected readings*. Harmondsworth, England: Penguin, 1967.

Witty, P. A. A study of one hundred gifted children. *University of Kansas Bulletin of Education,* 1930, *2*(8).

Witty, P. A. A genetic study of fifty gifted children. In G. M. Whipple (Ed.), *39th Yearbook* (Part 2). National Society for the Study of Education, 1940.

Wolfe, T. *The web and the rock*. New York: Harper & Row, 1939.

Wolfle, D. Diversity of talent. *American Psychologist,* 1960, *15,* 535–45.

Wolfle, D. National resources of ability. In A. H. Halsey (Ed.), *Ability and educational opportunity*. Paris: O.E.C.D., 1961.

Wolfle, D. (Ed.). *The discovery of talent*. Cambridge: Harvard University Press, 1969.

Yates, A. *The organization of schooling: A study of educational grouping practices*. London: Routledge & Kegan Paul, 1971.

Zach, L. The I.Q. debate. *Today's Education,* 1972, *61*(6), 40–43; 65–66; 68.

INDEX